Using simple economic reasoning, this book analyzes a broad range of global challenges including global warming, ozone shield depletion, acid rain, nuclear waste disposal, revolution dispersion, international terrorism, disease eradication, population growth, tropical deforestation, and peacemaking. These challenges are put into perspective in terms of scientific, economic, and political considerations. Many of these contingencies are shown to be solvable or reduceable without much explicit coordination among nations. Although there is no single panacea for these challenges, much can be done to tailor solutions. This book is intended for a wide audience drawn from the social sciences, including economics, environmental studies, political science, sociology, and public policy. It should also interest the general reader who wants to learn about global challenges.

Advance Praise for *Global Challenges*

"*Global Challenges* uses the theory of games to offer simple yet profound insights into the scope for international agreements on issues such as climate change, biodiversity loss, and acid rain. No other book offers nonspecialist readers a better understanding of the potential for solving apparently intractable international environmental problems."
– Charles Perrings, *University of York*

"Todd Sandler's *Global Challenges* offers the most accessible treatment to date of the complex ecological, economic and political web of connections that define the new international political order. It captures highly sophisticated relationships in cogent and carefully crafted arguments and explanations, and will be of wide use to students, teachers, and policy professionals."
– C. Ford Runge, *University of Minnesota*

"This book is chock full of clever and insightful examples of addressing environmental, political, and economic problems. What makes it especially valuable is that the examples are presented in a consistent framework so the reader is able to categorize the problems and understand common solutions."
– John Tschirhart, *University of Wyoming*

Global challenges

Global challenges

An approach to environmental, political, and economic problems

TODD SANDLER

Iowa State University

CAMBRIDGE
UNIVERSITY PRESS

337
521g

PUBLISHED BY THE PRESS SYNDICATE OF THE UNIVERSITY OF CAMBRIDGE
The Pitt Building, Trumpington Street, Cambridge CB2 1RP, United Kingdom

CAMBRIDGE UNIVERSITY PRESS
The Edinburgh Building, Cambridge CB2 2RU, United Kingdom
40 West 20th Street, New York, NY 10011–4211, USA
10 Stamford Road, Oakleigh, Melbourne 3166, Australia

First published 1997

Printed in the United States of America

Typeset in Times Roman   ⌐⌐ ℗

Library of Congress Cataloging-in-Publication Data
Sandler, Todd.
Global challenges : an approach to environmental, political, and
economic problems / Todd Sandler.
p.   cm.
Includes bibliographical references and index.
ISBN 0–521–58307–1 (hc). – ISBN 0–521–58749–2 (pbk.)
1. Economic policy – International cooperation.   2. Environmental
policy – International cooperation.   3. Competition, International.
I. Title.
HD87.S364   1997   94–48226
337 – dc21   CIP

*A catalog record for this book is available from
the British Library.*

ISBN 0 521 58307 1 hardback
ISBN 0 521 58749 2 paperback

To Carol, looking out of a window

Contents

Tables and figures

Tables

Figures

Preface

During the past fifty years, momentous changes in economic activities, technology, warfare, communications, information systems, and population have drawn the world's countries into a global community. Countries' borders, once secured through armies and artillery, are now invaded daily by pollutants, unleashed by economic activities at home and abroad. We live in an era during which the side effects of these activities have surpassed limits, beyond which stresses placed on the planet's ecosystems lead to permanent deterioration. In aggregation, economic activities have degraded the troposphere, stratosphere, high seas, rivers, watersheds, forests, and airsheds. The collective pursuit of economic well-being has thinned the stratospheric ozone shield and has heated the atmosphere. As little as thirty years ago, terms like ozone hole, acid rain, nuclear meltdown, nuclear-weapon proliferation, international terrorism, global warming, desertification, and biodiversity were foreign to most people. Traditionally, the next generation's well-being improves compared with that of preceding generations as knowledge, capital, and other assets are passed down. If environmental deterioration continues to destroy the earth's assets, this tradition will end.

Will these problems continue unabated? Will future cities be encapsulated in domes of concrete, steel, and glass, where a day in the country will involve watching a video and where residents look nostalgically out on an inhospitable environment? Significant challenges confront the global community, where actions taken today will limit the options of generations to come. With the recognition of these challenges have come pleas for larger decision-making jurisdictions in the form of regional and global governments to safeguard the environment and maintain the peace. In most cases, the nation-state has tended to break apart to form smaller decision units rather than larger superstates. Nationalism is still alive. Thus, to assess the feasible responses to potential crises confronting the planet, we must consider what nations are prepared to do on their own or in loose federations with, say, neighboring nations. Before we despair, we must remember that nations can and do take actions on their own and, at times, in conjunction with other nations. A multinational pollution pact cleaned up the Baltic Sea; the United States and Russia have joined forces to build a space station; and scientists worldwide coordinated efforts to monitor the encounter of Comet Shoemaker-Levy 9 with Jupiter in mid-July 1994. Although the problems that the world faces are varied and complex, not all require large collective responses. To ascertain which crises can be solved at the national level and which cannot, I must examine the underlying incentives associated with each exigency.

Perhaps the following parable sheds light. Suppose that a planet has but two nations that are long-standing enemies. Suppose further that they are threatened by a hostile alien race, capable of defeating either country but insufficiently strong to overcome their combined arsenals. Surely, the two nations will recognize their plight and put aside differences, at least temporarily, to coordinate a response. Next assume that the scenario is the same, except that two hundred nations must combine power to defeat the alien invader. Even one noncooperator would spell defeat and annihilation to all. Would action be sufficiently swift to ward off the disaster? Even in this case nations, if given convincing evidence that it would take every last one of them to coalesce forces under a general command, should rise to the occasion. For the second scenario time is more of a factor owing to the number of participants among whom efforts must be coordinated. A lone holdout can attempt to obtain better terms, which, in turn, could cause defeat as bargaining or coercion proceeds.

A number of alterations to the scenario could change incentives adversely, thereby limiting or eliminating an effective collective response. First, information may be incomplete, so that the required response to turn back the alien invasion is unknown. This uncertainty may lead to bickering in which nations less concerned or less convinced about the crisis take a wait-and-see attitude. Second, some nations may seek accommodation with the aliens, provided that a credible agreement is reached in which any attack spares them. Third, only a subgroup of nations – say 50% – represents the minimal-winning force so that nonparticipants can reap the safety from the efforts of others without putting their own forces in harm's way. In this last case, enough nations may seek to be among the nonparticipants that the aliens conquer all. This last consideration plagues many current challenges to the world community – for example, large cutbacks in carbon dioxide (CO_2) emissions by half of the nations may curb global warming sufficiently to put off crises well into the future for all nations. Unfortunately, too many nations may rely on the others to curb CO_2 emissions, so that minimal participation rates are not achieved.

This book is intended to put global crises in perspective by drawing on modern tools of economic analysis that emphasize incentive structures collective action, market failures, strategic interactions, information, and the role and need for institutions. A host of contingencies of an environmental, technological, economic, and strategic nature are considered. Although some challenges are particularly difficult to confront effectively, the harsh scenarios, now popular in science fiction movies and the media, may indeed be warded off in our lifetime and that of our children. It is crucial to identify the problems where action will be adequate without coordination, so that resources and efforts can be channeled to those problems where action will be inadequate without some centralized control. This book takes stock of what we know about pending crises and what the prognosis is for the future. The design of institutions to manage these crises is also addressed. When, however, nations can respond reasonably well on their own, additional centralized action is not typically justified in terms of net benefits.

Acknowledgments

In addition to the support of my home institution, Iowa State University, I have received support from the University of Newcastle, Australia, during May–June 1996 when I was a Visiting Professor under the Vice-Chancellor's Research Best Practice Scheme. I made revisions to the book while I was a Visiting Scholar at Keele University, UK, during 1996.

I greatly appreciate the editorial guidance and support of Scott Parris of Cambridge University Press. I have profited from comments provided by Ko Doeleman, C. Ford Runge, and a host of anonymous reviewers. I also thank the many professional people at Cambridge University Press who transformed the manuscript into a book.

I owe a debt of gratitude to Norman Myers and Dudley Luckett, who encouraged me in this project. Deb Moore helped me locate research materials and provided moral support. Anne Hrbek did a wonderful job in word processing the various drafts. Sue Streeter also assisted with the word processing.

I want to thank some coauthors who worked on various topics that I address in this book. These include James Murdoch, Walter Enders, Jon Cauley, Keith Sargent, Ko Doeleman, Richard Cornes, and Jyoti Khanna. Finally, I thank my wife, Jeannie Murdock, and my son, Tristan Jon, for their support and understanding during the writing of this book.

1 Apocalypse now or never?

With the end of the millennium approaching, the world is besieged by potential crises that require collective action, motivated for the good of the world community. These challenges involve global warming, a thinning ozone shield, contamination of water supplies, nuclear weapon proliferation, terrorism, antibiotic-resistant diseases, and increased income inequalities within and among nations. Are nations that cherish their autonomy prepared to cooperate in an unselfish fashion to confront collectively these challenges? An even more provocative question asks whether most of these challenges *really require* a "new world order," for which nations eschew nationalism to form supranational bodies to deal with crises. Classical economics rests on the principle that, when markets function properly, the uncoordinated actions of self-interested agents result in an efficient outcome, from which no one can be made better off without making someone else worse off. Roughly speaking, the selfish pursuit of one's well-being promotes an optimum outcome. Can this analogy be applied to the international level, so that the self-interested pursuits of a nation's well-being will lead to a global optimum? As shown below, market failures can spell difficulties for these principles at *both* the national and international levels, and it is these market failures that are behind many of the crises confronting the world today. But the existence of market failures does not necessarily mean that nations must form governments beyond the national level – that is, supranational governments – to confront these challenges successfully. At times, the proper incentives exist

1

to act to avert disaster; at other times, these incentives can be fostered without the need for tight federations of nations.

To illustrate the kinds of paradoxes that self-interested pursuits can pose for the welfare of the whole, I borrow an example from Richard Dawkins, the famed sociobiologist,[1] who inquires why trees are so tall in rain forests. As trees seek sunlight to preserve their species, they grow ever higher to vie with neighboring trees. The end result is the expenditure of energies that could be preserved if this natural competition could be restrained. An apt analogy is opposing alliances, locked in an arms race in an attempt to promote security through weapon acquisition. As arsenal upgrades are matched, the alliances grow weaker economically, but with no true gain in security. The resulting economic toll can be great, as the end of the Cold War has revealed. Another case involves nations' efforts to become more developed so as to raise their standard of living and that of their children. When the environmental consequences of this development are considered along with the economic gains, the net result may be a reduced living standard. Yet another example concerns a trade war in which nations impose ever more restrictive trade practices on one another in an attempt to gain a trade advantage. In the end, both nations not only fail to gain an advantage, but also hurt themselves in the process.

SOME CHALLENGES

In today's world, potential crises of both a regional and a global nature abound and stem from diverse sources. Nevertheless, these exigencies share a common factor: self-interested pursuits that have unintended negative consequences for others. For global warming, the actions of individuals to keep warm, to feed themselves, and to produce goods and services add to the atmospheric accumulation of greenhouse gases, most especially carbon dioxide. Keeping this problem from worsening in the decades to come, in light of population projections and growth scenarios for the developing world, may require coordinated actions on an unprecedented global scale. The burning of fossil fuels by power plants also releases sulfur di-

1. See Dawkins (1995).

oxide, which combines with water vapor to form acid rain and fog. As a consequence, acid precipitation poses transnational regional threats to lakes, rivers, forests, and manmade structures. Another potential crisis involves tropical deforestation, which has negative impacts on biodiversity and global warming. Tropical deforestation has been brought about, in part, by forest cultivators who have cleared vast tracts in order to scrape together a living. Yet another crisis concerns the release of chlorofluorocarbons (CFCs) that have depleted the stratospheric ozone shield, which absorbs much of the ultraviolet radiation of the sun. This absorptive shield protects humans and other organisms from skin cancers and other harmful consequences.

The growth of population and the drive toward development in the less developed countries (LDCs) will surely exacerbate some of these problems. In mid-1994, the world population stood at 5.6 billion with 1.2 billion in the developed countries and 4.4 billion in the LDCs.[2] During 1990–5, average annual growth of population was 0.5% in the former and 2.0% in the latter. Annual increases in world population are projected to be 94 million people until 1997; thereafter, over 90 million people are anticipated to be added yearly until well into the twenty-first century. Since much of this growth will be in the LDCs, even greater demands on the tropical forests, the atmosphere, the soils, and the watersheds are expected as these people attempt to survive. Pressures will be placed on already overcrowded cities as people leave rural areas for the promise of a better life. Africa and Asia will experience the greatest population and urban increases. The possible impact on global warming and acid rain can, perhaps, be appreciated by contemplating projected annual energy demand increases of 5–7% for the LDCs, as compared to 2–3% elsewhere. Thus, the greatest pressures on the environment will come from those countries where growth is essential to support an expanding population. In these countries, options are more limited for improving environmental quality unless living standards are increased sufficiently.

Not all global contingencies are tied to the environment or pressures brought by population growth on the environment. Despite

---

2. The facts in this paragraph come from the United Nations (UN) Population Fund (1994, 1–5) and United Nations (1992a).

the end to the Cold War, the world remains a hostile place with many challenges to peace. An obvious threat derives from ethnic crises that could spill over borders and entangle nations within and beyond a region of conflict. Another challenge is posed by the proliferation of nuclear weapons. Nations may not want to rely on the current nuclear powers for security when these powers can easily choose to ignore other nations' pleas when a security crisis arises. Popular opinion may dissuade a nation's leadership from honoring a pledge to protect another nation.

Possession of nuclear weapons may provide a nation with a sense of security and autonomy to pursue its own interests even if these interests are unpopular with the world community. The spread of nuclear weapons to nations harboring bitter animosities may mean that local disputes could escalate to a nuclear conflict. Imagine what the Bosnian conflict or the Iran–Iraq war would have been like if the warring factions had had nuclear bombs. Nuclear proliferation also raises the risk that weapons could land in the hands of terrorists or a rogue state. The possibility of accidental nuclear conflict, in which nations fire nuclear weapons because of a falsely perceived attack, also increases with proliferation. As rival nuclear powers are in closer proximity, the window shortens during which time a perceived attack must be characterized as real or imagined, and, in the former case, a retaliatory response taken.

Future wars increasingly may be fought over resources. In 1991, the Gulf War was due, in large part, to a dispute between Iraq and Kuwait over the ownership of an oil pool lying beneath the territories of both nations. Matters were made worse when Iraq perceived Kuwait as pumping and selling this oil at rates that exceeded agreed-upon Organization of Petroleum Exporting Countries (OPEC) quotas. As countries of OPEC surpassed quotas, their actions lowered the world price of oil, thus hurting all OPEC members. Thus, Iraq held Kuwait responsible for two grievances – depleting the disputed oil pool and reducing world oil prices. The rights to water may be the flashpoint to the next conflict in the Middle East and other trouble spots.

Borders made secure by armies may still be breached by pollutants that can cause environmental and human damages. A sufficiently lethal release of pollutants may cause enough devastation in a neighboring nation that the latter resorts to armed conflict to end the pollution threat. Pollution poses a real threat to lives and property. Simply asking another nation to stop its polluting activities may not be effective if the polluter anticipates significant costs from doing so. As the pollution example demonstrates, modern threats to security are complex and assume myriad forms; thus, the notion of security needs to be rethought.

Transnational terrorism poses another security concern. Terrorism is the premeditated use, or threat of use, of violence to achieve a political goal through intimidation or fear. The presence of a political objective is essential; threats of violence used to extort money with no underlying political motive do not constitute acts of terrorism. To create an atmosphere of fear and vulnerability, terrorists make their attacks appear to be random so that risks are perceived widely. Terrorism is not a new phenomenon. Consider the following incident: A time bomb explodes on Wall Street killing thirty-four, injuring over two hundred people, and causing millions of dollars in damages. Is this tomorrow's headlines? In fact, a TNT bomb planted in an unattended horse-drawn wagon did have these consequences on 16 September 1920 and represented the worst terrorist attack on US soil until the Oklahoma City bombing of the Alfred P. Murrah building on 19 April 1995. Since the late 1960s, terrorism differs from that of the past in one major way: the greater prevalence of transnational terrorism.[3] When a terrorist attack in one country involves victims, targets, institutions, governments, or citizens of another country, terrorism assumes a *transnational* character.

Why does terrorism present a significant threat to the world today? Consider the Unabomber's threat to blow up a commercial airplane leaving Los Angeles International Airport during the July Fourth weekend in 1995. Given the Unabomber's track record – seventeen years of successful bombings – the authorities had to take the claim seriously. The consequences were flight delays, disruption of the mail, and heightened anxiety, caused by a single individual who wanted to publicize his alleged grievances with a technology-based society. Modern society's dependence on technologically sophisticated infrastructure means that individuals or nations willing to resort to terrorism can create havoc. The sarin attack and sub-

3. On patterns of terrorism, see Mickolus (1980), Mickolus, Sandler, and Murdock (1989), and US Department of State (1994). For conceptual issues, definitions, and analysis, consult Wilkinson (1986) and Wilkinson and Stewart (1987).

sequent incidents on Tokyo subways underscore this vulnerability. Other high-profile terrorist events include the downing of Pan Am Flight 103 on 21 December 1988, the bombing of the World Trade Center on 26 February 1993, and the bombing of the US Marine barracks in Beirut on 23 October 1983.

Transnational terrorism is particularly attractive to its perpetrators, because few resources are needed to capture the world's attention. The cloak of secrecy can allow nations to employ or sponsor terrorism at relatively small costs in an attempt to destabilize an enemy without necessarily being tied to the act. The state sponsor's anonymity means that it can escape the consequences of retaliation. Terrorism is also attractive because it is so difficult to protect against – potential targets are ubiquitous. Even when effective means are developed to protect against one type of attack, terrorists have merely substituted their operations to an alternative less-protected target.[4] Unfortunately, terrorism often provides an advantage to the weak in their confrontation with the state. This advantage derives from the terrorists' use of secrecy and the minimal resources needed to attack so as to impose large political, economic, and human costs on a better-equipped adversary, who must guard all possible targets.

Nature also presents crises to the global community. Arguably, the most challenging of these crises is the appearance of new diseases, resistant to standard treatments. Even here, self-interested actions may have exacerbated the problem. The overuse of antibiotics may be behind the rapid appearance of antibiotic-resistant disease strains. Greater penetration of human activities by cultivators into the rain forests may be exposing humans to long-hidden viruses, such as Ebola and AIDS.

Economics also presents its own potential crisis from an ever-increasing income disparity among the world's nations. This disparity means that the poor nations will have to turn more often to the rich for assistance in coping with all forms of crises. Without this assistance, diseases that gain a foothold in the poor nations, where populations are more susceptible, can spread worldwide. The same may be true of revolutions. Environmental degradation in the

---

4. This transference or substitution is shown statistically for a host of protective measures by Enders and Sandler (1993). For example, the securing of US embassies coincided with morer assassinations and attacks against US officials when these people were in less-secured places.

poorer countries, which may not have the means to invest in newer, cleaner technologies, will spill over to the developed world.

THE ROLE OF TECHNOLOGY

Technology has become a two-edged sword in which beneficial aspects are often associated with potentially negative consequences that are tied to some of the global contingencies. A case in point corresponds to the information revolution in which vast amounts of data can be stored, organized, and retrieved readily. Computer networking allows individuals to interact and share this stored information. These same networks and information systems are vulnerable to computer viruses and other intruders that can destroy information or gain access to sensitive documents. Scanners can, for example, identify passwords sent over the Internet. Once a password is discovered, a spy program can be used to enter computer files to retrieve confidential files. Air travel promotes commercial, social, and other ties worldwide but is vulnerable to terrorists' skyjackings and bombings. A plane passenger can carry a deadly virus to cities near and far. During the Cold War era, nuclear technology was used to create weapons of mass destruction that kept peace between the superpowers. Now these same weapons are in danger of falling into the hands of terrorists or into the arsenal of a dictator bent on obtaining political concessions through blackmail. Technology applied to agriculture has created the Green Revolution, which has greatly increased crop yields but at the cost of insidious pollutants that befouled the air, the atmosphere, rivers, lakes, and groundwater. In industry, new chemical compounds – CFCs, halons, PCBs – have been applied in novel ways, but with dire consequences to the environment.

Advancements in communications mean that scientific and medical breakthroughs can be disseminated worldwide in record time. Such dissemination means that nations can save on research and development (R & D) expenditures by relying on the discoveries of others. This reliance weakens the incentives for engaging in basic research. If, in fact, every nation were to depend or "free ride" on the R & D findings of others, there would be no one engaging in this activity. Modern communication networks transmit news events worldwide. This media exposure may entice terrorists to engage in acts of transnational significance in the hope of making their grievances known to the world. Once broadcast by the media, novel forms of attack are often copied by others, thus leading to a contagion of similar attacks.

Despite its negative influences, technology has brought us the means to monitor the earth and its atmosphere in ways never dreamt possible. Thus, remote-sensing satellites and other scientific-measurement devices have identified holes in the stratospheric ozone layer at the higher latitudes, north and south. Atmospheric observatories atop Mauna Loa on the island of Hawaii assess the dispersion and accumulation of carbon dioxide, sulfur dioxide, and other atmospheric pollutants. On a regional basis, the Cooperative Programme for Monitoring and Evaluation of the Long-Range Transmission of Air Pollutants in Europe keeps track of transboundary air pollutants (sulfur and nitrogen oxides) based on data collected at various sites. The possible spread of deserts (i.e., desertification) and the loss of forests can be monitored with satellite-generated surveys. As humankind employs these monitoring technologies to ascertain the health of the planet, stresses on the biosphere that could lead to irreversible ecological disasters can be identified so that action can be taken.

Because nations are more willing to cooperate with one another when they are convinced that disaster is imminent, these monitoring devices can play a crucial role in averting disaster by indicating the consequences of inaction. Recall the alien attack scenario of the Preface. If nations can be convinced that their collective response is needed to avert catastrophe, then action can be expected. With these monitoring devices deployed, even subtle changes can be detected and made public. A common scenario for addressing a potential transnational crisis is to come to an agreement or convention that expresses a collective concern and that mandates further study. Monitoring technologies can then provide the data needed to determine the appropriate response. When, for example, nations were provided in 1985 with indisputable evidence that the ozone layer was thinning, they became willing to take actions to curb CFC emissions (see Chapter 4). As monitoring devices made clear that the thinning was worsening at a rate faster than originally predicted, nations augmented their actions. Gaining knowledge of the problem is one of the most effective motivators to cooperation; but, as in the alien scenario, it is essential that this information becomes available and is believed when action can still avert disaster.

MARKETS AND MARKET FAILURES

In a well-functioning market economy in which every activity has a price, property rights are defined and protected, competition is rigorous, and market information is complete, the unfettered pursuit of self-interest by individuals leads by an "invisible hand" to an efficient outcome. In such an ideal economy, Adam Smith and other classical economists recognized the need for government intervention in just four areas: defense, a justice system, education, and infrastructure. Infrastructure includes the social capital that provides for the functioning of markets for private exchange. Roads, communication networks, sewage treatment, and police are examples of this infrastructure.

Challenges at a national, regional, or global level can often be traced to a market failure in which participants' self-promoting actions do not achieve an efficient outcome, so that it is possible to increase the welfare of one or more individuals without harming someone else's welfare. The presence of market failures means that some form of intervention on a collective basis among the economic agents *may* be needed. Intervention may not be required when the concerned parties are prepared to negotiate an agreement without the presence of an outside authority. In the case of transnational crises, three kinds of market failures are germane.

Market failures can first result from an *externality*, which is an interdependency among two or more individuals or nations that is not taken into account by a market transaction. Although the term sounds esoteric, its concept is not. An apt example is the burning of leaves during the fall. This practice is an inexpensive means of disposing of yard waste but imposes costs on neighbors as their air quality is degraded. Asthma sufferers may experience severe costs; yet, the burners are typically not made to consider these neighborhood costs in their decision. If they were made to consider them, they may pay to have their yard waste disposed of by alternative means. On a transnational level, pollution that is exported to a neighboring state represents an externality. When, for example, electric power generation in one nation releases emissions that result in the deposition of acid rain in a downwind nation, a *transnational externality* or external effect exists. If the emitting nation is not required to compensate its downwind neighbor, then the emitter would naturally have no incentive to curb its polluting activity unless the recipient can retaliate with its own pollutant. From a social welfare viewpoint, too much production is taking place unless the externally imposed costs are included in the producer's operating expense.

Not all external effects are necessarily detrimental to third parties. In the case of scientific breakthroughs or technological innovations, the discovery can benefit the finders and others alike. Without the support of grants or subsidies by private foundations or governments, too little R & D may be undertaken. This anticipated underinvestment may explain why R & D has such high rates of return. In the United States, drug companies have relied on the externality argument to obtain government support to underwrite their R & D for new drugs and to convince the government that high profit rates are warranted to finance a large R & D budget. Many global crises – for example, the transmission of revolutions, the spillover of transnational pollutants, the spread of plagues – are examples of externalities.

Market failures may also be associated with public goods. The term *public good* does not necessarily imply that some government needs to provide the good, although that may be the case. Instead, it means that the good's benefits possess two properties that distinguish these goods from those that can be traded in markets. A public good's benefits can be received by payers and nonpayers alike once the good is provided. The provider cannot, therefore, keep a nonpayer from consuming the good's benefit, and this inability limits incentives on the part of users to finance the good's provision. If, for example, a nation were to clean up a polluted river shared with other nations and then were to request contributions to reimburse cleanup costs, it is likely that these voluntary contributions would be meager. Individuals are anticipated to take a free ride on the efforts of the providers. Next consider defense. If defense were not supported by taxes but by citizens' generosity, defense budgets would be very small indeed.

A second property of a public good is that its benefits are nonrival;

that is, one individual's consumption of the good does not detract, in the slightest, from the consumption opportunities still available to others from the same unit of the good. Again consider pollution cleanup. The cleansing of a river can be enjoyed by all nations along its banks; one nation's enjoyment of the cleaner river does not diminish the same benefits available to others. Analogously, activities that degrade the environment are public bads whose harms are non-rival among recipients and experienced by anyone who depends on the environmental asset. For the global community, a loss in biodiversity or the thinning of the ozone shield represents a public bad whose consequences spread to the ends of the earth regardless of whose action caused these outcomes.

A third source of market failures may stem from *property rights* that are either undefined or owned in common with unrestricted or open access. Markets, which allow for the voluntary exchange of property rights, can only operate if these rights are recognized and protected. When property rights are not recognized, there is little incentive to acquire a particular good. Suppose that a government decrees that the ownership of automobiles is only recognized and protected for the first ride from the dealership; thereafter, anyone can legally use any car he or she comes upon.[5] Once not in use, a car is then fair game for anyone needing transportation. Entrepreneurs who market devices for breaking into cars would do a booming business, while new car sales would plummet. The stock of cars would deteriorate rapidly, since there would be little gain from maintenance. The market for new cars would soon disappear. The landscape would be littered with broken-down cars with empty gas tanks.

Common ownership, *when coupled with open access*, would also lead to wasteful exploitation in which a user ignores the effects of his or her action on others. Open access to the commonly owned resource is a crucial ingredient of waste and inefficiency. Common-property institutions have developed that succeed in managing resources,[6] provided that the owners can limit exploitation to those

5. This example derives from Demsetz (1964). On property rights, also see Pejovich (1990).
6. Ostrom (1990) provides a fascinating treatment of common-property institutions. She shows that common-property arrangements can manage a resource efficiency under a wide variety of circumstances. She, however, recognizes that access must be restricted. Also, see a recent treatment in Cornes and Sandler (1996, 277–89).

within the group who abide by the rules. Many of the earth's greatest treasures – its oceans, its atmosphere, its groundwater, its fisheries – are owned in common *with open access* and, thus, are subject to wasteful exploitation. In many locations, the world's fisheries are an apt case. Because of the application of advanced technologies – satellite-position tracking, radar, sonar – and overharvesting, many fish species have had their populations reduced drastically. In some cases, some species can no longer be harvested commercially. The result of this overharvesting is shortsighted when short-run profits lead to long-run losses as a species is driven to extinction.

The earth's open-access common-property assets are under siege from industrial activities worldwide, resulting in a number of the global exigencies mentioned earlier. Although these assets have been threatened since the start of the industrial revolution, their plight appears more dire today owing to a number of factors. First, nations only acquired the means to monitor these stresses recently, so that we are now more aware of the problem. Second, many of these stresses – for example, atmospheric carbon dioxide – accumulate over time with earlier releases. Stocks of atmospheric pollutants, such as carbon dioxide, have now surpassed thresholds beyond which further accumulations may affect such things as the severity of hurricanes, the levels of the seas, or the pattern of rainfall. Third, population growth has increased these environmental demands and will continue to increase them into the foreseeable future. The poorer countries look to the past actions of the developed countries as a guide for development. These past pathways toward riches have not been paved in kindness to the environment. Any advice to the LDCs from the developed countries to limit economic expansion so as to protect the environment for the good of humanity appears hypocritical.

STANDARD REMEDIES

When market failures occur at the national level, the government is expected to regulate externalities, to provide public goods, to assign and enforce property rights, and to redistribute income. Governments may impose taxes or limits on some forms of pollutants to control externalities. Public goods are provided and financed through taxes. Consider the provision of an interstate highway system, which is supported by gasoline taxes, tire excise taxes, general taxes, and, in some instances, tolls. Public goods, such as national defense or pollution cleanup, are financed by general taxes. Modern economies depend on national and local governments for a host of public goods that would not necessarily be provided by individual actions, but are nevertheless needed. Property rights are protected by police and adjudicated in the courts. For public lands, property rights are granted through franchise as in the case of mineral rights. Property rights to the electromagnetic spectrum, a common property resource, are assigned by government agencies. Income redistribution is typically engineered through progressive income taxes, which take a higher percent of income from the rich, and by transfer payments or gifts.

Standard remedies for addressing market failures face insurmountable challenges if they were applied beyond the nation-state. Nations are loathe to empower a supranational body with the authority to collect taxes to regulate transnational externalities, to provide international public goods, to assign property rights, or to redistribute income. For starters, supranational governments do not currently exist. The European Union (EU) comes the closest to this ideal, but many obstacles remain to be overcome if a truly united Europe is to evolve. Recent experience is more consistent with the breakup of nations than the conglomeration of nations into larger decision-making units. Nations fiercely protect their autonomy despite some benefits from doing otherwise.

To date, the international judicial system has not been effective. At times, neighboring countries have allowed the World Court to hear a case and then have abided by the decision as in the *Trail Smelter* case concerning a transboundary pollution problem between Canada and the United States. But this is the exception rather than the rule. In general, the international judicial system is not a remedy to control international disputes and market failures, because it is virtually powerless to impose its decisions on nations. In fact, cases can be only heard provided the nations or parties agree to go to court. Since there is no recognized authority to enforce the Court's judgments, the Court must rely on the losing party to carry out the judgment, no matter how adverse. This is a bit much to expect. Libya's continued refusal to hand over two suspected terrorists to stand trial for their alleged bombing of Pan Am Flight 103 underscores the Court's lack of power. This same lack of power applies to the Court's ability to influence transboundary pollution. For example, the World Court is not equipped with the means to adjudicate in the global warming problem, which involves literally every country on earth.

COLLECTIVE ACTION AT THE SUPRANATIONAL LEVEL

The global community needs to be inventive in finding means that address global crises, while recognizing the persistence of the nation-state. Some form of collective action is needed. Transnational collective action refers to activities that require the coordination of efforts by two or more nations.[7] In essence, collective action involves group efforts meant to further the interests or well-being of the participants.

Can collective action be achieved to avert global crises, so that the world does not experience large-scale collapses of vital ecosystems, the escalation of terrorist threats, or the spread of world conflict? Far from being another book of prophetic doom, this book is intended to show that, although some crises will become worse before they improve, many crises can be averted by some form of collective action, provided that proper attention is paid to the incentives of the participants. Successful collective action requires that all participants perceive a net benefit. This simple realization is often forgotten. Consider the Law of the Seas Treaty. A provision of this treaty required states that mined the deep seabeds to pay a significant share of their revenue to the LDCs as an income redistribution device. Since the United States had nothing to gain and much to lose from this provision, the United States, a key player, refused to sign the treaty. Collective-action scenarios and solutions are explored here with a sense of realism in terms of what can be achieved given the likely institutions and expected behavior of nations. Thus, a vision of a global government unselfishly pursuing the good of humanity, although an admirable ideal, is not considered. Nations

---

7. The seminal work on collective action is Mancur Olson's (1965) *The Logic of Collective Action*. Updated treatments can be found in Hardin (1982) and Sandler (1992).

and their leadership are the likely agents in the foreseeable future when it comes to confronting global challenges. And thus they serve as our basic decision makers or agents.

GLOBAL AND REGIONAL TREATIES

Throughout the last half century, countries have relied on treaties as a means to achieve collective action. In Table 1.1, some of the key environmental treaties and conventions since 1959 are listed. An abbreviated, but descriptive, title of each treaty is given along with the date of formulation, the place(s), and the number of participating nations. The date of formulation is not the same as that on which the treaty takes effect. The latter is always after the drafting: For example, the Montreal Protocol protecting the ozone layer was drafted on 16 September 1987 but did not enter into force until 1 January 1989.

Have these treaties really improved the environment and averted disaster? The answer is mixed. Many of the treaties are more symbolic than substantive. For example, the Climate Change Convention pledged the nations to be concerned about global warming. It contains a nonbinding commitment from the developed countries, but not from the LDCs, to achieve 1990 CO_2 emission levels by the year 2000. The treaty is weak, since it contains no enforcement mechanisms except for world opinion. This opinion is unlikely to be much of a deterrent, especially because *most* developed countries have done little to meet the target (see Chapter 4). Furthermore, the commitment was stated more as an aim than a hard-and-fast target. As a general rule, the smaller the actual commitment, the larger the set of participants. A noteworthy exception to this general rule is the Montreal Protocol, which now includes over 150 nations and which commits its ratifiers to real cutbacks in the production and consumption of CFCs. All significant CFC producer and consumer nations were included at the outset, and this bolstered the Protocol's effectiveness. On a regional basis, the Helsinki Protocol (1985) to the Long-Range Transboundary Air Pollution Convention restricts sulfur emissions in Europe, while the Sofia Protocol (1988) to the same convention restricts nitrogen oxide emissions. For many of the participants,

Table 1.1. *Major environmental treaties and conventions*

Treaty or convention	Date formulated[a]	Place	Number of signatories and ratifiers
Antarctic Treaty	1959	Washington, DC	39
Nuclear Test Ban in the Atmosphere, Outer Space, and under Water	1963	Moscow	120
Wetlands of International Importance	1971	Ramsar, Iran	84
Prohibition of Biological and Toxin Weapons	1972	London, Moscow, Washington, DC	122
Protection of World Cultural and Natural Heritage	1972	Paris	120
Prevention of Marine Pollution by Dumping	1972	London, Mexico City, Moscow, Washington, DC	73
International Trade in Endangered Species	1973	Washington, DC	111
Prevention of Pollution from Ships	1978	London	65
Transboundary Air Pollution (Europe)[b]	1979	Geneva	29
Conservation of Migratory Species	1979	Bonn	47
Conservation of Antarctic Marine Life	1980	Canberra	27
UN Law of the Sea	1982	Montego Bay, Jamaica	126

these two protocols merely codified reductions that the parties had already accomplished independently or were soon to achieve (see Chapter 4). A primary benefit, derived from these collective agreements, was the pressure that the majority exerted on other European nations to follow their example. A secondary benefit was to demonstrate that collective agreements at the transnational level could be attained within a system that preserves the nation-state. It remains to be seen to what extent these successful treaties can serve as a blueprint for other global crises, such as global warming, where participation has much greater costs in terms of economic losses. Much of the book's analysis will be focused on examining this and related issues.

Table 1.1. *Major environmental treaties and conventions*

Treaty or convention	Date formulated[a]	Place	Number of signatories and ratifiers
Vienna Convention Protecting the Ozone Layer	1985	Vienna	103
Early Notification of Nuclear Accident	1986	Vienna	80
Assistance for a Nuclear Accident	1986	Vienna	82
Montreal Protocol on the Ozone Layer[c]	1987	Montreal	96
Control of Transboundary Hazardous Waste Movement	1989	Basel	58
Convention on Biological Diversity	1992	Nairobi	140
Convention of Climate Change	1993	New York	143

[a] The date formulated does not correspond to the date on which the treaty goes into effect.
[b] Four protocols putting limits on emissions were subsequently formulated to curb sulfur and nitrogen oxide emissions. Tough limits on sulfur emissions have been incorporated in the 1994 Oslo Protocol to strengthen the Helsinki Protocol (see Chapters 4 and 5).
[c] Future protocols mandated the elimination of emissions by 2000.
Source: World Resources Institute (1992, tables 25.1 and 25.2); World Resources Institute (1994, tables 24.1 and 24.2).

Nations have also resorted to treaties to outlaw some forms of terrorism. In Table 1.2, selected international treaties and conventions concerning transnational terrorism are listed. Although the international community was quick to respond to the escalation of transnational terrorism in the late 1960s by drafting and signing these treaties, forbidden acts – skyjackings, kidnappings, attacks against diplomats – continued at more or less the same pace after the institution of these conventions and resolutions. In fact, sophisticated statistical analysis indicates that these treaties had no effect whatsoever on the number of events that they sought to reduce (see Chapter 4).[8] Treaties have been less effective in curbing interna-

8. See Enders, Sandler, and Cauley (1990).

Table 1.2. *Selected international treaties and conventions relating to terrorism*

Treaty or convention	Date drafted	Place
Convention on the Suppression of Unlawful Seizure of Aircraft	16 Dec. 1970	The Hague
Convention on the Suppression of Unlawful Acts against the Safety of Civil Aviation (Sabotage)	23 Sept. 1971	Montreal
Convention on the Prevention and Punishment of Crimes against Internationally Protected Persons	14 Dec. 1973	UN, New York
European Convention on the Suppression of Terrorism	27 Jan. 1977	Strasbourg
UN General Assembly Resolution 2551: Hijacking	12 Dec. 1969	UN, New York
UN General Assembly Resolution 32/148: Hostage Taking	16 Dec. 1977	UN, New York
UN Security Council Resolution 286: Hijacking	9 Sept. 1970	UN, New York

Source: Alexander, Browne, and Nanes (1979). Complete texts for these treaties are contained in this source.

tional terrorism than in ameliorating environmental pollution. Unlike environmental treaties, many of the key players – the nations that sponsored terrorism – did not participate. Furthermore, the terrorists themselves were neither party to the treaty nor under the control of treaty nations. In contrast, polluting firms could be placed under state control: For the Helsinki Protocol on sulfur emissions, the major polluters were state-owned or state-regulated power-generating plants. Antiterrorism treaties never provided a means for enforcing their provisions. If an infraction occurred, it was up to the victim state to take appropriate steps – for example, the United States' retaliatory raid against Libya in April 1986. Instances arose in which countries reneged on their treaty pledge or, worse yet, supported terrorists covertly.

The failure of terrorism treaties to have any real impact means that alternative forms of international collective action are needed for addressing transnational terrorism. To date, nations have relied on their own measures to thwart terrorism through intelligence gathering, retribution attacks, protective measures, and rigorous prosecution of suspected terrorists. This has led to an inefficient system in which nations duplicate one another's actions and work at cross-purposes in trying to deflect the attack elsewhere rather than deterring the attack altogether. The differing experiences associated with environmental and terrorism treaties indicate a common theme throughout this book – the inability to use what works for one kind of global crisis on another kind of global crisis.

SOME KEY ISSUES

At a transnational level, effective action can be fostered if the participants' incentives are kept in mind. Take the case of sulfur emissions that fall as acid rain or that degrade ambient air quality. Most countries are motivated to control polluters, because the lion's share of their emissions are not exported to downwind neighbors but, instead, befoul the nation's own soil, lakes, and air (Chapter 4). Nations are, thus, more willing to form collectives to do something and to pressure others to do something. There is little need to expend scarce resources in trying to bring about a collective response – it will come about naturally. Global warming, however, presents an entirely different scenario, insofar as local consequences of a nation's greenhouse emissions are not discernible from global consequences. Moreover, from a nation's viewpoint, the benefits of curbing its emissions are swamped by the associated costs. Each nation wants to free ride on the efforts of others. Global warming is the type of problem where efforts to bring about effective collective action are sorely needed.

The interrelationship among global challenges is another crucial consideration when determining the proper course of action.[9] For example, CFC emissions, which deplete the ozone layer, also contribute to global warming, while sulfur emissions, which cause acid rain, increase the reflective ability of clouds, thus reducing global warming. Even the appearance of some deadly viruses may be traced to population pressures that have led to the destruction of rain forests where these viruses lie in wait. Given these and other interrelationships, the incentives behind a number of global exigencies must be addressed simultaneously if effective collective responses are to be found.

9. Interrelationships among pending environmental crises are discussed in Myers (1992a) and Sandler and Sargent (1995).

Another crucial interrelationship concerns the impact that the increased inequality among the rich and poor nations will have on the global community's ability to address challenges. Between 1960 and 1991, the distribution of income among nations has become markedly more unequal, despite phenomenal growth displayed by some developing nations. In 1991, the richest 20% of nations received 85% of the world income, up from 70% in 1960; the poorest 20% received just 1.4% of this income, down from 2.3% in 1960.[10] This increased inequality has mixed implications for diverting global disasters, as shown in Chapter 7. Greater inequality can lead to revolutions, plagues, and pollutants that disperse globally. Such negative outcomes are well known, but less obvious positive outcomes may arise.

For some challenges, the greatest or best effort, not the cumulative effort, determines the provision of a public good that benefits the world community. Consider the curing of AIDS or the finding of a vaccine against Ebola. It matters not who finds the cure or vaccine first, since, once it is discovered, all nations can profit. These kinds of breakthroughs require huge resource allocations that only the richest nations can afford to support. In such cases, skewed income distributions provide these countries with the means for carrying on these research efforts. Many of the most frightening global crises have solutions that depend on a best effort (see Chapters 2, 3, and 7). By solving or alleviating such crises, the rich will, partly, redistribute their wealth through a free ride for the poorer countries. Already the Center for Disease Control in Atlanta, Georgia, is providing a free ride to the world in tracking and identifying new diseases and the reappearance of old ones. The United States assumes this role because of a concern for its own citizens; but everyone benefits from these actions.

Economic growth may provide the best means for curbing population growth, since improvements in education, health, and living standards are typically associated with reduced fertility rates and less population growth. Moreover, a society's value and demands for the environment appear to respond positively to increased income. Higher per-capita income levels allow a nation's people to turn their attention to protecting the environment for their children. It is dif-

---

10. For an in-depth study of the world's income distribution, see UN Development Programme (1992, 1994).

ficult to pay much heed to the environment when economic growth is needed to ensure one's survival. Advanced countries, such as the United States, allocate vast sums to supporting the environment.

Many of the exigencies confronting the planet today are of an intergenerational character, since the actions of one generation affect or constrain the choices of subsequent generations. Biodiversity, global warming, ozone depletion, nuclear waste containment, and space exploration are but a few examples. For example, the decision to pursue nuclear-fission power meant that future generations would have to dispose of highly radioactive wastes, whose potentially harmful effects last hundreds of thousands of years. Short-run solutions to such problems, while improving the well-being of the current generation, may limit choices and even impoverish future generations. Decisions are needed to induce cooperation among nations in a sufficiently farsighted fashion to adjust for the impact on subsequent generations (see Chapters 3 and 5).

To elicit cooperation among nations, certain preconditions must be present. There must be reasonable certainty that action is needed to avert catastrophic consequences. Nations must also perceive a net benefit from their cooperation. If the nations whose actions are most responsible for the crisis assume a leadership role, then this, too, fosters collective action. Even the need for a threshold effort may be conducive to achieving a collective response among a minimal-sized coalition. Challenges with significant localized influences are the easiest to confront. These and other issues are considered in Chapters 4 and 5, where designing effective collective responses is addressed. Evolutionary aspects of collective action are considered in Chapter 6, where a nation's response to the actions of other nations is examined over time.

PURPOSE OF THE BOOK

The essential purpose of this book is to use modern tools and concepts of economics to put global and regional challenges into perspective. This book is meant to be provocative in the hope of stimulating discussion and thought on what the world faces in terms of challenges and what can be done to avert any resulting crises. An essential purpose is to identify a host of potential crises and their causes, while being careful to delineate differences and similarities among them. Since an economic way of thinking is employed, incentives of the participants are a primary concern. Nations are assumed to behave to further their own interests, not the good of the world. If world welfare is to be furthered by a collective response, then there must be sufficient gains in such actions to motivate the participants. I am not interested in drawing a utopian ideal in which a benevolent world achieves the greatest good for current and future generations, since such scenarios are not realistic. Instead, I am concerned with how nations are likely to confront the challenges on the horizon and whether institutions could be tailored to their selfish behavior to avert disaster. The task at hand is much more difficult than putting forward an ideal, but unobtainable, blueprint for global harmony – some idyllic scene worthy of the greatest Baroque masters. If nations and individuals acted with the interests of others in mind, then the world would not be challenged by the potential crises of today.

PLAN OF THE BOOK

The remainder of the book contains seven chapters. In Chapter 2, essential concepts and tools are presented that are used throughout the book to conceptualize the study of global crises. Elementary concepts of game theory and collective action are addressed. This presentation is at a basic level; intuition and understanding are emphasized. Intergenerational aspects are presented in Chapter 3 and are among the most complex and interesting factors connected to today's challenges, since the consequences of today's actions are often irreversible for the foreseeable future. A host of different global problems – tropical deforestation, population growth, global warming, ozone depletion, acid rain, transnational terrorism, peacekeeping – are investigated in Chapter 4. The design of institutional structures for addressing transnational problems is addressed in Chapter 5. In Chapter 6, evolutionary issues are examined as to whether nations will change with time so as to coordinate better their actions. The effects of inequality among nations are studied in Chapter 7 to determine the effects of growing inequality among nations on global challenges. Chapter 8 contains key conclusions.

2   Global interdependencies: Basic tools and principles

Markets are heralded as effective means for coordinating production and exchange with minimal interference on the part of government. If, for example, there is a sudden increased demand for rocket scientists, then today's rocket scientists will begin to receive higher salaries, which will transmit a signal to others to acquire the requisite training as earnings are now greater compared to other similarly skilled professionals. In a well-functioning market economy, high wages and/or profits direct resources and efforts to what society values highly relative to its costs. As mentioned earlier, markets will not function properly when property rights are not defined or protected, or else external effects and/or public goods are present. In these situations, incentives are often perverse so that self-interested actions need not achieve a desirable or efficient assignment of resources.

Consider surface-level ozone in our cities' air caused primarily by automobile emissions of nitrogen oxides (NO_x). Reducing these emissions is a pure public good, since a given cutback is enjoyed by all (nonexcludability applies), no matter who has reduced them. The benefits from this reduction are also nonrival, because one person can breathe the cleaner air without adding NO_x pollutants that would limit another's enjoyment of the improved air quality. It is in your private interests to free ride on the curtailment of others. Suppose that I were to conduct a survey to ascertain what the cleaner air is worth to you so that I could advise a government about its pollution policy. Your response would surely depend on the manner in which the questions are phrased. If the survey convinced you that your response would be unrelated to a later payment demand, you might either exaggerate the gain to convince the government to provide the reduction, or else you might say anything by not taking the survey seriously. If, however, I reframed the questions so that you were convinced that your answers would be used to assign your payments – say, on your electric bill – you might be motivated to understate your payments.[1] In either case, ascertaining the true value of a public good is a difficult task, requiring a good deal of cleverness on the part of the advisor. Without this information, the government would not know how much of the cleanup to provide.

This chapter concerns an in-depth study of the problems involved with market failures and their evaluation. For these failures, a common theme applies: Individual rationality or pursuit of self-interest does *not* typically result in an efficient outcome. Even in well-defined groups, members' rational actions may end in undesirable outcomes or losses for the overall interests of the group.[2] Take the thirteen nations known as the Organization of Petroleum Exporting Countries (OPEC) cartel, which agreed to restrict oil supply in the hope of raising price and sale revenues. Such actions led to a fourfold increase in the price of a barrel of oil during the early 1970s. The world was in a panic with dire predictions of financial ruin for the industrial countries, but this crisis never materialized as incentives worked to the advantage of the world and against OPEC. Each OPEC country had an incentive to increase its individualized profit beyond those of the agreement by exceeding their assigned production limits (quotas) and underpricing other members. As cartel members engaged in these cheating responses, and as high-profit margins led non-OPEC countries to discover new oil fields, the market price for oil plummeted, and oil profits for each cartel country and, hence, for OPEC became less than had the members honored their pledges. Worldwide crises were avoided, and the real price of

1. On these contingent valuation approaches, see the survey books by Cummings, Brookshire, and Schulze (1986) and Mitchell and Carson (1989). There is a large literature, and these are good sources to use to get one's bearings. Also see Smith (1993) for some recent concerns.
2. Olson (1965) and Sandler (1992).

oil (adjusting for general inflation) is not much higher today than at the start of the OPEC-engineered price rise. The individually rational responses of the OPEC members *did not further* the common good of OPEC.

Strategic behavior, whereby your choice depends on that of others, is behind the understanding of market failures and global challenges that are frequently the manifestation of these failures. Interactive choices that cause agents' (people's or nations') payoffs to be interdependent are known as *strategic*.[3] Strategic behavior also involves a *recognition* of this interdependency; that is, one player or agent thinks that the other player will act in a certain way, and so the first player acts on this belief. Moreover, the other player anticipates the first player's belief-based action and, in turn, acts on this belief, and so it goes. The beliefs of the players are like the reflections of an object placed between two facing mirrors – an infinite regress. In the cartel example, each cartel member may break an agreement, because each believes that the others believe that it will break the agreement, so that it too should break the agreement to maximize its net payments.

A second purpose of this chapter is to introduce the reader to some simple, but important, tools of game theory. These tools facilitate an understanding of what drives many of the looming contingencies that challenge nations, regions, and the world today. Since I view game theory as a means of organizing thinking about the underlying motivations of nations and other participants in crises, and not as an end in itself, the treatment here is brief and intended to provide some useful principles.[4] These principles are germane to fathoming not only the anticipated response of participants, but also the manner to redesign institutions or interactions to promote more desirable responses. Just because people or nations may trash the environment, this does not mean that the situation must be accepted. Sometimes simple actions can change the incentive structures so that even self-centered players act in a way that furthers the common good.

3. Dixit and Nalebuff (1991) provide an accessible treatment for strategic thinking and analysis.
4. For a more in-depth treatment, consult Binmore (1992) or other standard sources.

"HE MADE ME DO IT": THE PRISONERS' DILEMMA

A significant number of global crises have the configuration of pay-offs among the players, and therefore the perverse incentive structure, as that of the *Prisoners' Dilemma*. The storyline behind this so-called dilemma goes as follows: Suppose that an armed robbery is committed by two individuals matching the description of two suspects, who were in the vicinity of the holdup. The true culpability of the suspects is immaterial to the game or its anticipated outcome. Shortly after the crime, the suspects are apprehended and brought before a district attorney, who possesses insufficient evidence to convict them unless she can convince at least one of the suspects to confess. Because a handgun turned up during a search of their car's trunk, she has sufficient evidence to convict them of possessing a handgun without a permit, which carries a 1-year jail sentence. Further suppose that the maximum sentence for armed robbery is 9 years. The prisoners are interrogated separately, in which they are offered the following deal: a much-reduced sentence of just 2 months if one of them confesses and the companion does not, or a reduced sentence of 5 years apiece if both confess. In the case of a single confessor, the nonconfessor receives the maximum sentence allowable. Even though the district attorney cannot convict on the robbery charge and it is in the suspects' collective interests not to turn state's evidence, it is likely that both will confess, claiming that the companion made him or her do it. But why?

To explain this answer, I must explore the underlying configuration of payments and its implication for identifying the anticipated strategy or choice of the suspects. In Figure 2.1, the matrix indicates the jail sentences for the four possible strategy combinations of the suspects: no confessions (cell *d*), just prisoner *A* confesses (cell *b*), just prisoner *B* confesses (cell *c*), and both prisoners confess (cell *a*). The first payoff (or prison sentence) in each cell of the matrix is that of prisoner *A*, whereas the second payoff is that of prisoner *B*. The rows denote the two strategies of prisoner *A*, whereas the columns indicate the two strategies of prisoner *B*. Mutual confession is the anticipated outcome, because the payoffs for, say, prisoner *A* are larger for confessing than the *corresponding* payoffs for not confessing. That is, 5 years is a better sentence than 9 years, and 2

B's strategy / A's strategy	Confess	Do not confess
Confess	* a 5 years, 5 years	b 2 months, 9 years
Do not confess	c 9 years, 2 months	d 1 year, 1 year

Figure 2.1. Prisoners' Dilemma.

months is a better sentence than 1 year. If, therefore, prisoner *A* cannot depend on his or her counterpart to keep quiet, then confessing is *A*'s optimal response for dealing with the uncertain reaction of one's counterpart. A strategy, such as confessing, that provides a greater payoff regardless of the other player's action is termed a *dominant strategy* and figures prominently throughout the book.

The mutual confession strategy combination, cell *a* in Figure 2.1, has an asterisk to denote a *Nash* equilibrium, a concept discovered by John Nash, a recipient of the 1994 Nobel Prize in Economics. At a Nash equilibrium, neither player would *unilaterally* alter his or her strategy if given the opportunity: If, at cell *a*, player *A* (or *B*) alone changes to not confessing or withdrawing the confession, then his or her payoff is reduced by the addition of 4 years of prison time. Although playing one's dominant strategy leads to an equilibrium, from which neither player would regret his action *alone*, both players could be made better off if they *both* changed their strategy. Such undesirable equilibria are shown to characterize many global challenges. Can the Prisoners' Dilemma be spotted easily when many payoff combinations are associated even with the simple two-person, two-strategy game? One means for limiting the number of alternative payoff configurations so as to identify the Prisoners' Dilemmas readily is to rank ordinally the payoffs from highest to lowest in terms of desirability, as accomplished in Figure 2.2 for the payoffs of Figure 2.1. The best payoff (a 2-month sentence) is assigned a 4, the next best a 3, and so on. Any two-person payoff matrix of payoffs that possesses the same ordinal payoff pattern as Figure 2.2 is a Prisoners' Dilemma. All other payoff arrangements – and there

A's strategy \ B's strategy	Confess	Do not confess
Confess	2, 2	4, 1
Do not confess	1, 4	3, 3

Figure 2.2. Ordinal form of Prisoners' Dilemma.

are seventy-seven *other* distinct ordinal alternatives – constitute a different game.

In Figure 2.3 an arms race scenario is depicted for two adversarial nations.[5] Each can limit or escalate its arms expenditures, leading to four strategy combinations: (1) both nations escalate arms acquisition, (2) nation *A* escalates arms acquisition, while nation *B* limits arms, (3) nation *B* escalates arms acquisition, while nation *A* limits arms, and (4) both nations limit arms. The worst scenario is to limit arms when the opponent escalates, thus leaving the disarming nation vulnerable. The next-to-worst payoff occurs when both nations escalate, since the nations' expenditures on weapons do not improve their security vis-à-vis their opponent. The next-to-best payoff applies to mutual disarmament, while the best payoff involves arming when one's opponent disarms. The hypothetical payoffs in Figure 2.3 are consistent with this scenario. If this matrix's payoffs are changed to its ordinal payoff form, then the pattern is the Prisoners' Dilemma with a dominant strategy to escalate arms acquisition, thus resulting in a Nash equilibrium with an arms race. When locked in an arms race, neither nation wants unilaterally to disarm, thus perpetuating a costly deadlock that is difficult to escape, aptly illustrated by the length of the Cold War.

An analogous game situation could characterize two superpowers engaged in espionage activities, especially if each is aware of the other's activities. Expenditures on spying may increase over time, but the nations' security may not really improve. Both nations are

5. Arms races are analyzed in greater detail by Brito and Intriligator (1995) and Sandler and Hartley (1995). Both of these works contain extensive bibliographies on the subject.

A's strategy \ B's strategy	Escalate arms	Limit arms
Escalate arms	* -6, -6	10, -14
Limit arms	-14, 10	4, 4

Figure 2.3. Arms race Prisoners' Dilemma.

likely to be better off if both could agree to stop spying on one another. The honoring of treaties may also fit a Prisoners' Dilemma scenario. Suppose that two nations pledge to retaliate against any country tied to sponsoring a terrorist act directed at the people or property of a treaty signatory. Suppose further that a terrorist event injures the interests of nation A, which calls upon nation B to join it in a retaliatory raid against nation C, suspected of sponsoring the incident. Nation B knows that it would gain much of the retaliatory benefits of nation A's raid, if successful, whether it participates or not. Participation, however, involves costs: putting its commando forces in harm's way and attracting a revenge incident.[6] Thus, nation B may refuse to join in. In an attempt to save face, it may claim that the evidence is unconvincing. Does this sound familiar? The US retaliatory air strike on Libya during the morning of 15 April 1986 was based on alleged evidence linking Libya to the 5 April 1986 bombing of the La Belle Discotheque in West Berlin that killed 3 and injured 231.[7] Sixty-four Americans were among the casualties. Except for Israel and the United Kingdom, other countries distanced themselves from the raid. France went so far as requiring the planes not to fly over its air space, thus significantly complicating and jeopardizing the mission. Treaties concerned with controlling pollution, sharing information, taking military action, and dividing profits may follow Prisoners' Dilemma payoff structures.

The Prisoners' Dilemma may apply to any number of participants

6. There has been much speculation that the downing of Pan Am Flight 103 over Lockerbie, Scotland, on 21 December 1988 was a revenge attack for the Libyan retaliatory raid.
7. On the Libyan raid and the La Belle Discotheque bombing, see Mickolus et al. (1989, 2: 365–7, 373–4). On the effectiveness of the raid, see Enders and Sandler (1993).

that seek a collective response, in which the gain from reneging on one's pledged action can give the defector a short-term advantage over cooperation. For illustrative purposes, consider eight nations whose pollution activities are causing a decrease in every nation's environmental quality. Let these nations contemplate an across-the-board 10% reduction in pollution emissions through, say, a curtailment in production. To simplify the presentation, assume that each nation is identical in size in terms of its polluting activities and that each places the same value on a cleaner environment. Each country must decide whether or not to curb emissions by 10%. Assume that this curtailment in output loses the nation profits of 5, while improving its environment and those of the other seven nations by benefits valued at 3 apiece. That is, a 10% reduction in any nation confers a benefit of 3 *on each and every nation*, so that a public good scenario of nonrivalry and nonexcludability of benefits applies.

In Figure 2.4, the associated game matrix is displayed, in which the columns refer to the actions of the other seven nations, and the rows denote the strategy of the ith representative nation. The payoffs listed in each of sixteen cells are those of nation i, based on its decision to cut pollution or not and the decisions of the other nations. The payoffs in Figure 2.4 are computed as follows. Consider the top row of payoffs, representing nation i's free-rider response when it relies on the pollution-reducing efforts of the other nations. *Each* nation that reduces pollution gives nation i a gain of 3 without any associated costs. If, for example, four nations participate in pollution cutbacks, then nation i gains 12 ($= 4 \times 3$), as indicated. Next consider the bottom row, corresponding to nation i cutting its emissions by 10%. If only nation i cuts emissions, then it receives -2, which equals its benefits of 3 less its curtailment costs (or lost profits) of 5. If, however, another nation also reduces its emissions, then nation i receives 1, which equals its benefits of 6 ($= 2 \times 3$) less its costs of 5. Gross benefits are 6, because the nation's reduction *and* that of another nation provide 3 in benefits apiece. The other net payoffs to nation i in the bottom row are computed in an identical fashion.

Given this payoff pattern, how will nation i or any nation be expected to respond? The payoffs in the top row are always 2 greater than the corresponding payoffs in the bottom row; hence, nation i has a dominant strategy not to reduce emissions. Since nation i is

Number of pollution-reducing nations other than nation i

	0	1	2	3	4	5	6	7
Nation i does not cut pollution by 10%	0	3	6	9	12	15	18	21
Nation i cuts pollution by 10%	−2	1	4	7	10	13	16	19

Figure 2.4. Eight-nation Prisoners' Dilemma.

representative of any of the eight nations in this stylized game, each is expected not to curtail emissions – a classic *n*-person Prisoners' Dilemma applies. The so-called Nash equilibrium has no one reducing their emissions. But how can this scenario be changed? Suppose that an enforcer materializes that punishes any nonparticipant by 3. (Any punishment greater than 2 will work.) This would change the numbers in the top row of Figure 2.4 to -3, 0, 3, 6, and so on. With this change, the bottom row's payoffs are now larger than the corresponding payoffs in the top row. Each nation would comply with the agreement.

This enforcement scenario illustrates the problem plaguing many international agreements or protocols – that is, the absence of an enforcer that removes the gain from reneging on an agreement. The presence of an enforcement mechanism acts like a public good, whose benefits are themselves nonexcludable and nonrival. As such, the institution of such a mechanism poses its own Prisoners' Dilemma.[8] This is well illustrated by the absence of such mechanisms to back up United Nations conventions and resolutions, violated daily. When, for example, North Korea was in violation of the nuclear weapons nonproliferation treaty in 1995, the United States' appeal to the international community to join it to sanction North Korea met with silence. Finally, the United States had to take a tough stance on its own.

Let us step back for a moment and consider more mundane cases of Prisoners' Dilemmas and enforcement possibilities in our own lives. Suppose that you are short of cash and borrow $100 from a friend. Though most people do not attempt to calculate a game matrix of payoffs as to whether or not to reimburse the friend, if you were to make such a calculation, then a Prisoners' Dilemma might apply. Your best option might be to borrow the money and not pay it back, especially if you do not value your friendship more than the loan. In many cases, the loss of friendship acts like an enforcement mechanism by reducing the payoffs from reneging on the loan, so that meeting your payment obligation gives a higher payoff. Next let us ignore friendship by having you borrow the money from a

8. In an interesting paper, Heckatorn (1989) explores free riding with and without the imposition of an enforcement mechanism. Free riding on the enforcement decision is called second-order free riding, while standard free riding is called first-order free riding by Heckatorn.

loan shark. If you do not pay on time, a warning is sent, followed swiftly by an enforcer who might break your nose or worse. Faced with this contingency, most people will pay back the loan. Even if the cost to the loan shark of punishing you outweighs the payment due, it is in his or her long-term interest to do so, because it sends a message to others, who might consider not reimbursing a loan with interest. The Mafia clearly understands these game-theoretic principles.

In other daily examples, enforcement may assume other less drastic, but no less effective, forms. Take a marriage engagement, where the woman has more to lose in many cultures if the pledged vows are not exchanged. The nonrefundable engagement ring, if expensive enough, may change the man's payoffs from reneging on the promise to favoring going through with the marriage in the case of second thoughts.[9] When a person seeks a loan through a commercial bank, collateral serves the role of "enforcer." In short, society has created conventions to circumvent the Prisoners' Dilemma in some exchanges.

Next suppose that a firm pledges to refund your money if you are not satisfied with its product. What keeps the firm from going back on its pledge when you bring the soiled item back and say that you did not like it? The primary enforcer is the importance of the firm's reputation for meeting its commitments. Maintenance of its untarnished reputation means your future business and that of others. Continual interactions, especially in a Prisoners' Dilemma, bring a whole new dimension to the problem. In particular, the short-run gains from reneging on your promise must be weighed against the long-term losses from smaller exchanges or no exchanges whatsoever (also see Chapter 6 for further analysis).

By analogy, these day-to-day instances indicate how nations may also successfully confront Prisoners' Dilemmas. First, nations that have fostered friendships with one another are less likely to perceive there to be gains from reneging on agreements. Trade linkages and other channels of interaction are essential avenues toward world peace and international cooperation, because these linkages make defection on agreements more costly. Isolationists fail to realize that trade generates positive impacts beyond the issue of job creation

---

9. On this engagement example and other fascinating examples, see Schelling (1980).

A's strategy \ B's strategy	Do not Contribute	Contribute
Do not Contribute	* 0, 0	0, −8
Contribute	−8, 0	* 4, 4

Figure 2.5. An Assurance game.

and destruction. Second, repeated interactions and long-standing relationships are supportive of nations passing up the short-run temptation of not executing a commitment. This is true even if the pledge had been made by a previous administration or regime. Third, nations that gain the most in the long term from international agreements may assume the role of an enforcer, as the United States has done in recent years. To maintain this role, the enforcer must see sufficient *long-term* gains from transmitting the right signal to would-be defectors. Fourth, nations might take "hostages," analogous to the engagement ring, to induce compliance. When the United States pledged to retaliate on behalf of Western Europe in case of a nuclear attack during the Cold War, the stationing of well over a half million troops in Europe served as the "hostages" that cemented US interests to European security. The United States' European investments and citizens residing in Western Europe also served as collateral.

OTHER GAMES AND THEIR APPLICABILITY

Even though Prisoners' Dilemmas have become almost synonymous with international relations, many other game structures, whose attributes differ, may apply in some situations. Another game form that proves useful in many applications is that of the Assurance game[10] depicted in Figure 2.5. In the game depicted, each player has two strategies: to contribute one or no unit of the public good. The payoffs depicted derive from a public good contribution scenario *in*

10. Assurance games are discussed by Runge (1984), Sandler (1992), and Sen (1967).

which both players must contribute a unit of the public good before the players receive a benefit of 6 from *each* unit contributed; that is, a minimal cumulative effort of two units must be achieved before benefits flow. To contribute a unit, an individual must pay a cost of 8. If both contribute a unit, then each receives a net payoff of 4, equal to the total benefits of 12 ($= 6 \times 2$), derived from two units, less unit cost of 8. If, however, only a single player contributes, then the contributor expends his costs but receives no benefits, since the threshold effort of two units has not been attained. Moreover, the free rider gets nothing; hence, the payoffs to the players for a single unit are -8 and 0, or 0 and -8, depending on who contributes. Suppose that two nations face an invasion (military or viral) that requires the full efforts of both to turn it back successfully. This scenario would abide by the payoff patterns, but not necessarily the numbers, of Figure 2.5 and, as such, would be an Assurance game. Another case would be two neighboring states battling a forest fire currently confined to only one state, but which may spread to the other state if not contained. Neither state has the resources to contain the blaze alone, but they can put it out together.

The Assurance game differs from a Prisoners' Dilemma in a number of fundamental ways. First, there is no dominant strategy that yields higher payoffs regardless of the other player's strategy. Focus on player A's payoffs for the four strategy combinations in Figure 2.5. This player's contributing payoff of -8 is less than the corresponding payoff of 0 associated with not contributing, while his or her contributing payoff of 4 is greater than the corresponding payoff of 0 associated with not contributing. Thus, neither strategic choice dominates. Second, there is no single Nash equilibrium, since both cells marked with an asterisk are equilibria. In either of these equilibria, neither player would desire to change strategy unilaterally, insofar as $0 > -8$ and $4 > 0$ for both players' payoff comparisons at these equilibria. Third, unlike the Prisoners' Dilemma, contracts are *self-enforcing*, because if one player cooperates (contributes), it is also in the interest of the other player to cooperate (contribute), as $4 > 0$. There is no reason in the Assurance game to gain an advantage by breaking a promise, and, hence, Assurance game structures can be supportive of a cooperative response.

In Figure 2.5, the cooperative response, where both players contribute, has much to recommend it over the noncooperative equilibrium, where neither player contributes. In this regard, the cooperative equilibrium gives everyone a higher payoff than does the noncooperative equilibrium. The greater is the difference between the cooperative and noncooperative payoffs, the more likely it is that the lower right-hand equilibrium will prevail. If in Figure 2.5, the 0 payoffs were all changed to −6, then the contribution equilibrium has a greater attraction, since the relative gains over cooperation failure are greater. Reconsider the forest fire or invasion scenarios where the states or nations must both exert their full efforts to win the battle. Losing the battle is likely to result in a loss consistent with a payoff of −6 that is less than 0 but greater than −8, associated with losing and expending efforts in a lost cause. If, therefore, the consequences of losing are severe enough, the non-contribution equilibrium may not possess any attraction. This is reminiscent of the example in the Preface when nations must unite to turn back an invader. The same kind of collaborative action was motivated during the 1991 Midwest floods in the United States, where threatened property owners and others chose to sandbag rather than free ride. The lesson is clear: The right underlying game can be very conducive to cooperation.

A third important game for analyzing global crises is that of Chicken. This game derives its name from the following tale. Two cars traveling from opposite directions are speeding toward one another down the middle of the road. Neither driver wants to be the first to swerve out of the path of the other oncoming car. If no one swerves (cooperates), then the outcome is disastrous so that mutual-defection (noncooperation) payoffs are the lowest. The best payoff results for the driver who manages to hold his or her ground while forcing the other driver to swerve. The swerver then receives the next-to-worst payoff, owing to embarrassment. If both swerve (cooperate), then the payoffs are below the best but above those associated with swerving first (that is, being chicken) or being in a head-on collision. If the above scenario is put into a game matrix with ordinal payoffs (that is, 4 for best, . . . , 1 for worst), then Figure 2.6 displays the trademark matrix for Chicken.

If Figure 2.6 is contrasted with the ordinal representation of the Prisoners' Dilemma in Figure 2.2, then the essential difference concerns a switching of the 1s with the 2s. This switch implies some important strategic differences between the two games. As for the

A's strategy \ B's strategy	Hold one's Ground	Swerve
Hold one's Ground	1, 1	*a* * 4, 2 *b*
Swerve	* *c* 2, 4	3, 3 *d*

Figure 2.6. Classic Chicken game – ordinal payoffs.

Assurance game, there is no dominant strategy with Chicken, since 2 > 1, but 3 < 4; thus, the strategic choice of the players is uncertain. Additionally, there are two Nash equilibria, highlighted by the asterisks. For each of these equilibria, one driver swerves and one holds the path. Once at one of these equilibria, neither player would want unilaterally to change his or her strategy. That is, consider cell *c* where player *A* receives 2 and player *B* receives 4 as ordinal payoffs. If player *A* could change to holding his or her ground, *given that B* holds his or her ground, then player *A* would go from an ordinal payoff of 2 to that of 1. If, similarly, player *B* could change to swerving, given that player *A* swerves, then player *B*'s ordinal payoff would fall from 4 to 3. Thus, cell *c* is an equilibrium. Unlike the Prisoners' Dilemma where no one cooperates in equilibrium, it is in at least one participant's interest to cooperate. Someone will do something, and, for some global problems, this is enough.

To motivate the relevancy of the Chicken game, I consider a couple of modern potential crises. Suppose that nations of equal strength have massed their troops along their common border over a dispute. Further suppose that each side perceives that war would result in a protracted battle with much death and destruction and no victor. Neither nation wants, however, to be the first to back down. Nevertheless, backing down is not so bad if they both back down and is better than going to war in any case. The best scenario from each nation's viewpoint occurs when it holds its ground and its opponent backs down. The payoff pattern is that of Chicken, and, at least, one nation should ultimately back down. Next consider what would happen if the strength of the adversaries were not equal, as

A's strategy \ B's strategy	Do not Contribute	Contribute
Do not Contribute	a * -5, -5	* b 6, -2
Contribute	* c -2, 6	d 4, 4

Figure 2.7. Chicken game for public goods.

was the case during 1990–1 for Desert Shield prior to the Gulf War. If country A is the United States, then it perceived a better payoff from holding its ground than backing down when Iraq held its ground. Not only did the United States possess air superiority,[11] but also its tanks had twice the targeting range of that of the Iraqi tanks. US tanks could spot and destroy an Iraqi tank prior to the latter even knowing that it was in the enemy's sights. Friendly fire posed one of the greatest dangers of the Gulf War. With unequal players, the stronger player has a dominant strategy to hold its ground even if it means war. In the early morning hours of 16 January 1991, the United States acted on its ultimatum and bombed Baghdad. The outcome of the Gulf War is history – the "mother of all battles" was a rout! Apparently, Saddam Hussein did not view the payoffs as unequal and stood his ground.

As another example of Chicken, consider two nations that face a common pollution threat, whose alleviation or cleanup is a public good, as depicted in Figure 2.7. Unlike the minimal-effort case presented earlier, *each* nation's efforts to remove the pollutant (that is, to contribute) provides 6 in benefits at a cost of 8 to just the provider. If, for example, both nations contribute their full efforts to the public good, each gets a net benefit of 4 ($= 6 \times 2 - 8$) as costs of 8 are deducted from the cumulative benefits of 12. When, however, only one nation contributes, the free rider gets 6 while the contributor receives -2 ($= 6 - 8$). The current game in Figure 2.7 differs from the Prisoners' Dilemma, because the status-quo payoffs from doing nothing give each nation a loss of 5. The status-quo

11. See, for example, Schultz and Pfaltzgraff (1992).

payoff is worse from either nation's viewpoint than being the "sucker," who provides the free ride. By converting these payoffs into their ordinal or ranked equivalence, the reader can establish that the underlying game is that of Chicken, so that some nation is anticipated to do something.

This example makes an important point about public goods and global challenges in general: The payoff pattern may favor some kind of action, especially if doing nothing can lead to a bad state of affairs. Potential crises concerning diseases, insidious pollutants, natural disasters, and contagious revolutions (for example, Islamic fundamentalism) may be viewed by many nations as having dire status-quo outcome payoffs if no defensive actions are taken. This then bodes well for the world community to achieve some action.

Thus far, nations have been treated as identical in most of the above examples. Consider a small, but crucial, alteration to the payoffs in Figure 2.7. Suppose that everything is the same except for the status-quo payoff to nation A. In particular, change the -5 to -1 for nation A in Figure 2.7 (not shown). This can occur if, say, nation A is farther away from the site of the resulting disaster, so that its losses of -1 are less than the losses from being the sucker who provides the free ride. In this new game matrix, country A has a dominant strategy to free ride and rely on B's efforts, since $-1 > -2$ and $6 > 4$. The only equilibrium is cell b where nation B averts the crisis and nation A does nothing. For many potential crises, proximity may affect the relative sizes of the status-quo payoffs – for example, nations in the higher latitudes have more to fear during the springtime from a widening ozone-shield hole than do nations nearer the equator. Similarly, nations neighboring another that is experiencing a fundamentalist revolution have more to dread than do nations more distant.

EXTERNAL EFFECTS: FURTHER CONSIDERATIONS

In Chapter 1, the reader was introduced to an externality or external effect in which the action of an individual or nation creates a cost or a benefit for another, and this cost or benefit *is not taken into account by the market price.* When a country fires up a coal-burning power plant, the country receives energy to drive its machines and to heat and cool its houses. In addition, pollutants (sulfur dioxide, particulates) are emitted through smokestacks. Harm imposed by these pollutants on the country's residents and those in downwind countries is not reflected in the price of the electricity, determined by the forces of demand and supply.

There are a number of remedies for taking account of external effects. First, a government can impose taxes for harmful external effects and subsidies for beneficial external effects. The logic of these taxes or subsidies is to make the provider account for not only the private costs and benefits of the activity, but also the external costs and benefits. For external cost, the ideal tax would equal the additional damage created by the activity on anyone affected by the unpriced side effects.[12] If the proper taxes or subsidies are assigned, then they *internalize the externality*, which is a fancy way of saying that the provider of the activity is made to account for the unintended consequences. Second, the government can determine the level of the externality-producing activity to allow and then provide permits that can be traded among the polluters. This latter remedy has the advantage of relying on the markets for permits to ensure that, no matter how these permits are initially assigned, they will eventually end up in the hands of those who value them the most. These are the firms whose activities are valued the most relative to the associated cost by society. Third, the government can set limits or quotas for pollution levels. If these levels were to match those associated with the ideal tax or subsidy, then resources would be directed to their best uses. Fourth, the courts can assign the rights to an externality-free environment to the potential recipient of the externality and allow the externality generator to bribe this recipient into accepting a certain amount of the external effect. Or the externality generator can be granted the right to produce the external effect, and the recipient of this effect can bribe the generator to limit its activity. For either property right assignment, the outcome of this bargaining process will be efficient in the sense that resources go to their best uses, provided that only a few parties are involved.[13]

12. These and other remedies are discussed more fully in Baumol and Oates (1988) and Cornes and Sandler (1996).
13. This bargaining outcome is known as the Coase (1960) Theorem. If bargaining costs are high, bargaining may not be a feasible outcome.

Of course, the initial assignment of rights has tremendous income distribution and fairness consequences. Fifth, the government can choose to do nothing and just let the external effect remain unattended. This is the best policy when the gains achieved from correcting or internalizing the external effect are less than the costs from doing so.

Each of the above remedies has its advantages and disadvantages. A big drawback concerns getting the information to, say, assign the taxes or subsidies. If you were to ask someone harmed by an external effect how much they had suffered, it would be in their interests to exaggerate if they anticipated that their answers would lead either to compensation or to curtail the harmful activity. Although the bargaining solution has much to recommend it, it may prove difficult or too costly to implement for large numbers of participants. For more localized pollution problems involving neighboring nations, bargaining may, however, be an ideal means of confronting externalities.

The correction of transnational externalities faces severe obstacles because the required infrastructure does not currently exist to implement the standard remedies. The provision of this infrastructure is, arguably, one of the greatest challenges confronting the world community if nations are really going to be secure from the harmful acts of other nations.[14] Just as nations control external effects in order to direct resources to their most-valued use, the global community must develop similar measures.

Externalities come in many shapes, sizes, and types. Some of these distinctions prove useful throughout the book. *Unidirectional external effects* flow from a generator to a recipient, with no returning external effect produced by the recipient. River pollution is typically unidirectional. Even terrorism that spills over from one region – for example, the Middle East – to another is unidirectional because the recipient region does not necessarily generate a return flow of external effects. In contrast, a *reciprocal externality* includes external effects that flow in a return direction between two or more persons or nations.

Reciprocity may provide incentives to do something about external effects, because the participants have leverage over one another.

---

14. This point is well made in Myers (1995).

Take the case where two families live in next-door apartments that have thin walls. Family *A* listens to heavy metal rock and roll played loudly during the late evening, while family *B* enjoys Wagnerian arias played at full volume during the morning. An accommodation is likely, since each family has its own means of sanctions that it would enjoy administering. At an international level, Canada has received air pollution from the United States, while the United States has experienced water pollution from Canada. On a number of occasions, these countries have been able to achieve accommodations.

The neighbors and the Canada–United States examples highlight another important distinction – small-numbers versus large-numbers external effects. The former involves a small number of generators *and* recipients, while the latter involves a large number of generators *or* recipients, or both. From an international perspective, pollution dumped on the open seas is a large-numbers externality, while pollution released in lakes is typically a small-numbers externality. Large-numbers externalities are more complicated to correct than small-numbers externalities, because a greater number of interdependencies must be identified, valued, and compensated. For large-numbers externalities, bargains must be struck with all relevant parties, because a few important holdouts can undo the efforts of everyone else. Suppose that all CFC-producer nations except the United States agree to eliminate CFC production. By expanding its CFC production capacity, the United States could limit greatly the overall effects of the other producers to curb ozone depletion.

The nature of the reciprocity also changes for large-numbers externalities, where some generators may view the effects of their actions on themselves and on others as being small compared to the actions of everyone else. In fact, they may think that their impact is inconsequential, thus justifying their continued generation of the external effect. In a national park, visitors often question why they are forbidden from picking a flower or taking home a stone as a souvenir. They wonder how a single flower or stone would be missed. From the time that humans have escaped the earth's gravity, they have treated the orbital bands as places to leave unwanted debris or spent satellites. These objects are now so numerous that they pose lethal threats to the astronauts who will construct a manned space station. For small-numbers reciprocal externalities, the interdependency is, however, much clearer to the participants.

Intergenerational externalities constitute another important class of external effects in which the uncompensated interdependency is among generations. From an intergenerational perspective, these externalities are unidirectional, since an earlier generation's actions can influence a future generation but not the other way around. The release of high-level radiation, the loss of biodiversity, and global warming are intergenerational externalities.

PUBLIC GOODS

Public goods are an important market failure that characterizes global problems concerned with, for example, the removal of pollution, the elimination of diseases, the accumulation of knowledge, the provision of security, and the forecasting of disasters. With their nonexcludable benefits, pure public goods are not readily supplied by market exchanges. Why pay for something that you are going to receive anyway? These goods' nonrival benefits mean that exclusion may not make sense, insofar as extending the benefits to another consumer is costless. Returning to Figure 2.4, one can see that public good contributions can pose a Prisoners' Dilemma, especially when the benefits per unit to the provider are less than the cost per unit provided. In Figure 2.7, contributing to a public good did not imply a Prisoners' Dilemma. In fact, many different games may be relevant to public goods.

The class of public goods is large and can vary in terms of the degree of nonrivalry and the extent of nonexcludability. An important subclass includes *club* goods, which possess partially rival benefits that can be excluded at a sufficiently small cost to permit visits to be monitored and charged a toll.[15] Rivalry of benefits among users assumes the form of crowding or congestion, which results in a decrease in the quality of the shared good as users at any given time increase. As traffic on a highway increases, crowding takes the form

---

15. Club goods were first analyzed by Buchanan (1965), Olson (1965), and Tiebout (1956). For a recent survey on club goods, see Sandler and Tschirhart (1997).

of slower commutes and a greater risk of an accident. Even the electromagnetic spectrum is a club good, whose congestion takes the form of signal interference as bandwidths are made smaller to accommodate more users. In national parks, crowding may result in longer queues to view vistas, more traffic on park roadways, and more encounters on nature trails. Communication networks (for example, the INTELSAT communication system of satellites),[16] orbital bands in outer space, nature preserves, commando squads, and infrastructure (for example, the Chunnel linking the United Kingdom and France) are further examples of club goods. Club goods can be provided by the members and financed through tolls that charge for the crowding costs. Unlike pure public goods, club goods can be allocated efficiently without the need of a government, because the exclusion mechanism can force payment based on tastes. Users, whose tastes for the good are greater, will visit more often and be charged accordingly. Club arrangements may be an important means for nations to meet some public good needs without sacrificing sovereignty. For example, INTELSAT is run like a private corporation with no need for a supranational government.

To illustrate that incentive structures may be quite supportive for providing a public good, I again consider the two-person contribution scenario.[17] But this time I assume that each unit provided gives 6 in benefits to the provider and to the other individual, at a cost of 4 to the provider. That is, per-unit benefits now exceed per-unit costs. In Figure 2.8, the resulting game payoffs are indicated. This game is "incentive-compatible" because each individual has a dominant strategy to contribute to the public good, because $2 > 0$ and $8 > 6$, so that the contributor is satisfied with his or her action regardless of how the other player responds. One can justify contributing in isolation, even though a free ride is conferred on others. Each player can be expected to support the equilibrium indicated by the asterisk. When, for example, the United States discovered in 1987 that the gains from banning CFCs production, even in isolation, far outweighed the associated costs (see Chapter 4 for details), its incentives corresponded to those of either player of Figure 2.8.

16. INTELSAT is analyzed as a club in Sandler and Schulze (1981, 1985).
17. Public goods can be viewed as incentive structures. The manner in which public goods are allocated can affect the extent of nonrivalry and nonexcludability and, as such, the goods' incentive structure (Cornes and Sandler 1994a).

A's strategy ＼ B's strategy	Do not Contribute	Contribute
Do not Contribute	0, 0	6, 2
Contribute	2, 6	* 8, 8

Figure 2.8. Incentive-compatible public good.

Sometimes, information needs to be gathered, as in the CFC case, before one or more countries view the payoffs as conducive to action. Once this information is revealed, the media can serve an important purpose in educating the country's citizens on the overall net gains from a contemplated action, despite losses to one or two special interests.

PUBLIC GOODS WITH SELECTIVE INCENTIVES

Some public goods provide more than one type of benefit that can differ in terms of their nonrivalry and nonexcludable aspects. Suppose that a nation is developing a scientific breakthrough that can benefit humankind, while giving the developing nation specific knowledge, useful for it but not for others. This private knowledge may make contributing to the public good a dominant strategy from the developer's viewpoint. The private benefits are "selective incentives" that can motivate action.[18] Next consider why individuals actually lead revolutions when the consequences can be unimaginable punishment. To an oppressed citizenry, these rebel leaders can provide huge public benefits by ridding it of a tyrant. Even though these public benefits may support some rebel action, the anticipated gains to the revolution leaders from obtaining power, fame, revenge, and wealth must outweigh the expected punishments from being caught. When the United States assumes the role of the world's police force, it is similarly motivated not only by the "global good," but also by

18. Olson (1965) first stressed these selective incentives. Also see Cornes and Sandler (1984, 1994b).

its own standing in the world community and by threats posed to its interests.

Private selective incentives must be facilitated by the world community if it wants to encourage more global public goods being provided without the need for elaborate or costly supranational structures. As another instance of private incentives, consider why nations develop commando squads that can crisis manage a terrorist hostage incident. When attacks are domestic, the benefits from deploying the squad are primarily country-specific; when, however, attacks are foreign and involve some of the nation's citizens, the benefits from deploying the squad are both country-specific and international. Nations confronting significant domestic threats are more apt to have a commando squad that can be used at home and abroad. Other instances of public goods with selective incentives include foreign aid and the control of airborne pollutants. For the former, the donor nation can tie aid to demands on the recipients, while, for the latter, curbing the pollutant includes an improvement in the nation's ambient air quality.

PUBLIC SUPPLY AGGREGATION CONSIDERATIONS

Earlier, the public good contribution scenario was shown to be consistent with alternative game forms. The relationship between a public good problem and its underlying game depends, in part, on the manner in which individual actions contribute to the total level of the public good. The association between individual contributions and the total quantity of the public good is known as the *technology of public supply aggregation*.[19] Most often a summation technology is assumed so that each individual's or nation's contributions boost the good's total level and benefits. Additionally, the contribution of one individual can substitute for that of another on a one-to-one basis – it matters not who is contributing. In Figure 2.4, payoffs are consistent with a summation technology in which each new unit adds 3 in benefits to each and every person. Benefit totals grow with

19. Hirshleifer (1983) refers to the technology of public supply as the social composition function.

contribution and do not depend on a threshold level being reached or on the largest or smallest contribution.

When public contributions abide by a summation technology, a Prisoners' Dilemma or a Chicken game is apt to apply. In such scenarios, the wealthiest individual often provides the free ride for the others and, in doing so, is exploited by the small individuals. A summation technology is also associated with undersupply of the public good, because contributors only care about their own additional benefits relative to the additional costs when determining how much to contribute. Redistributing income to the richer contributors to increase their contribution may be totally undone by the resulting drop in contributions from the poorer individuals who have lost real income.[20]

Next consider the weakest-link technology in which the *total* public good level is identical to the smallest provision level of the contributors.[21] If, out of ten people, the smallest contribution is two units, then all ten people consume two units even if some give fifteen and others twenty units. Prophylactic measures taken to forestall the spread of a disease, a fire, or a pollutant adhere to this technology. Security in these cases is solely determined by the weakest effort. The ability to keep a secret from being learned depends on the willpower of the most talkative member. During a conventional war, the strength of the weakest ally along the front determines whether or not the enemy can break through and gain the advantage. A project that depends on the integrity of the whole is only as strong as its weakest part; thus, the lowest section of a levee determines the flooding danger for the entire river valley. Weakest-link technologies are invariably associated with an Assurance game as in Figure 2.5. At the equilibria, players match one another's contributions, because there is no gain, just costs, from exceeding the minimal contributions. If one individual contributes toward the public good, the other individual has much to gain by also contributing the same amount so that positive benefits will be achieved. A weakest-link technology can be conducive to promoting a coordinated response. When each one is pulling his or her weight, a free rider spoils

20. On the neutrality of income redistribution for a summation technology, see Sandler (1992, 18, 60, 77–8). Also see Cornes (1993) and Vicary (1990).
21. On weakest-link technology, see Cornes (1993), Conybeare, Murdoch, and Sandler (1994), Hirshleifer (1983), and Vicary (1990).

it for everyone, especially for him- or herself. With this technology, a redistribution of income that promotes equality can raise the overall level of provision. This follows because the level of matching behavior is expected to increase as resource endowments are equalized, especially if tastes are similar. Among pending global crises, the containment of revolutions corresponds to a weakest-link technology. The same is true for the spread of diseases or the containment of nuclear radiation.

In stark contrast to weakest-link, the best-shot technology equates public good provision to the largest individualized effort. If, for example, ten individuals contribute from one to ten units to the public good, the quantity of the public good will be ten, or the highest individual contribution level. The discovery of a cure for a disease is an example of the best-shot technology, as is the more imaginary example of slaying a dragon. Other examples include the achievement of a research breakthrough or the intelligence gathered in an espionage operation. The best-shot technology may also apply to an offensive alliance that initiates an attack, since the ally inflicting the heaviest damage may well determine the outcome of the war. For nuclear waste containment, the first nation to develop a safe long-term containment procedure can share this insight with all other nations. When a rogue nation or terrorist group, bent on world destabilization, is neutralized, the neutralizing nation's actions provide a public good in terms of augmented security that abides by a best-shot technology. The race to find a cure for Ebola, AIDS, and antibiotic-resistant tuberculosis as well as the effort to discover an environment-friendly pesticide are global crises that adhere to a best-shot technology, where the first over the line wins for everyone. For best-shot public goods, it is in everyone's interests to take a free ride, except for the best-endowed individual with the wherewithal to get the job done.

For equally endowed individuals, who should act is more ambiguous. Suppose that two individuals are contemplating whether or not to contribute to a public good that abides by a best-shot aggregation. Only a single unit is required to achieve the public good, so that each of two individuals has two strategic options: Contribute one unit or do not contribute. Suppose that the first unit contributed gives a benefit of 6 to both individuals, but that a second unit adds no benefit. Since each person can provide only a single unit by as-

B's strategy / A's strategy	Do not Contribute	Contribute
Do not Contribute	0, 0	* 6, 2
Contribute	* 2, 6	2, 2

Figure 2.9. Best-shot Coordination game.

sumption, the first unit provided denotes the best shot. Further suppose that each unit costs 4 to provide. In Figure 2.9, the associated *Coordination* game is depicted and contains no dominant strategy for either individual. Payoffs are computed as before – for example, if player *A* contributes and player *B* does not, then *A* receives a net payoff of 2 (= 6 − 4) and *B* receives the free-riding payoff of 6. For individual *A*, not contributing gives 0 or 6 depending on *B*'s strategy, while contributing gives 2 regardless of *B*'s strategy. Equilibria correspond to one individual contributing and the other taking a free ride. In this game of equals, it is anyone's guess as to who will do the providing. If the same scenario included ten potential contributors, only one contributor is needed, and that contributor could be anyone.

Next suppose that player *A* has a higher payoff than that of player *B* from the public good. For example, assume that player *A* receives 8 from the public good at a cost of 4 if he or she contributes. In Figure 2.9, 8 then replaces 6 in the top row and 4 (= 8 − 4) replaces *A*'s payoffs of 2 in the bottom row. Player *A* needs greater assurance that *B* will contribute for player *A* to shirk its role as contributor. On average, player *A* has more to gain from contributing than does player *B*. If player *A* were to receive additional private benefits from contributing to the public good, then he or she has even more incentives to contribute, so that the lower-left cell becomes focal. Uncertainty is partly resolved when payoffs are heterogeneous, favoring one individual over another.

This example has much to say about global challenges that abide by a best-shot technology. Action is less ambiguous and *more likely* if the players' payoffs are *unequal*. If demand for a public good increases with income, as is typically the case, then wealthier players will gain the most and are the most likely to act. A skewed income distribution that favors some individuals (or nations) over others is conducive to a best-shot type of action. This theme is important in Chapter 6.

There are numerous technologies that are less stark than the three presented above. A weaker-link technology of public supply means that weaker players' actions (or smaller contribution levels) have a greater effect than stronger players' actions, but actions above the smallest have some payoff. Matching behavior is not strictly required. Controlling pests or weeds is a weaker-link example. In contrast, a better-shot technology of public supply implies that the largest action has the greatest impact, but all actions can assist. Spreading knowledge or culture are examples.[22] A final technology is that of weighted sum, where actions are weighted and then added up, so that some players' actions might be more effective.

Each underlying technology of public supply can have different game structures and, hence, different predicted outcomes in terms of cooperation. These technologies play an important role in studying global exigencies, since the prognosis for curing these concerns can hinge on whether the technology is conducive to collective action. At times, institutions can be designed to foster cooperation if the aggregation technology is better understood. If, for example, a problem is a weakest-link one, such as trying to contain the spread of heterosexual AIDS, the media can provide information on how society is only as safe as the least-protected couple. Institutions that promote income equality would help weakest-link crises but not best-shot crises.

CONCLUDING REMARKS

This chapter has introduced the reader to some elementary notions of game theory and market failures. My approach is to apply these concepts in a simple manner to demonstrate which challenges are resistant to a solution and which possess the proper incentive struc-

---

22. On weaker-link and better-shot technologies, see Cornes (1993) and Cornes and Sandler (1996).

ture to be solved with little assistance. Public goods and externalities are prevalent at a number of jurisdictional levels. For example, smoke from one state, county, or region can foul the air of another within the *same* nation. In these cases, the injured party can use the courts to sue for compensation or request a higher level of government to regulate the external effect. Public goods that affect the citizens of an entire country are provided by the central government – for example, national defense, pollution control, disease control, and space exploration. When these public goods and external effects transcend nation-state borders, nations may need to cooperate if these challenges are to be confronted successfully. Since nations cherish their autonomy and do not sacrifice it readily to supranational governments that could impose decisions that they may view as unacceptable, transnational cooperation in loose, ad hoc arrangements appears more feasible. In this latter case, nations are like game players that must choose their strategies based on their beliefs about the likely choices of others.

There are at least four means for approaching global challenges. The optimist expects nations to combine with others and to accomplish whatever is best for the collective, no matter the consequences to these nations' autonomy or interests. Another approach rules out all attempts to do something as too wishful. Still another argues that there are no crises: there is no ozone hole, acid rain does no harm, there is no world hunger, terrorism poses no threat to world stability, and there are no plagues of the twentieth century. Finally, there is the pragmatic approach that recognizes that cooperation can be fostered and some headway made. This is the approach taken here. In doing so, nations are viewed as calculating entities that serve their interests. By identifying what promotes and inhibits collective action among these calculating nations, I show which global issues pose the greatest challenge.

Some readers may object to my use of rational-actor and game-theoretic concepts to address global concerns. While this approach is not the only means for studying global challenges, it does provide some insights on how nations might act. When these insights are combined with those from other approaches, a more informed understanding of global challenges should emerge.

3 For our children's children

Decisions today may have implications well into the future and, as such, may influence the well-being of generations to come. For the world fisheries, harvesting decisions today can destabilize marine ecosystems and even drive some species into extinction, thus affecting the welfare of all subsequent generations. The application of modern technologies – satellite global positioning systems, radar – have severely depleted some species' stock and, thus, have imperiled the commercial viability of these species.[1] As another instance, consider biodiversity, where the existence of large numbers of species adds to the heritage of humankind. The stability of ecosystems depends in part on the presence of multiple species fulfilling similar functions, since disruption to the population of some species can be compensated by other species expanding to assume needed functions previously provided by the depleted population. Biodiversity is dependent on habitat, so that land conversion in the species-rich tropics can have serious consequences for the number of species. If biodiversity is to be preserved, then the current generation in a tropical country must be sufficiently farsighted to account for the impact of their land-allocation decisions on future generations at home and abroad. This is a tall order. Storage of high-level nuclear wastes, such as plutonium, is a prime example of how decisions today can impact the well-being of generations for millennia to come. Given

---

1. For a general interest piece on the world's imperiled fish, see Safina (1995). Dasgupta and Heal (1979) contains economic models of fisheries.

the long half-life of plutonium-239 (24,000 years), nuclear waste repositories would have to protect the environment from nuclear contamination for literally hundreds of thousands of years.[2]

Many of the global problems confronting the world today possess significant intergenerational impacts. In addition to the examples above, current exigencies with significant intergenerational implications include the depletion of the ozone shield, the contamination of watersheds, the loss of culture, the destruction of wetlands, the buildup of greenhouse gases, land degradation, and the appearance of antibiotic-resistant diseases. Once intergenerational considerations are raised, collective action, whereby individuals coordinate actions to further the interests of the group, must be considered on at least three levels: within a nation, among nations, and among generations. If neighboring nations work in unison to limit a mutual pollution problem, but do not properly adjust for the consequences to the unborn, then decisions are likely to have inefficient consequences when viewed over the long run, despite the coordination at the supranational level.

Intergenerational challenges raise concerns in terms of the efficient allocation of resources *and* the equitable distribution of income among generations. Decisions today can significantly affect the range of choices or constraints that future generations will inherit. In economic parlance, decisions of a current generation influence the production possibilities of future generations. As for global problems generally, one needs to identify which challenges are apt to be solved with reasonably farsighted outcomes and which will not. Can markets always be expected to yield reasonably farsighted and efficient outcomes? What influences do political institutions and systems have on the achievement of intergenerationally friendly results? For example, are democracies anticipated to have greater intergenerational awareness than authoritarian regimes? These and related questions are addressed in this chapter. The presence of benefits to the *current* generation is a crucial consideration that promotes more farsighted collective outcomes from an intergenerational perspective. Other factors – altruism and sufficient certainty – can also foster more efficient and farsighted outcomes.

---

2. This is the safe containment period for spent fuel rods (Miller, 1994, 61). On other long-term persistent pollutants, see Opschoor and Pearce (1991).

IRREVERSIBILITIES AND FIRST-MOVER ADVANTAGE

When a global challenge has an intergenerational dimension, the sequencing of the generations becomes a crucial consideration. In game-theory terminology, the present generation has a *first-mover advantage* because it gets to choose its play prior to subsequent generations. In chess, the player who draws white and moves first has a slight competitive advantage over an equally skilled opponent who draws black. In ticktacktoe, however, a skilled player has a decided first-mover advantage, since he or she can always win or at least draw. Lest the reader believe that moving first is always advantageous, the games of paper-scissors-stone or matching pennies indicate a clear second-mover advantage, because the second mover can always defeat the opponent once his or her move is revealed. If, for example, the first player chooses scissors, then the second player can counter with stone (which breaks scissors) to win. Such games are only interesting when moves are simultaneous, so that second-mover advantages are removed. Politics can also present a second-mover advantage in which a candidate can match an opponent's announced platform on issues favorable to the largest majority and oppose the opponent's platform on any issue unfavorable to a majority. This strategy can produce a platform with greater overall popular support.[3] Second-mover advantages are particularly relevant for situations where the participants coexist.

A current generation possesses a first-mover advantage in the sense that it can choose an agenda or pathway that best serves its own purposes, even though these purposes may be at odds with those of future generations. To appreciate this first-mover advantage, consider choices with respect to the environment, such as the building of a dam that requires flooding the Grand Canyon. Once the Grand Canyon is flooded, the original beauty can never be restored even if a subsequent generation decides to drain it. The flooding decision is irreversible.[4] The ordering of the generations grants earlier generations these irreversible decisions, which are manifes-

---

3. On second-mover advantage and political parties, see Downs (1957) and Mueller (1989, 183–5).
4. The irreversibility of economic decisions is discussed in Arrow and Kurz (1970a, 1970b), Elster (1979), and elsewhere.

tations of the first-mover advantage. Irreversibilities can be for either the good or the bad of subsequent generations. Actions of the present generation that reduce the earth's biodiversity or that increase its atmospheric concentration of greenhouse gases are irreversible into the foreseeable future. Other decisions – the clearing of tropical forests, the depletion of the ozone shield, the release of toxic wastes – may be reversible with time, but not before subsequent generations suffer the adverse consequences.

To avert dire future consequences, the present generation can also engage in decisions that benefit all subsequent generations, such as curing a disease, attaining a technological breakthrough, containing nuclear wastes, or introducing environmentally friendly technologies (for example, longer-lived lightbulbs). When these beneficial side effects or externalities are experienced by a future generation, a second-mover advantage is then conferred on this future generation, since it may benefit without necessarily expending the development resources. The ultimate question concerns what promotes the current generation to undertake a farsighted decision that confers these intergenerational public benefits to subsequent generations. If we were to know this answer, then we would be in a better position to provide the proper preconditions for more efficient intergenerational decision making.

At least three factors appear crucial. The first has to do with the level and share of benefits experienced by the current generation. In terms of public good analysis, there must be sufficient generation-specific benefits to motivate the current generation's action, even if the cost is solely borne by it.[5] Consider the hunt for a cure for a plague. A present generation, ravaged by a disease such as AIDS or polio, stands to gain large benefits from uncovering a cure and would allocate significant resources. This is not to say that even greater resources would be applied if future generations, yet to be born, could also make their preferences known and support the decision. Not only is the level of benefits to the current generation important, but so, too, is its *share* of benefits. The greater is its intergenerational share of resulting benefits, the greater is its stake

5. This implies that the group is privileged in the sense of Olson's (1965) collective-action principles. A privileged group contains at least one individual or coalition (generation) whose benefits from collective action exceed the associated costs, even if these costs are solely borne by the individual or coalition (Sandler 1992, 9–11).

in underwriting the expense of the action. The current generation's
share of the derived benefits would be greatly enhanced if patents
or other similar instruments would enable the discoverers to gain
royalties on their breakthrough. In essence, patents protect the dis-
covering generation's property rights and, in doing so, motivate action for the good of the present and future. Extremely risky
investments that require a tremendous resource commitment, such
as finding a cure for AIDS, would need longer patent-protection
periods than those that are standard. With long-term patent protection, the current generation can assign the disposition of posthumous
earnings to designated heirs. Another important insight concerns the
discoverer's need to share the proceeds from the royalties among
all of the major research teams within the current generation. This
action would foster cooperation among the teams, since everyone
would have a piece of the action, so that research efforts could be
better focused. Of course, the discoverer should be given the lion's
share of the royalties; there needs to be a greater prize for success
to motivate all teams sufficiently.

A second factor, which may be supportive of a present generation
undertaking an investment beneficial to future generations, concerns
the technology of public supply aggregation, presented in Chapter
2. The provision of intergenerational public assets may be more successful if they involve a "best-shot" technology in which the *maxi-
mal effort* indicates the amount of the asset provided, as in curing a
disease. In this scenario, the largest effort beyond a threshold, rather
than the cumulative effort, determines the provision level. Typically,
the best-endowed or wealthiest potential participant is the one most
apt to achieve the best shot.[6] In an intergenerational context, the
current generation is traditionally the wealthiest of all preceding
generations and, as such, is in a better position than earlier generations to achieve the breakthrough. Crises-averting behavior that
abides by best-shot technology is promoted over time by the increasing well-being of future generations. Of course, this proposition depends on the increasing well-being of future generations, which may
change, as shown later, if the current generation passes a smaller
asset pool onto the next generation. Such an underlying technology

6. On best-shot public goods and income distribution, see Hirshleifer (1983), Cornes
(1993), and Sandler (1992).

would also lend support to research teams within the present generation pooling efforts rather than working independently.

Altruism is a third consideration that can motivate a current generation to undertake farsighted actions on its behalf and that of future generations. Altruism exists when the current generation cares enough for the welfare of future generations to curb its own consumption in favor of increased consumption by its children and their children's children.[7] Quite simply, altruism motivates the current generation to partake in more intergenerationally aware actions, because its members get greater benefits from such actions. Thus, altruism reinforces the first supporting factor, concerned with the decision-making generation's level and share of benefits, but this is not to say that altruism can by itself ensure farsighted decisions. Altruism may be insufficiently strong and involve only the next generation, while the required decision may affect generations well into the future. Additionally, the current generation cannot truly know what a future generation really desires. Although the current generation can attempt to shape these future generations' tastes through indoctrination, it cannot absolutely determine these tastes. Anyone with children knows this all too well.

Even though the above factors can mitigate the myopia involving intergenerational collective action, many obstacles will always exist that inhibit efficient decisions for global contingencies. Perhaps the best way to understand the potential for market failures and inefficient choice when intergenerational decisions are tied to potential crises is to consider the allocation of property rights among generations arising from the natural progression of generations. In Chapter 1, property right assignment and enforcement were shown to be a necessary ingredient for the functioning of markets as illustrated by the protection of property rights to cars. When intergenerational decisions are made today, the current generation holds the property rights to the earth's assets, even though today's actions will affect the future generations. If, however, these future generations could influence current decisions prior to their birth, then they may wish to trade their future endowments (or inheritance) with the current generation to influence the latter's choice. In practice, this trade is

---

7. There is a large literature on altruism in the economics profession. Recent contributions include Schulze, Brookshire, and Sandler (1981) and Howarth and Norgaard (1990, 1995).

difficult or impossible to accomplish unless the generations overlap sometime during their lifetime, so that a subsequent generation can later reimburse the preceding generation for its investment. Such trades are really impossible when relevant generations are greatly separated in time, as shown later in the chapter. Even under the best of circumstances, some inefficient decisions will occur from an intergenerational perspective, because outcomes that could improve the well-being of all generations concerned will not be consummated. In essence, potentially important markets are missing, a theme stressed often.

Another potential problem associated with intergenerational decisions concerns *"incoherent dynamic choice"* in which a society seeks its best-ranked alternative, but chooses instead the worst-ranked alternative by the end of a sequence of decisions.[8] This phenomenon may result from a change either in circumstances or in tastes and may be behind some global concerns. To illustrate an example of incoherent dynamic choice, I consider the adoption of nuclear power as an energy source. In Figure 3.1, n_1 and n_2 represent points in time when the current and subsequent generations, respectively, must make key decisions concerning nuclear energy. At the first decision point, n_1, the current generation must decide between never trying nuclear energy (choice c) and trying it and leaving the decision whether to keep it for a later time, n_2. Consequently, at the second decision point, n_2, the subsequent generation must decide either to keep nuclear energy (choice b) despite the waste containment and other problems or to give it up (choice a). At n_1, the two-generation society most prefers option a, then option c, and last option b. When the decision is made at n_1, the first generation chooses to try nuclear energy in the hope of attaining its most desirable choice, option a. However, once decision node n_2 is reached, the second generation may have no chance to choose option a over option b, because the economy has become reliant upon nuclear energy and no alternative exists in the near term. In such a scenario, dynamic choice is said to be incoherent because society has finished with its least desirable choice, option b. Any potentially addictive behavior is consistent with incoherent dynamic choice. For example,

---

8. Incoherent dynamic choice is put forward by Hammond (1976) and is related to time-inconsistent choice where a sequence of choices that a decision maker intends to follow is changed as the game proceeds.

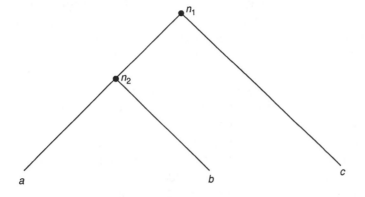

a – use nuclear energy until it appears to create
    significant environmental problems

b – become a habitual user of nuclear energy
    despite potential environmental problems

c – do not use nuclear energy

Figure 3.1. Decision tree.

society's heavy reliance on fossil fuels since the industrial revolution
has made it very difficult to switch to alternative energy sources at
subsequent dates, despite the dangers of global warming and acid
rain. Society's addiction to energy-wasteful lifestyles is another instance of incoherent dynamic choice.

In order to avoid incoherent dynamic choice as displayed in Figure 3.1, the first generation has at least two possible strategies: (1)
it can make a sophisticated choice based on the whole decision tree
and choose option *c* from the outset by foreseeing the consequences
of seeking option *a*; or (2) it may precommit its behavior so as to
create a new option whereby it tries nuclear energy but provides for
a means to facilitate easy transition to an alternative energy supply
if necessary. Neither option is anticipated unless the first generation
displays an unusual degree of altruism and farsightedness to future
generations. The precommitment strategy is akin to Ulysses' in-
structing his crew to bind him to the mast so that he could hear the
songs of the Sirens without jumping overboard to his death.[9] For

9 On this example, see Elster (1979).

governments, constitutional amendments can bind legislatures to the mast, as in the case of the proposed balanced-budget amendment or the forbidding of negotiations with hostage-taking terrorists.

Some decisions with respect to global contingencies may be partly reversible but at a high cost. Consider tropical forests where a reforestation program could involve the planting of fast-growing tree plantations in the tropics to replace forests cleared by shifted cultivators, wood harvesters, or cattle ranchers (see Chapter 4). Such programs are currently under consideration.[10] Only a partial fix is evident, because, although reforestation will sequester carbon (thereby alleviating global warming worldwide) and provide localized benefits (for example, erosion control) for the host and neighboring countries, it will not replenish the biodiversity lost with the cleared forests. Thousands and even millions of years are needed for nature to create thousands of new species. There is also the matter as to who will underwrite such a reforestation program. It should clearly be those who stand to gain. The host country has a significant stake in such programs owing to localized benefits, but the global community, both present and future, also gains from the sequestering of carbon and needs to help finance the reforestation. But global support faces a major impediment, since carbon sequestration represents a global pure public good, so that nations will try to free ride on the generosity of others. Consequently, reforestation is unlikely to be supported by very many nations.

Any geoengineering project used to offset a global crisis (for example, seeding the oceans with iron filings to increase carbon absorption) will confront this free-rider problem, thus limiting, in practice, the ability of a subsequent generation to reverse a decision by an earlier generation. Some headway against free riding can be achieved if countries can substitute their support for geoengineering projects, such as reforestation, for other actions, viewed as more costly. In recent years, some developed countries would have prefered to plant trees in the tropics if this activity were to count as an offset to limits on greenhouse gas emissions. If this proposed substitution leads to an equal reduction in global-warming potential but at a lower cost, then it is a desirable option. More localized geoen-

10. Reforestation programs are discussed by Myers and Goreau (1991) and Sandler (1993).

gineering projects involving the acidity of soils and lakes may, however, be implemented if the financing is needed from only one nation or neighboring nations. But first such geoengineering programs must be shown to be feasible from an economic and scientific basis.

A final aspect of reversibility concerns uncertainty. For many environmental problems, the threshold beyond which the environmental asset begins to deteriorate may not be known in advance. Similarly, the precise relationship between the pollutant and the degradation of the asset may not be known and may behave erratically, so that significant environmental losses are only experienced past some threshold. The sudden appearance of the "ozone hole" over the South Pole in 1985 might be a case in point (see Chapter 4). If the current generation were better informed about the pitfalls of its pollution practices, then this generation may be more cautious, because of the realization that it would itself experience some of the costs from an environmental catastrophe. When, however, the danger limits are unknown and are unlikely to occur during its lifetime, the generation may then place very small weight on these environmental costs. In this latter case, once the pitfalls are revealed, it may then be too late to reverse the consequences.

Uncertainty is germane to many of the environmental crises that confront the current generation. Global warming is a prime example because the precise relationship between atmospheric accumulation of carbon and the rise in mean global temperature is still poorly understood and will be so for some time to come. While scientific observation can document the increase in atmospheric levels of CO_2,[11] the effect of these levels on temperature and rainfall is very complex. Many factors intervene that make calibration of this relationship particularly difficult. The role of the oceans on temperature fluctuations and rainfall is just becoming understood. Additionally, other pollutants, such as sulfur, may have an offsetting influence on global warming by increasing the reflectivity of clouds. These uncertainties limit the motivation of the current generation to act, because until the uncertainties are resolved, the problem is likely to be viewed as one for future generations to solve.

11. From 1970 to the early 1990s, fossil fuel–related emissions of CO_2 grew by 50%. For this same period, atmospheric levels of CO_2 increased by approximately 10% (Ausubel, Victor, and Wernick 1995).

THE ROLE OF DISCOUNTING ON
IRREVERSIBLE DECISIONS

It is instructive first to consider the justification for the practice of discounting future earnings for investment decisions affecting just the present generation. Suppose that an investor has \$100 to leave on deposit in the bank for a year. If the interest rate, i, is 10% then this investment will be worth

$$\$100 + \$100i = \$100(1 + i) = \$110 \tag{1}$$

at the end of a year when i equals 10%. If, instead, the investor were given the option of receiving \$110 in a year's time in return for a sum of money sacrificed *today*, the investor would not sacrifice \$110, since he or she gives up the use of this payment for a year and must be compensated for this forgone opportunity cost – the lost interest earnings. Equation (1) indicates that the value of \$110 a year from now is worth \$110/$(1 + i)$ or \$100 today. That is, the *present value* of \$110 in a year's time is \$100, since \$100 today would be equal to \$110 if left on deposit. In general, the present value (PV) is related to the future value (payment) one year hence (FV) as follows:

$$PV = FV/(1 + i). \tag{2}$$

A higher interest rate implies a smaller present value for a given future payment, because a sum deposited today would earn more, thus a greater opportunity cost of waiting is relevant.

Formula (2) can be generalized to allow for more years of waiting, a changing interest rate, or interest compounding. Only the first generalization is addressed. Suppose that \$100 is left on deposit for two years, at which time this principal will have grown to

$$\$100(1 + i) + \$100(1 + i)i = \$100(1 + i)^2 = \$121 \tag{3}$$

when i equals 10%. If, therefore, asked to forgo the use of \$100 for two years, an investor must be paid \$121 at the end of two years if the interest rate remained steady at 10%. In general, the present value (PV) of FV dollars in t years from now equals

$$PV = FV/(1 + i)^t. \tag{4}$$

The longer the wait, the smaller the future value of the promised sum t years from now.

Next consider the implication that discounting has when the consequences of a decision, in terms of expected future costs, are postponed far into the future. Suppose that a nuclear accident is anticipated to occur in a thousand years from a decision today. Further suppose that this accident will require $1 billion to clean up after it occurs. If discounting is practiced, the present value of $1 billion a thousand years from now is worth

$$\$1,000,000,000/(1 + i)^{1000}, \tag{5}$$

which, for an interest rate of 10%, is a modest amount of money since the discount factor of $1/(1 + 0.10)^{1000}$ is near zero. For example, this discount factor is approximately $1/(1.76$ trillion$)$ after a mere 320 years! The practice of discounting means that even future catastrophes may be given little value by the current generation if the costs are not anticipated until a far distant date.

In reality, the practice of discounting only requires that the nuclear plant insures itself against anticipated future losses by putting aside money or assets today equal to the present value in equation (5) that can grow in value to cover this future contingency.[12] In the above example, only a small amount is needed despite the $1 billion of future damages. While it is reasonable to assume that banking and insurance institutions will exist to justify this discounting procedure over the current generation's lifetime, it is more doubtful when the period of discounting involves hundreds or even thousands of generations into the future. Standard cost-benefit analysis requires that the value of the current investment necessary to cover future anticipated damages be included as part of the decision process to internalize the intergenerational externality so as to ensure economic efficiency.

Whether or not the money will actually be available in the future when needed depends on the existence of institutions that may not be there when the contingency occurs. This existence issue calls into question standard cost-benefit procedures when contingencies are very far off. The practice of discounting confers on the current gen-

---

12. The material in this paragraph draws from Schulze et al. (1981). For the debate on social discount rates and the responsibility toward future generations, see Page (1977), Sandler and Smith (1976, 1977, 1982), and Sen (1982).

eration a significant first-mover advantage that could induce it to adopt decisions that could result in global crises for future generations. As such, irreversible decisions may be adopted when the current generation believes that only a far-distant generation may suffer the eventual consequences. When one considers that uncertainty provides yet another source of discounting through the probability rate, the current generation, if not properly informed and if sufficiently impatient (possessing a high interest rate), may adopt technologies that could prove disastrous. Another relevant consideration involves a human tendency to undervalue what these future costs might be. If, for example, a future generation places a greater value on its environmental amenities, perhaps because of greater scarcity, then today's estimates of tomorrow's damages may be much too small. The farther away that tomorrow is, the greater is this undervaluation.

At least two policy conclusions follow. First, further thought must be given to the practice of discounting especially when long-term consequences are relevant. The standard discounting practice means that the current generation will place little value on potential disasters in the far-off future. This raises concerns as to whether discounting is ethically sound from an intergenerational perspective. The current generation, as steward of the earth's assets, should have some responsibility to future generations. Second, uncertainty augments the difficulty associated with discounting. Actions to gather information prior to making decisions limit this uncertainty and support more farsighted decision making. Recent transnational environmental agreements (for example, the Vienna Convention on Ozone Depleting Substances, the Long-Range Transboundary Air Pollution Treaty) required an information-gathering period prior to framing protocols to limit emissions.

SUSTAINABLE GROWTH

In recent years, it has become fashionable to speak of sustainable economic growth, which concerns the responsibility that the current generation has to future generations. Myriad definitions coexist for the concept of sustainable growth; a universally acceptable definition does not yet exist.[13] The nearest thing to such a definition is to describe growth as sustainable if it does not limit the options still available to the future. The preservation of these options may be presented in vastly different fashions – for example, as constant real consumption through time, or as a constant welfare level through time. Maintenance of a constant welfare level among generations may require decisions that sacrifice the current generation's consumption to achieve larger consumption levels for the next generation. Investment decisions regarding the capital stock are behind the notion of sustainable growth.

Weak sustainability requires that changes in the total capital stock, accounting for new investment through savings and capital losses through depreciation, be greater than or equal to zero.[14] Total capital stock includes man-made capital (for example, machines), human capital (for example, accumulated knowledge, embodied training), and natural capital (for example, the forests, the ozone layer, natural resource stocks). With a weak sustainability rule, it is permissible to exhaust some of the natural capital endowment so long as the *overall* capital stock is maintained.[15] Thus, the present generation can make choices that use up some of the natural or environmental capital provided that the proceeds from this consumed stock finance offsetting increases in other capital stocks, so that subsequent generations possess the wherewithal to achieve similar levels of welfare.

Strong sustainability is more restrictive and requires, in addition to weak sustainability, that *the change in natural capital is never negative*, so that the environmental stocks are maintained undiminished from generation to generation.[16] The strong sustainability rule

13. The reader can gain a flavor for these alternative definitions by consulting the following articles: Howarth and Norgaard (1995), Pearce and Atkinson (1995), Solow (1986), and Toman, Pezzey, and Krautkraemer (1995).
14. This weak sustainability condition can result in a constant consumption level through time and is known as the Hick-Page-Hartwick-Solow rule (Pearce and Atkinson 1995).
15. The manner in which diverse capital stocks are aggregated to give a single overall measure has not been addressed in the literature. This measurement problem is a crucial concern, especially in the case of natural capital since no agreed-upon technique currently exists. No one has devised a value for a watershed or other forms of natural capital. Unless the various forms of capital can be measured and made comparable in, say, value terms, the notion of sustainability will remain nonoperational.
16. On the strong sustainability, consult Pearce and Atkinson (1995) and Toman et al. (1995).

limits greatly the present generation's first-mover advantage and its exercise of property rights to the environment. When the strong sustainability rule applies, irreversible decisions with respect to natural capital are not permitted. These decisions are, however, allowed with weak sustainability, provided that other forms of capital increase sufficiently. With weak sustainability, the present generation maintains its first-mover advantage and can pursue its well-being with fewer impediments. The current generation is unlikely to feel bound to a strong sustainability criterion.

When sustainable growth is considered, intergenerational equity or distribution considerations must be included along with efficiency considerations. If markets were functioning and no markets were missing (that is, there are no external effects within or among generations), then an efficient outcome is assured even in an intergenerational sense. As long as property rights are assigned, the precondition for well-functioning markets is fulfilled. These well-functioning markets are not, however, sufficient to support sustainability, inasmuch as the assignment of property rights *among* the generations or the intergenerational distribution issue is also germane. To include these distributional issues, one must address the value that society attaches to alternative distributions of welfare among the generations. This calls for an ethical judgment beyond that of putting into practice policies that improve the well-being of one generation if it is not at the expense of another generation.[17] If sustainable growth is mandated, then the practice of discounting needs to be reexamined, since this practice biases decisions in favor of the current generation. As such, nonsustainable growth can result as capital stocks are driven down in the process of putting most weight on the wishes of the present generation.

The study of sustainable growth has a long way to go before it provides an operational concept that can guide policy making. At this juncture, sustainability indicates that decision makers need to be aware of more than intragenerational efficiency, because even efficient acts performed by one generation may have important consequences for the choices available to future generations. If sustainable growth could direct policy, global and regional environmental

17. This efficiency criterion is known as intergenerational Pareto efficiency (Sandler and Smith 1976).

Table 3.1. *Taxonomy of public good problems*

	Local or regional	Global
Intragenerational	Tropical deforestation (soil erosion) Peacekeeping Knowledge (geoclimatic specific) Desertification Acid rain Terrorism Containment of revolution Weather forecasting Disease containment Flow pollutants Highways Forest fire suppression	Tropical deforestation (ecotourism) Peacekeeping Knowledge (basic, generic) Disease containment Flow pollutants Transnational terrorism Satellite communication networks Genetic engineering
Intergenerational	Tropical deforestation (watersheds) Ocean pollution Stock pollutants Knowledge (agricultural research) Acid rain Desertification Collapse of local ecosystems Lake and river pollution Wetlands	Tropical deforestation (biodiversity) Disease eradication Nuclear waste storage Space exploration Ozone depletion Global warming Stock pollutants Knowledge (new technologies) Overuse of antibiotics Electromagnetic spectrum Genetic engineering

challenges would surely diminish in number. They will not disappear, because the presence of intergenerational consequences may not be known until much later, as in the case of CFC emissions. In today's political climate, decision making takes a short-run view that all but ignores future generations.

AN EXPANDED TAXONOMY FOR PUBLIC GOODS

Public goods' benefits can be nonrival and nonexcludable not only over space – say, among nations – but also over generations. In Table 3.1, public goods are pigeonholed based on geographical and temporal considerations, so that these goods are identified as local or global, and as intragenerational or intergenerational. For example, peacekeeping has implications at either the regional or global level depending on the dispute and typically affects just the current generation. In contrast, disease eradication, nuclear waste storage, space exploration, ozone depletion, genetic engineering, and the others listed provide nonrival benefits to the world, now and into the future. Such public goods are "intergenerational global public goods." The curbing of desertification, the reduction of acid rain, the preservation of wetlands, and the accumulation of stock pollutants (for example, lead, dioxins, polychlorinated biphenyls) tend to affect multiple generations within a well-defined region. Other public goods – weather forecasting, highways, curbing localized terrorism, forest fire suppression – possess benefits that are regional for just the current generation.

There are a number of characteristics of Table 3.1 worth highlighting. First, and foremost, many of the global challenges confronting the world today have public good characteristics. Second, as shown in the lower two cells of Table 3.1, some of these challenges are intergenerationally public as current decisions affect today's and tomorrow's people. Consequently, the relevant marginal benefits calculations involve current and future generations, thereby justifying the expenditure of a greater marginal cost than had future generations' marginal benefits been excluded. Unless these benefits are included, these intergenerational public goods are likely to be undersupplied. Third, some potential crises have multiple attributes that fit into more than one category. Tropical deforestation involves public good characteristics, in terms of soil erosion, ecotourism, watersheds, and biodiversity, that fit into each of the four categories. Public goods with these multiple attributes may be particularly difficult to assign resources efficiently.

As Table 3.1 illustrates, public goods and public bads[18] can have both a spatial and temporal dimension. Although supranational cooperation, if practiced, attempts to rectify the spatial problem by extending decision making to include the affected collective of nations, inefficiency may remain. Decisions by a supranational institution may still result in underprovision of the public good, be-

---

18. Public bads are simply public goods whose "benefits" give negative satisfaction, as in the case of air pollution.

cause the future generations' benefits from the public good are neither accounted for nor revealed.

Is there any means to alleviate the provision problem with respect to these intergenerational public goods? Decision-making bodies that include a wide age range among their members will contain some overlapping generations and, in doing so, should include an intergenerational perspective. If these overlapping generations possess some altruism toward future generations, this will also place some weight on the future benefits, derived from providing an intergenerational public good or averting an intergenerational disaster. Limiting the practice of discounting can also support more farsighted intergenerational public good provision decisions. But since the unborn cannot truly make their preferences known and trade future endowments with the current generation, a complete fix to the problem is, of course, infeasible. To date, decisions have not been farsighted, as evident from the large number of intergenerational concerns that challenge the world today.

AUTHORITARIAN VERSUS DEMOCRATIC REGIMES

When allocation of resources for public goods is considered, the form of the political institution may play a vital role.[19] Are authoritarian or democratic systems more likely to be supportive of public goods that benefit either the current generation or future generations? Based on reasoning drawn from public choice and collective-action theory, democracies may be viewed more favorably for the provision of certain public goods, especially those that protect the environment. Consider public goods whose benefits are confined to the present generation. Mancur Olson characterizes autocracies as maximizing tax revenues and maintaining their monopoly rights over these taxes. According to Olson, "he [the autocrat] will then spend money on public goods up to the point where his last dollar of expenditures on public goods generates a dollar's increase in his *share*

19. This issue is analyzed by Congleton (1992), Murdoch and Sandler (1997), Neher (1976), Olson (1993), and Schulze et al. (1981). This section draws insights, in part, from these works.

of the national income."[20] If, for example, the public good adds $5 million to national income and the ruler's take is one-fifth of national income, then he or she would expend up to $1 million, the net gain ($5,000,000 × 0.2) for providing the public good. An authoritarian regime is, however, likely to spend vast sums to avert terrorism or civil unrest, since the direct gain to the autocrat is great owing to his or her high share *and* large resulting payoff. Autocratic regimes need to appear in control.

In a democracy, the majority of voters command a share in the gain from a public good based on the majority's relative size. A large majority may be supportive of public goods because the majority's *relative* share is large. Thus, public goods that promote growth (for example, training, research and development, the discovery of new technologies) should receive much support in a democracy. There are, however, some offsetting factors. In a representative democracy where the majority chooses its decision makers as opposed to a direct democracy where issues are decided by referendum, the representatives make policies to win reelection.[21] As such, they may place different weights on members of their constituency. Lobbies may exercise undue influence on the provision of some public goods that benefit a very small segment of the population. Such lobbies are less concerned about the public good's effect on national income, insofar as their share of any adverse income effect is relatively small.[22] If these lobbies are environmentally oriented, then this will augment the provision of environmental public goods.

Next consider intergenerational public goods – in particular, those that protect the environment. Will autocracies differ from democracies in their provision of these public goods and in their willingness to participate in international environmental agreements that protect the earth's assets? Based on Olson's argument, autocrats should be suspicious of environmental protocols (for example, the Montreal Protocol on Protecting the Ozone Layer) that could impose taxes or else mandate contributions or financial assistance to other countries. Such policies cut into autocrats' tax revenues. Autocracies have on average shorter lengths of rule than democracies, and this factor

20. Olson (1993, 569).
21. This view was made famous by Downs (1957).
22. This argument derives from the analysis in Olson (1982).

reinforces autocracies' short-run focus.[23] If, moreover, no short-run augmentation in taxable income is anticipated from curbing emissions, then autocracies will not be too keen to support such environmental measures. Democracies, may, however, favor these measures, since voters as a group are interested in things other than income – for example, good health and a pleasant environment. Recent studies show that political freedom is a significant influence determining participation in international environmental agreements and the institution of domestic laws that protect the environment.[24] These same studies indicate that environmental protection responded favorably to increases in income; voters apparently demanded more environmental amenities as their incomes rose. Other things equal, rich democratic countries are anticipated to be the greatest patrons of the environment.

In a related analysis, Roger Congleton also put forward a convincing case that democratic governments will support the environment to a greater extent than autocratic regimes.[25] He argues that authoritarian governments face a higher price when trading national income against environmental quality. Because an autocrat receives a much greater share of national income than a median or average voter in a democracy, the opportunity cost, in terms of lost income, is much greater for the autocrat when instituting environmental safeguards. The short office length for autocrats also reinforces their greater opportunity cost, because they put more value on current benefits as compared with future benefits, which could come from an improved environment. Finally, autocrats tend to be more risk accepting than the average voter and, thus, should show less interest in buying insurance against environmental disasters by expending resources today to improve environmental quality tomorrow.[26]

This suggests that environmental-based crises may be more avoidable if the number of democracies is greater. Trends since the late 1980s in the growth of democracies may create an environmental

---

23. See, for example, the study on the length of African authoritarian regimes by Bienen and van der Walle (1989) where the average term was about four years.
24. Examples include Congleton (1992), Murdoch and Sandler (1997), and Murdoch, Sandler, and Sargent (1997).
25. See Congleton (1992).
26. This hypothesis of risk-loving behavior follows because authoritarian leaders are willing to assume positions in dangerous environments that have relatively short tenures.

dividend as nations become more willing to protect the environment through domestic laws and their participation in international environmental agreements. This growth of democracies may also foster transnational cooperation regarding environmental contingencies.

There is yet another reason for supposing that democracies might promote more farsighted decisions than authoritarian regimes. Although future generations are initially disenfranchised when a democratic decision with long-run consequences is reached, these generations can vote on options at a later date after they are born and attain voting age. In an intergenerational context, a democratic ethic is consistent with reexamination of issues as the constituency changes with time. The need to provide future generations with maneuverability is, therefore, essential under the democratic ethic. Suppose that the current generation must decide the repository strategy for storing high-level nuclear waste. Suppose further that just two strategies are available: (1) put the waste in glass and steel canisters that are then stored in mined repositories drilled into stable geological structures, or (2) put the waste in lined canisters that are dropped into the deep seabeds. For the second option, the canisters will eventually be encased in stone through the natural geological process. Process 1 provides significant maneuverability for a subsequent generation, because the canisters can be easily recovered and then stored or disposed of differently if better methods become available. In contrast, process 2 does not lend itself to recoverability and, hence, limits greatly the options of a subsequent generation to pursue alternative storage procedures. Process 1 is more in keeping than process 2 with permitting the future generation to recontract. An authoritarian government should have little interest in preserving maneuverability and recontracting, since future decision makers may be individuals who have overthrown the current regime. Authoritarian regimes should have little reluctance to choose irreversible outcomes.

THE IMPACT OF INCOME INEQUALITY ON INTERGENERATIONAL CHOICE

Income inequality as it relates to the sequence of generations can play a role in the manner in which public goods are provided and global crises avoided. As a general principle, the current generation, barring significant destruction of the environment by earlier generations, is better off than preceding generations.[27] By the same token, future generations are anticipated to be better off than the current generation. This general tendency for the improving well-being of future generations depends on economic growth being sustainable. If crises-averting actions were positively related to income, then richer (future) generations would be more inclined to provide this action. Empirical findings to date show that environmental preservation is income normal – for example, the demand for preservation rises with income *within* a generation.[28] However, the income elasticity or responsiveness of environmental preservation has not been well documented thus far. If environmental assets were income elastic, then a 10% increase in income would result in a greater than 10% increase in activities to preserve the environment.

The ability of humankind to confront crises may depend on the underlying technology of public supply aggregation. First consider a best-shot technology. As argued in Chapter 2, the richest participant is the most apt to provide the public good for the best-shot scenario. Each succeeding generation may be in an improved position, owing to its enhanced endowments, to provide public goods so as to avert crises if a best-shot technology applies, as it does for some of the world's greatest challenges – for example, finding a cure for the e-virus strain of AIDS, whose infection rate is increasing at an alarming rate. Thus, the increasing wealth of succeeding generations bodes well for confronting some kinds of crises. However, if, with nonsustainability, the current generation were to pass on fewer assets to a subsequent generation, then this would hamper the next generation's ability to achieve important breakthroughs and best-shot public goods.

Of course, alternative underlying technologies may apply to different global crises. By way of contrast, consider a weakest-link technology in which the least-well-off generation's contribution to the crisis-averting public good determines the overall level of safety for

27. Comparing the well-being among generations would be greatly enhanced if national income accounting procedures were extended to include environmental transactions. Depreciation of environment assets would be entered as losses in income.
28. For example, see Congleton (1992), Murdoch and Sandler (1997), and Murdoch et al. (1997).

all subsequent generations. The construction of dikes or seawalls abides by the weakest-link technology, as do measures to control the spread of diseases or revolutions. The current generation's actions may then be pivotal in determining the overall security afforded to the society, both present and future. The increasing wealth of future generations may play no role in improving on a small effort by an earlier generation for the weakest-link case.

Crisis-averting public goods that depend on a summation technology are determined by the *cumulative* efforts of all of the generations. Crises that are dependent on, say, the accumulation of a stock pollutant, such as global warming, are associated with a summation technology. In this case, the greenhouse gas emissions of all generations contribute to the problem, and a redistribution of income among the generations, if possible, would not necessarily change the overall levels of greenhouse gases in the atmosphere over a particular time horizon, unlike the best-shot or weakest-link cases.[29] Intergenerational income distribution could, however, influence the *time profile* of greenhouse gas accumulation in the atmosphere. If income were positively related to *greenhouse gas emission reductions*, then the growth of wealth with subsequent generations would mean more atmospheric accumulation of these gases in the near term when generations are poorer. This works to the detriment of all future generations. Increases in population could reverse this tendency as more people must stay warm in winter and cool in summer.

Because the current generation is generally more impoverished than future generations, this also inhibits the assignment of sufficient resources to the provision of intergenerational *pure* public goods. This follows because the richest generations that stand to gain the most from these intergenerational public goods are not there initially to make the allocation decision. There may be little that one can do to rectify this problem. If, instead, the public good is impure and generates benefits that differ between the current and future generations, then the current generation will be more motivated to contribute as *near-term* nonrival benefits increase in their relative importance.

---

29. Technically speaking, public good provision level is neutral with respect to redistributing income among the contributing generations. See, for example, Cornes and Sandler (1996, chapter 6), Sandler (1992), and Warr (1983).

For one class of intergenerational public goods, income inequality within and among the generations has really no role to play. This class consists of intergenerational club goods, whose benefits are excludable and partially rival within and among generations.[30] At any moment in time, such goods display rivalry in the form of crowding as users detract from the quality of the experience of other users. At a national park, the number of visitors creates crowding in numerous ways – for example, longer commute time between scenic vistas, increased noise levels, and decreased solitude. This crowding or rivalry applies to just the current users. Another form of rivalry – depreciation due to utilization – affects the current *and* future generation of users. Consider a nature preserve, such as the Great Barrier Reef off the Queensland Coast in Australia. Once visits at a given time surpass the "carrying capacity" of the reef, the reef's environment begins to deteriorate from visitation. This may arise as swimmers interfere with the fish or as boats release pollution. Intergenerational club goods can be managed efficiently by a collective of members, called an "intergenerational club," that charges users a toll or fee based on crowding *and* depreciation losses that their visits impose on the membership.

Essentially, highways and other forms of infrastructure are intergenerational club goods that can be managed in the same fashion, provided that tolls charge for both crowding and depreciation. Road user charges in the United States have failed to run these highway clubs effectively, because tolls based on the number of axles and miles traveled accounted for crowding but did not adjust for depreciation. The latter depends on vehicle weight; road depreciation rises exponentially with vehicle weight. Tolls based on axles increase proportionally as the vehicle length increases, but weight and the resulting road surface damages rise more than proportionally to vehicle length. Incentives were perverse, so that trucking firms switched to heavier vehicles to minimize tolls and other fees. Thus, US road revenues from user fees were insufficient to finance maintenance and replacement, thereby resulting in a fast-deteriorating infrastructure.[31] Some bridges (for example, a bridge on the New York State Throughway) even collapsed, with loss of life. Cities and

---

30. On intergenerational club goods, see Sandler (1982) and Cornes and Sandler (1996).
31. See Lipsman (1994), Sandler (1982), and Congressional Budget Office (1992).

even countries are other examples of intergenerational clubs that can be maintained by members and passed down among generations.

If the proper tolls that account for intergenerational and intragenerational congestion costs are collected and used to finance provision and maintenance, then the club can be maintained by its members and passed from one generation to the next. Intergenerational club goods are distinguished from other public goods by the presence of an exclusion mechanism, which allows for the collection of fees based on revealed tastes through use. For national parks, the nature enthusiast would display his or her strong demand for the amenity by visiting more often and would be charged accordingly in total tolls. Income within and among generations surely motivates the visitation rate, but this consideration is accounted for by total toll payments. Toll proceeds are earmarked to maintain and to provide the club good, passed among the generations. One generation can reimburse an earlier generation's investment through equity shares, sold as the club good is transferred. The value of these equity shares depends on the residual value of the club good. If a generation were myopic and ran down the club good's value through depreciation and collected tolls that did not reflect this depreciation, then the generation would receive less in payments to support its retirement when the asset is traded to the next generation. Many assets – universities, churches, national parks, jungle tracts, nature preserves, scenic wonders, lakes – are intergenerational club goods. Club arrangements have a significant role to play in managing some intergenerational assets, provided that exclusion can be practiced at a reasonable cost.

MISSING MARKETS AND INTERGENERATIONAL CHOICE

As discussed earlier, generations may not always be able to rely on markets to promote efficient decision making. This is particularly true when investment decisions under risks are considered in an intergenerational context. To illustrate the possible difficulties, I consider a couple of scenarios where an earlier generation must decide whether or not to invest to protect a future generation from a possible disaster. A few stylized examples establish some of the crucial considerations as to whether an earlier generation would be motivated to insure a future generation against danger. This type of situation relates to numerous current contingencies. For global warming, actions to limit greenhouse gases today can insure against dire consequences tomorrow. By maintaining biodiversity, a current generation provides a future generation with genetic material that may prove useful in developing pest-resistant crops or even a cure for a plague.

Consider two overlapping generations for which generation 1 must decide in period 1 whether or not to invest in a safeguard – heightening a levee – to protect against flooding during a subsequent period.[32] Suppose that, if the flood occurs in the second period, it destroys the endowment only of generation 2. That is, generation 1 is unscathed during flooding, because it has retired to higher ground! Flooding in the second period occurs with a 50–50 chance that is only revealed at the start of period 2. Further suppose that generation 1 lives for two periods, while generation 2 lives for just the second period during which the two generations overlap. Generation 1 receives an endowment of 10 in the first period, while generation 2 receives an endowment of 10 in the second period. The levee, which must be provided in period 1 if at all, costs 5 to heighten. At the start of period 2, it is assumed to be too late to heighten the levee once the information of a pending flood is revealed, since investment takes time. This storyline accords with reality where the protecting investment has to be anticipated prior to the time when it is known to be required. For instance, building seawalls may protect future generations from rising seas as polar ice caps melt due to global warming. Additionally, developing new antibiotics may guard the next generation from the consequences (for example, antibiotic-resistant bacteria) of overusing existing antibiotics.

In this stylized game, generation 2 decides whether or not to compensate generation 1 for its investment in the levee *once the uncertainty is resolved* at the start of the second period. If, at that time, the flood becomes a certainty, then generation 2 will reimburse generation 1 with generation 2's anticipated flood losses of 10. If, how-

---

32. This section draws on an example and analysis in Amsberg (1995). The analysis is extended and modified.

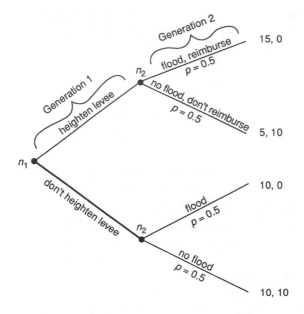

Figure 3.2. Intergenerational competitive case.

ever, the flood does not materialize, generation 2 does not reimburse generation 1 for having raised the levee. Assume further that *both generations are risk averse*, so that they prefer 10 with certainty to a gamble with an expected value of 10.

In Figure 3.2, the scenario is translated into a simple two-period game tree, where n_1 is the decision node at the outset of the first period for generation 1, and n_2 is the decision node at the outset of the second period for generation 2. The game can end in four ways: Generation 1 can heighten the levee and either be reimbursed or not by generation 2, or generation 1 does not heighten the levee and either the flood comes or it does not. At the four endpoints, the payoff on the left is that of generation 1, while the payoff on the right is that of generation 2. As shown, generation 1 decides the levee's height and generation 2 decides reimbursement based on generation 1's actions and the resolved uncertainty. When generation 1 decides its investment option, it does not know nature's future "play" since the flood probability is 50%. If generation 1 were to heighten the levee and the flood came, it would receive 10 for its investment of 5. Given its endowment of 10, generation 1's net payoff is then 15 as indicated. If, instead, it heightens the levee and no flood occurs, it will be left with 5 after paying the levee cost of 5. At these two top endpoints of Figure 3.2, generation 2 gets 0 after compensating the first generation or 10 if no compensation is required. In the lower half of the tree, generation 1 gets 10 regardless of the flood, while generation 2's fortune hinges on the draw from nature.

The game scenario of Figure 3.2 is called competitive because both generations optimize without coordinating actions and generation 2 pays generation 1 the full value of its potential losses when protection is provided and later needed. The bet posed to the two generations is actuarially fair. For the competitive case, generation 1's decision whether or not to heighten the levee depends on how it values the *certain* payoff of 10 that is assured by not heightening the levee versus the expected payoff of $10(= 0.5 \times 15 + 0.5 \times 5)$ associated with heightening the levee. A risk-averse first generation would not heighten the levee – thus, the thicker branch emanating from n_1 shows its preferred course of action.

The competitive solution results in underinsurance and inefficiency, inasmuch as generation 2 would prefer to pay generation 1 the costs of the levee, 5, to insure against the gamble of a flood wiping out its endowment. This can be illustrated with the help of Figure 3.3, which displays a "coordinated" equilibrium where generation 2 trades with generation 1 so as to limit its risk. Figure 3.3 differs from Figure 3.2 since generation 2 commits to reimburse generation 1 regardless of what is revealed at node n_2. The payoffs for the bottom two endpoints of Figure 3.3 are the same as Figure 3.2, but the top payoffs are different. By committing to reimbursement of costs if the levee is heightened, generation 2 pays 5 in either state of nature and holds onto a net payoff of 5, while generation 1 holds onto its endowment of 10. If generation 2 could engineer this exchange with generation 1, the certain payoff of 5 for generation 2 provided through the insurance of heightening the levee is preferred to the gamble of not raising the levee with its expected value of $5(= 0.5 \times 0 + 0.5 \times 10)$. The thicker branches emanating from n_1 and n_2 indicate the equilibrium path. Given the natural sequencing of generations, the required trade for the coordinated equilibrium cannot typically be achieved, and consequently, the necessary insur-

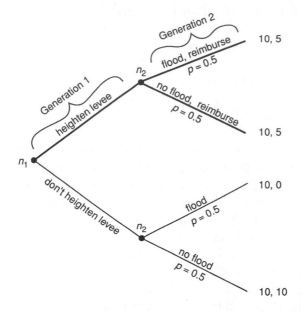

Figure 3.3. Intergenerational coordinated case.

ance market is missing. Generation 2 is not around when generation 1 must decide the insurance investment.

On the other hand, the *missing-market dilemma may be ameliorated if generation 1 also suffers from the disaster.* Return to the example depicted in Figure 3.2, but now suppose that generation 1 loses half of its endowment if a flood were to ensue in period 2 and the levee is not heightened. This change is accounted for by altering only generation 1's payoff from 10 to 5 in the third payoff pair from the top of Figure 3.2 (not shown). A gamble for generation 1 is now tied to either decision. Raising the levee gives generation 1 a greater expected payoff and is thus preferred because the potential gain is greater and the downside risk is the same in either gamble. This case indicates that when the decision-making generation has *a stake* in the decision, a more efficient intergenerational decision might result. But this stake must be sufficiently high. If the loss to generation 1 from an unprotected flood were small, say, 1, then it may not pay to protect, since the option of not heightening the levee provides greater certainty from which a risk-averse agent would be willing to sacrifice some average return.

Circumstances sometimes tie overlapping generations together in terms of shared risks, thus simulating an intergenerational insurance market trade, similar to the coordinated solution. Suppose that generation 1 must sell its lowland houses to generation 2 at the start of period 2, prior to moving to the highlands where generation 1 lives on the proceeds during its retirement. The values of these houses depend, in part, on the risk of flooding which can be reduced by the levee. Raising the levee in period 1 can then be capitalized into housing values, thus giving motivation to generation 1 to insure the risk for both generations. In consequence, generation 1's efforts can be reimbursed by generation 2, thus achieving the sought-after intergenerational trade. Generations can also be tied by altruism, since the risk to a subsequent generation will then be partly reflected in the objective function of the parenting generation. If the generations are sufficiently *near* in time to allow the insurance decision to be tied to a traded commodity or to altruism, then the missing-market problem may be, at least, partially addressed. Problems are more insurmountable as additional generations need to be linked.

Suppose that three generations must be linked in which generations 1 and 2 overlap in period 2 and generations 2 and 3 overlap in period 3, but generations 1 and 3 do not coexist. Generation 2 must, therefore, be the link that ties together the generations. Further suppose that the contingency only occurs in period 3, if at all, and jeopardizes generation 3. If the investment must be made by generation 1 in period 1, as in the case of nuclear waste containment, then even a coordinated solution between generations 2 and 3 would pose problems. This follows because generation 2 would have an incentive to take advantage of generation 1 by not reimbursing its investment. This could be true even if generation 2 partly shared in the risk represented by the contingency.[33] Coordinated solutions for three or more generations can only be achieved when each generation faces sufficient risks for the contingencies. *Shared risk and propinquity are the crucial considerations for avoiding missing insurance markets.* By propinquity, I mean that the investment decision

---

33. See Doeleman and Sandler (1996) for an explicit model and demonstration.

is sufficiently near in time to when the contingency may occur so that overlapping generations are involved. Even a single break in the chain is sufficient to spoil coordination efforts.

Consider the dikes in Holland. The conditions for coordination are satisfied because every pair of overlapping generations shares the risks of being flooded. Coordination is, thus, achieved. Risks are also shared for acid rain and ozone shield depletion, so that inter-generational coordination has been achievable. However, risks are not shared for the overuse of antibiotics, insofar as the abusing generation may not experience a cost. The storage of high-level nuclear wastes also proves problematic, because short-term fixes (for example, placing the wastes in fifty-year-lifetime canisters and dumping them off the coast) transfer the risks from the current generation to a future generation. Additionally, global warming and lost biodiversity may not involve shared risks among the generations.

INSTITUTIONAL ASPECTS

Since Chapter 5 is devoted to the structure of institutions to achieve farsighted and efficient decisions for confronting global crises, only a few remarks are needed here. Institutions must bind the generations together so as to make farsighted decisions regarding crises that influence a sequence of generations. This can be fostered if institutional decision makers include representatives from *all* concurrent generations in proportion to their numbers in the population. Thus, decision-making bodies need to have all age cohorts represented. Trades among the generations can be supported through bequests to the future generations and pensions granted to the retiring generation. The role of transnational institutions in promoting altruism is another consideration. Western cultures tend to favor their children, while many Eastern cultures appear to favor their ancestors. For the former, bequests may be used by the present generation to motivate the next generation to certain courses of action, while, for the latter, care of one's elders may motivate the earlier generation to provide a hospitable environment for its caretakers. How these differences are resolved by supranational structures that include nations with diverse altruistic orientations to the future generations is an important, but unstudied, question. Anything that provides the deciding generation with an interest in the decision will encourage more-farsighted action, even though some of the benefits ensue after its death. If these supranational bodies are to abide by democratic principles, then decisions must preserve maneuverability for future generations to recontract.

CONCLUDING REMARKS

A number of conclusions follow from this chapter's analysis. First, crises *with consequences for both* the present and future generations are more likely to support farsighted collective action as compared with those with implications for just the future generations. The greater the share of these benefits going to the present generation, the more appropriate will be its response. Second, crises with the greatest uncertainty and more-distant consequences are the most difficult to resolve. Any action that increases the propinquity (for example, resolution of uncertainty) between the decision-making generation and the generation experiencing the consequences will promote more-farsighted policies. Third, political institutions that include a representative sample of overlapping generations should be in an improved position to further the interests of future generations. Fourth, if currently traded commodities can capitalize on future generations' value to decisions made today, as was the case for lowland houses threatened by flooding and intergenerational clubs, more efficient intergenerational decisions can be achieved. Shared risks and propinquity between the decision-making generation and the affected generation are the crucial concerns for avoiding missing insurance markets. Fifth, the technology of public supply and the provision of crisis-avoiding public goods can be related to income distribution among generations. In resolving crises, a best-shot technology favors the general tendency for the present generation to be wealthier than their predecessors, while a weakest-link technology does not favor this tendency. Sixth, while altruism cannot completely rectify the misallocation of resources among generations, it can ameliorate this misallocation. Seventh, no matter how well collective action is promoted through international cooperation, some misallocation of resources will remain owing to intergenerational considerations associated with most global challenges.

4   Global house

In their desire to attract readers, the news media and popular magazines have characterized the world as besieged by a host of challenges from deteriorating environments, diminishing resources, spreading hostilities, expanding populations, increasing inequality, emerging plagues, and escalating terrorism. For environmental concerns, in particular, one is often left with the impression that seemingly different problems – ozone shield depletion, global warming, acid rain – stem from the same sources. Most people cannot answer whether ozone depletion is related or not to the global-warming problem.[1] If all of these contingencies were due to the same source, then a single solution could serve as a panacea. Global challenges would be easy to address. Unfortunately, the world and its contingencies are far more complicated so that no panacea exists. Similarities are present among the environment crises, but crucial differences that influence the prognosis and the appropriate intervention, if any, are also present. Consider ozone depletion from chlorofluorocarbons (CFCs) emissions and global warming from the release of greenhouse gases (GHGs). CFCs are an extremely efficient GHG that add to global warming, but, given their relatively small concentration in the atmosphere, the primary damage from

---

1. This is aptly illustrated by a front-page article in the *Sydney Morning Herald* on 5 June 1996, whose headline read, "Australia places jobs before ozone." In fact, the article had nothing to do with ozone, but was about Australia's position at the then upcoming Geneva conference on climate change. Australian concerns over job losses were with respect to curbing greenhouse gases, not chlorofluorocarbons.

CFCs is in terms of depleting the protective ozone layer. Other GHGs – CO_2, methane, nitrous oxide – trap solar energy in the atmosphere, thereby heating the planet but without degrading the ozone shield. CFCs production and consumption are concentrated within relatively few countries, while GHG emissions are widespread, involving virtually every nation. From a strategic viewpoint, global warming is associated with greater incentives to free ride on the emission-reducing efforts of others. Other essential differences exist that can explain why progress is made for some problems but not for others.

By analyzing diverse examples of global concerns, this chapter highlights the similarities and, more important, the crucial differences among global challenges. Environmental difficulties are, particularly, fascinating to analyze, since ecosystems are interdependent so that imbalances and stresses associated with, say, the forests can spill over to influence other ecosystems – for example, watersheds and soils. Nations truly reside in a global house, passed from generation to generation, where some contingencies are isolated to one or two rooms (nations), while others may influence the integrity of the entire house. This latter set of contingencies can be especially troublesome for the world community to control. Remote-sensing satellites and other monitoring tools have enabled the world to gain a better appreciation that activities and their impacts are not always confined to the place of origin.

Although diverse problems are examined, some generalizations follow from the analysis. First, incentives are supportive for nations independently to confront *some* regional and global difficulties without the need for more-centralized direction. Second, when coordination is required, the prognosis for effective collective action is better when fewer nations are needed to address the exigency. Third, the acquisition of information concerning the costs and benefits from actions reduces uncertainty and greatly improves the chances of an effective response. Research, evaluation, and understanding must precede any action plan. Fourth, the greater the localized benefits relative to transnational benefits coming from a nation's action, the greater the likelihood that such actions will be undertaken. Fifth, differences among global exigencies limit severely the ability to apply effective means for dealing with one challenge to others. In this respect, global challenges are like cancers: Cures for one kind of cancer may prove ineffective in treating other forms. Sixth, the dire forecasts for global collapse unless nations sacrifice their autonomy to a global order are exaggerated. When coordination is needed, loose federations are best tried first. These federations can be later tightened if warranted. Seventh, today's treaties, while promising, tend to codify actions that nations were already doing; as such, they do not represent a true global consciousness.

Each of the selected problems analyzed in this chapter possesses myriad aspects. A thorough investigation of each challenge could easily fill volumes. Thus, the analysis must be eclectic. To characterize each problem, I select among the facts to highlight crucial similarities and differences.

PEOPLE AND MORE PEOPLE

Population growth is tied to many of the environment-based concerns challenging the world today, including tropical deforestation, desertification, and global warming. In countries with rapid population growth, population expansion may represent a market failure in which an individual's pursuit of his or her well-being leads to an outcome from which everyone's well-being could be improved. That is, when deciding whether or not to have another child, a couple weighs the costs and benefits to them, while ignoring external costs in terms of crowding and increased genvironmental pressures that another child may impose on others. Even if parents appreciated the societal benefits that their decision to limit family size might have, there is no assurance that their restraint would be emulated by others unless the government enforces or rewards this restraint. Given this likely lack of restraint of others, couples decide to do what seems best to them, thus ignoring any costs to society at large. At the international level, countries with rapidly expanding populations are loath to listen to other nations that argue for population control, since this advice impinges on the nation's sovereignty.

Some selected population indicators are given in Table 4.1. In mid-1994, the world population stood at 5.67 billion with approximately 1.24 billion in developed countries and 4.43 billion in LDCs (see the second column of Table 4.1). Population amounts are also indicated for the regions of the world in this second column. By

Table 4.1. *Population indicators*

Region	Population (millions) 1994	Population (millions) 2025	Average growth rate 1990–5	Urban growth rate (percent) 1990–5	Fertility rate 1990–5
Africa	681.7	1,582.5	2.9	4.6	6.0
Asia	3,233.0	4,900.3	1.8	3.5	3.2
Europe	512.0	541.8	0.3	0.7	1.7
Latin America	457.7	701.6	1.8	2.6	3.1
North America	282.7	360.5	1.1	1.3	2.0
Oceania	27.5	41.3	1.5	1.6	2.5
USSR (former)	284.5	344.5	0.5	1.1	2.3
Developed countries	1,237.6	1,403.3	0.5	0.9	1.9
LDCs	4,427.9	7,069.2	2.0	3.7	3.6
World	5,665.5	8,472.5	1.7	2.7	3.3

Source: UN Population Fund (1994, 55–9).

2025, population is anticipated to increase to 8.47 billion, with 1.40 billion in developed countries and 7.07 billion in LDCs (see the third column of Table 4.1, where projected regional breakdowns are also given). Population first reached one billion in 1800. It then took 130 years to reach two billion people in 1930, thirty years to reach three billion in 1960, fourteen years to reach four billion in 1974, and thirteen years to reach five billion in 1987. In just eleven years, the six billion mark will be attained in 1998.[2] Thereafter, another billion people will be added every eleven years until 2021, from which time it will take fourteen years to reach nine billion, thirty-three years to reach ten billion, and seventy-two years to reach eleven billion. These projections are based on a medium-range scenario. Annual average growth rates indicate that much of the growth is in the LDCs, where population increases have been quadruple that of the rest of the world (the fourth column of Table 4.1). LDCs' fertility rates are almost double those of the developed world (the rightmost column of Table 4.1). In addition, the rate of urban growth was 0.9% in developed countries compared with 3.7% in LDCs during 1990–5

2. On population growth, see UN Population Fund (1994), UN Development Programme (1992, 1994), Haub (1995), and Myers (1992b, 1993, 1994, 1995). The information in this paragraph draws from these sources.

(the fifth column of Table 4.1). These population indicators are dis-
aggregated by region in Table 4.1. Approximately 60% of the increase in population, anticipated in the 1990s, will be in the tropical
countries. Africa has the highest projected growth rate, followed by
Asia and Latin America.

Many factors contributed to this population explosion in the
1990s. Population growth is more a consequence of the fall in death
rates worldwide, owing to improvements in public health, medicines,
and nutrition, than a consequence of the increase in birth rates. This
decrease in death rates resulted in an unprecedented increase in life
expectancy. In agrarian developing countries, children are an economic asset and a source of social security, so that birth rates remained high. For such countries, the fall in death rates when
combined with the high fertility rate meant large increases in population size. In the United States and other developed countries,
social security and other similar government programs led to a decrease in birth rates.

Population expansion becomes a problem when strains are placed
on the soils, the forests, the water supplies, the fisheries, and the
atmosphere that degrade these natural assets permanently. Sustainable development implies that the economy is able to satisfy the
requirements of the current generation without reducing the ability
of subsequent generations to meet their own needs (see Chapter 3).
Once an ecosystem's "carrying capacity" is surpassed, stresses on
the system cause a permanent degradation. Prior to this capacity
being reached, an ecosystem is able to absorb the pollutants without
being noticeably impaired. Pressures on a host of ecosystems are
predicted to exceed carrying capacity as population expands. For
example, the demand for water is anticipated to double between
1971 and 2000.[3] Fuelwood gatherers have reduced tropical woodlands and savannas in Indonesia, Ghana, Sudan, Nepal, Northern
India, Pakistan, Bangladesh, Sri Lanka, Myanmar, Thailand, Viet-
nam, and the Philippines.[4] As the woodlands are razed by individuals seeking to survive, deserts have spread, and, then, still greater
demands are placed on the remaining forests and grasslands. Ac-

3. See Myers (1993, 1995).
4. On fuelwood gathering, see Myers (1992b, 115–26) and Repetto and Gillis (1988). On
   other related concerns, consult Hyde and Newman (1991) and Sandler (1993).

cording to Norman Myers,[5] one-half of all wood cut worldwide is used annually as fuel, with more than 80% of this cutting taking place in the LDCs. The high urban growth rates in the LDCs are often associated with increased poverty as people leave their rural backgrounds and huddle in the expanding metropolises. By the year 2010, there is expected to be over five hundred cities of a million or more people, with twenty-six of them exceeding ten million people. Many of these new million-plus cities will be in the LDCs, which will need massive public investments to supply the required infrastructure.[6] LDCs have a particularly difficult time in financing the urban infrastructure needed to accommodate this rural exodus.

The spread of deserts (that is, desertification) is not only due to the woodgatherers. The expansion of arable lands has meant the use of marginal lands that often cannot support more than a few harvests. In the tropical countries, "shifted cultivators" have also added to the problem by destroying rain forests for agricultural activities that are unsustainable, because the soil is nutrient poor once leaf litter from the rain-forest canopy is eliminated through clearing, burning, or decay. As shown later, the shifted cultivators are now responsible for more forest damage than the other agents of deforestation combined. Increases in livestock to feed an expanding population also contribute in some places to desertification and the destruction of ecosystems. A vicious circle is apparent: Population growth in the LDCs put stresses on the environment, which, in turn, eliminate habitats, thereby placing augmented demands on the remaining habitats.

A recent strain of analysis has focused on the determinants of "endogenous" growth, or growth promoted by economic decision.[7] Investment in human capital – education, training, improved health care – appears to be a primary determinant of endogenous growth in LDCs and elsewhere. Other essential determinants are investment, technology transfer from abroad, R & D levels, and the competitiveness of the economy vis-à-vis the rest of the world. Countries

5. Myers (1992b, 116).
6. Rabinovitch and Leitman (1996). The World Resources Institute (1996) documents some of the difficulties associated with this urban growth.
7. The endogenous growth literature has blossomed in recent years; references include Barro (1991), De Long and Summers (1991), Grossman and Krueger (1995), Rivera-Batiz and Romer (1991), and Stokey (1991).

that are pressured to feed, clothe, and house expanding populations find it difficult to save and support investment; hence, economic growth suffers. Fertility rates tend to vary opposite to a country's income per capita and education levels.[8] Education provides women with improved job opportunities and salaries, which motivate family planning. Education also prepares women for understanding contraceptive devices and for negotiating family choices with spouses and other family members. More modest population growth, when combined with income growth, will lead to greater income per capita, which can serve as a check to further population growth.

Recent findings indicate that economic growth and environmental degradation are not necessarily positively related; economic growth need not lead to environmental losses. An inverted U-shape relationship applies in which environmental quality is sacrificed with growth at low income per capita levels, but is augmented with growth at high income per capita levels.[9] After a threshold income per capita is achieved, the demand for environmental preservation varies positively with income per capita, so that demands for environmental quality are generally classified as income normal;[10] that is, increased income per capita is associated with greater demands for an improved environment beyond the threshold. A recent study estimated that pollution levels tend to fall for most countries after their income per capita exceeds $8,000.[11] While this insight is promising, the reader must remember that most LDCs are nowhere near this $8,000 level and, more important, are unlikely to reach this level for some time to come, especially if population growth is not curtailed.

Population growth worldwide has slowed somewhat from 2.1% per annum in 1970 to 1.7% per annum in 1991.[12] Unfortunately, only 0.1% of this drop came since 1977 and growth rates remain high in the LDCs. Energy demands in the LDCs are anticipated to increase at 5% to 7% per annum, compared with 2% to 3% in other places.[13] These energy demands can lead to increased acid rain, greater global warming, spreading deforestation, and growing desertification. For

8. UN Population Fund (1994).
9. World Bank (1992).
10. Murdoch, Sandler, and Sargent (1994).
11. Grossman and Krueger (1995).
12. UN Population Fund (1993).
13. UN Population Fund (1994).

the tropical countries, acid rain may represent a particularly devastating problem, because trees may be more susceptible to the stresses that acid rain can cause for nutrient intake. Even if traditional causes of tropical deforestation are curtailed, economic development in LDCs may bring an even greater forest destruction through pollutants.

Population pressures cannot be ignored when examining responses to environmental challenges. Population control at the national level must be solved first if collective responses at the international level are to succeed. Higher living standards coupled with greater investment in human capital seem to be the most effective means for motivating individuals to curb population expansion. Nations will not permit others to dictate their population policies. Nevertheless, these policies link the world community insofar as unchecked population growth creates transnational external effects: when, for example, tropical deforestation reduces the world biodiversity and the reservoir of carbon. Another example of a linked policy occurs when cleared hillsides limit watershed storage causing flooding in neighboring nations. As the planet's ecosystems are strained, increased demands are expected to create escalating harmful effects.

TROPICAL DEFORESTATION

Tropical forests house over half of the world's species of plants and animals, so that the clearing of these forests would have a significant impact on the earth's genetic diversity. In addition, these forests sequester significant amounts of carbon, which would, if released, accelerate global warming. Tropical forests also provide a bequest value that the current generation worldwide derives from passing an asset on to a future generation. When a generation derives satisfaction in its lifetime from bequeathing an asset to the next generation, a "bequest value" is present. Thus, tropical forests yield some global public goods. But these forests also give rise to localized public and private outputs to the host nations and their neighbors. Private or host-nation specific benefits include timber and nontimber products. For the host nation and nearby states, rain forests provide local public goods in terms of watersheds, erosion control, localized cli-

Table 4.2. *Tropical deforestation: Selected countries*

Country	Total forest extent 1990 (000 hectares)	Annual deforestation 1981–90 (percent)	Equivalent CO_2 1991 (000 metric tons)	Percent of world total
Brazil	561,107	0.6	970,000	28.5
Indonesia	109,549	1.0	330,000	9.7
Zaire	113,275	0.6	280,000	8.2
Bolivia	49,317	1.1	140,000	4.1
Myanmar	28,858	1.2	120,000	3.5
Philippines	7,811	2.9	110,000	3.2
Malaysia	17,583	1.8	110,000	3.2
Colombia	54,084	0.6	100,000	2.9
Peru	67,906	0.4	94,000	2.8
Thailand	12,735	2.9	91,000	2.7
Ecuador	11,962	1.7	68,000	2.0
Mexico	48,586	1.2	50,000	1.5
Gabon	18,235	0.6	47,000	1.4
Sudan	42,976	1.0	38,000	1.1
Laos	13,173	0.9	36,000	1.1
Cambodia	12,163	1.0	34,000	1.0
Zambia	32,301	1.0	33,000	1.0
Vietnam	8,312	1.4	33,000	1.0
Nicaragua	6,013	1.7	32,000	0.9
Total	1,161,884	—	2,706,000	79.6
World	1,756,299	0.8	3,400,000	100.0

Source: World Resources Institute (1994, tables 19.1, 23.2) and author's calculations.

mate effects, and nutrient recycling. In short, the preservation of tropical forests produces multiple outputs, whose influences or benefit range affect people near and far. Host-nation specific benefits can provide an important motivation for preservation, since without the forests these localized public and private benefits would be lost. Nearby countries have an interest to strike bargains with the host nation to support preservation activities to the extent that they derive benefits from the forests. Global public benefits, as discussed later, constitute the greatest problem when preservation is an issue.

Table 4.2 helps put recent tropical deforestation into perspective. In the tropical countries, forest types include rain, moist deciduous, hill and mountain, dry deciduous, very dry, and desert. Greater than 80% of tropical forests are rain and moist deciduous. At this juncture, the second and third columns of Table 4.2, displaying the 1990 extent of forests and the annual deforestation percentage for 1981–90, respectively, are relevant. The nineteen countries that experienced the greatest deforestation in 1991 are listed in the first column. On average, the world lost about 0.8% of its tropical forest each year during 1981–90. Estimates of tropical deforestation differ among sources;[14] some experts put annual tropical deforestation in recent years at about 2% per annum.[15] Latin America and Asia still possess about 60% of their original forest endowments, while Africa just less than 50%. If current rates of exploitation continue, then tropical forests may virtually disappear in fifty to one hundred years, depending on which estimate one consults. Some countries (Costa Rica, Ivory Coast, Madagascar), where tropical deforestation has been much greater a few years back, are no longer in the top group, because remaining forest tracts are so reduced. In 1991, the three largest countries with tropical deforestation were in Latin America, Asia, and Africa.

Tropical biodiversity provides people with important benefits; for example, one-quarter of all prescription drugs sold in the United States are derived from tropical plants. This biodiversity also provides genetic material useful in genetic engineering for creating, for instance, more pest-resistant crops; there is also no telling what future cures could be found from these tropical plants. Additionally, tropical plants and animals involve crucial interrelationships with species elsewhere. A fascinating instance involves songbirds that protect crops in the United States by feeding on insects.[16] Many of these songbirds migrate to Central and South America for the winter. If these birds' winter habitats are reduced through tropical deforestation, their numbers will dwindle. Insect pests will then experience a population explosion, thus causing widespread crop losses in the United States. To curb this damage, farmers may resort to more pesticides which, in turn, create their own harmful effects. The health of the temperate zone is linked to the tropics.

Myriad activities are responsible for tropical deforestation. One account listed four primary actions as resulting in the clearing of 142,000 square kilometers (sq km) in 1989: Wood harvesting ac-

---

14. World Resources Institute (1990, table 19.1) listed greater percentage decreases in forests for many of these nations in the 1980s.
15. Myers (1992b).
16. Myers (1992b, 59–60).

counted for 45,000 sq km; cattle ranching in South America, 15,000 sq km; the provision of infrastructure, 12,000 sq km; and shifted cultivators, 70,000 sq km.[17] Shifted cultivators pose the greatest threat today, because poverty drives these individuals to slash and burn the forests to scrape out a subsistence. Burning the forests to make way for crops often destroys much of the nutrients, leaving the soil unable to sustain more than a couple of harvests before these shifted cultivators move deeper into the rain forests. Given the soil's poor nutrient base as well as the short-term interests of the farmers, there is little incentive to make longer-term investments in terms of fertilizers to augment the soil's fertility. Projected population growth will add to the numbers of the shifted cultivators and their ravage of the tropical forests.

The underlying causes of these forest-destroying activities are rooted in misdirected government policies, population pressures, and collective action problems. In many tropical nations, forests are public lands managed by government officials who have allocated few resources to protect the forests from wanton exploitation. These officials often grant short-run concessions to logging companies in return for a fraction of the wood's value. A prime example is Indonesia.[18] Given the short-term nature of the contract, often involving only a few years, these companies have no incentive to manage the forest resource in a renewable fashion by planting trees for future harvests.[19] Another misdirected policy involves the institution of land-tenure policies requiring the forest lands to be improved – often meaning cleared – by the would-be owners in order to gain title. Yet another misdirected policy is the subsidization of agricultural uses that are unprofitable without significant government outlays. Until recently, Brazil paid huge subsidies to cattle ranchers to sustain a losing proposition. Unnecessary infrastructure – for example, the Trans-Amazon highway – can also destroy large forest tracts and make it even more difficult to control the shifted cultivators, who then have better access to the forests.

These misdirected policies can be corrected if the governments of the tropical countries begin to comprehend the losses that they im-

17. Myers (1992c, 17–19). Also see Myers (1994).
18. Gillis (1988).
19. Hyde and Newman (1991).

pose on their own people, present and future, through these policies. In addition, the developed and neighboring countries must pay for the benefits that they derive from the existence of these tropical forests. Payments from the developed countries for preserved bio-diversity, carbon sequestration, ecotourism, bequest value, and other benefits could defray the opportunity and enforcement costs incurred by host nations for preservation. Consider the case of bio-diversity, which has global public good properties. The biodiversity contained in a tropical forest provides nonrival benefits to the host country's people as well as to people worldwide, inasmuch as one nation's use of the associated gene pool does not necessarily detract from the benefits available to other nations from the same gene pool. If biodiversity is maintained, then its potential benefits – new cures – may be available to everyone, so that the benefits of biodiversity are partly nonexcludable. As a global public good, biodiversity is expected to be plagued by free riders in the form of nations that derive benefits but do not want to pay the host nations for the value received. For example, the preservation of the polar bear benefits people worldwide, regardless of whether or not they support its survival. In the past, developed countries that used genetic material taken from the tropical forests felt no obligation to pay royalties to the host nations, especially if the material was subsequently synthesized. This policy is clearly hypocritical on the part of countries, such as the United States, that have argued in the case of intellectual goods – books, inventions, scientific findings – that property rights must be protected and royalties paid or else too little of these goods will be produced. In the same way, host nations for genetic diversity need to be motivated to preserve their forest endowment; they need a stake in the action.[20] Preservation requires resources.

Developed countries have the knowledge to discover the drugs and, therefore, to profit from preservation of biodiversity even if royalties have to be paid. At the Earth Summit in Rio during June 1992, the United States refused to sign the Convention on Biological Diversity treaty (drafted on 22 May 1992 in Nairobi), which sought to protect the tropical nations' property rights to genetic material gathered from their forests. During the Clinton administration, how-

20. Sandler (1993) and Sedjo (1992).

ever, this position was reversed and the treaty signed. Unfortunately, as of early 1996, the United States has not ratified this convention.[21] A greater stake is clearly needed for the tropical nations if sufficient biodiversity is to be protected. In addition, the residents of these nations must themselves reveal a demand for preservation, so that elected officials are driven to protect forest resources. Such demands often come with increased income and well-being; it is difficult to allocate resources to preserving the environment when daily survival is an all-consuming activity. An "environmental dividend" may derive from efforts by the developed nations to improve the welfare of the LDCs through aid, provided that the aid lifts the condition of the general population and does not end up in the bottomless pockets of government officials. Misuse of foreign aid constitutes a serious roadblock and must be addressed if income redistribution is to serve as an effective policy.

A second global public good comes from the tropical forests' store of carbon. When this carbon is released through the clearing and burning of the forests, a public bad is experienced worldwide. In the fourth column of Table 4.2, I list the equivalent CO_2 emissions in thousands of metric tons from land-use changes in 1991 due to forest conversion. The rightmost column indicates the percentage of the world total emissions of CO_2 from land-use change attributable to the countries listed. In 1991, land-use changes released 3,400,000 thousand metric tons of CO_2 into the atmosphere, while emissions from industrial activities released 22,673,000 thousand metric tons. Although industrial processes accounted for higher levels of greenhouse gases, tropical deforestation was the second greatest source of these greenhouse gases, accounting for about 13% of the total CO_2 emissions.[22] Clearly, the developed countries have an interest in curbing tropical deforestation from a global-warming perspective. The connection between tropical deforestation and global warming underscores the interrelationship among global challenges.

21. Fridtjof Nansen Institute (1996, 169).
22. In the latest World Resources Institute publication (1996, 328), the 1991 land-use-change release of CO_2 is recalculated as 4,100,000 thousand metric tons, while the 1991 industrial release of CO_2 is recalculated as 22,614,000 thousand metric tons. With these new figures, deforestation accounts for approximately 15.3% of CO_2 emissions.

Not all of the benefits of these forests are global public goods; many are either private goods or public goods whose benefits are either specific to the host nation or to neighboring nations. Benefits from private goods (fruits and nuts), watersheds, reduced soil erosion, tourism, and localized climate effects provide an incentive for the host countries to preserve some of their own forests and for neighboring states to reach agreements over support payments. For tropical forests, markets and negotiations among neighboring countries can account for these localized benefits, but are unable to account for the global public goods, where the inclination is to free ride on the efforts of others to protect the forests. But even here there is hope, since the developed countries have much to gain from the preservation of the forests. Moreover, the bargaining advantage is decidedly with the nations that host the tropical forest due, in large part, to their first-mover advantage, given that they can control the forests' destiny. Developed countries must consider the shrinking nature of the forests as they stall in reaching an accommodation to assist in the support of forest preservation. Since the developed countries have the wherewithal now to exploit the genetic material of the forests, waiting means that fewer potential gains will come once a bargain is struck. Additionally, people in the richer countries have a greater demand to curb environmental degradation, owing to the positive relationship between income and the demand for environmental quality.

To clarify the notion about first-mover advantage in the case of a shrinking forest, consider two children – Pedro and Peter – bargaining over shares of a shaved-ice cone on a hot summer day. Every second that passes leaves less of the treat. Suppose that Pedro holds the cone and must be satisfied with the agreement before any trade is consummated. Further suppose that he can take licks during the negotiations. Peter will obviously get nothing unless his offer is sufficiently attractive. If he stalls long enough, what remains might have little or no value.

Table 4.2 indicates how tropical deforestation is concentrated in a few key countries. Just three – Brazil, Indonesia, Zaire – account for over 46% of the land-use carbon emissions in 1991. Since agreements among a few nations are often easier to accomplish and more meaningful than those among a large number, developed countries that value the tropical forest the most have an opportunity to curtail deforestation by striking bargains with those nations with the largest forest tracts and the greatest deforestation activities. In attempting to reach an accommodation, the developed countries must recognize that they are in a poor bargaining position owing to the shrinking nature of the forests and their impatience to do something sooner than later. New trees can be planted to replace deforested trees, but the lost biodiversity cannot be replenished through replanted forests – once lost, biodiversity is gone forever or, at least, for a very long time. Perhaps, the best agreement would be for the tropical nations to receive payments from the developed countries for the benefits that the latter derive from the forests' existence.[23] Any such agreements will surely be insufficient, because other developed countries will free ride on those that value the forests the greatest; nevertheless, some improvement in resource allocation is still better than none.

Unlike some global crises (for example, global warming), tropical deforestation provides a large share of localized benefits to the host nations that will motivate some conservation as forest tracts shrink. It is easy to extrapolate dire forecasts about the tropical forests based on past linear trends, leading some conservationists to predict that tropical forests will disappear in a mere fifty years. The value of forests may increase as their stocks dwindle, and this augmented value could curb future decreases. For this to occur, the value of these remaining forests must rise faster than the increased value of land development. Population growth will increase this latter value and inhibit conservation. In many ways, population control is an essential ingredient in saving tropical forests.

Countries such as Brazil have become aware of some misdirected policies and have taken steps to rectify these policies. Even population pressures on the forests can be checked domestically through resource allocation, provided that the tropical nation sees a net benefit from doing so. If the forests only benefited the developed countries, then the outlook would be bleaker, but localized benefits will motivate some preservation by the host nations.

---

23. On the problems with swapping debt for forest tracts, a solution favored by some
    conservationists, see Pearce et al. (1995).

GLOBAL WARMING

Of the many global challenges confronting the planet, global warming is perhaps the most difficult to solve through either national action or transnational cooperation. Global warming stems from a greenhouse effect as trapped gases in the earth's atmosphere let sunlight through but absorb and capture infrared radiation, thereby raising the mean temperature. Gases with this property are called greenhouse gases (GHGs) and include carbon dioxide (CO_2), CFCs, methane (NH_4), and nitrous oxide (N_2O). The bulk of the atmosphere is comprised of oxygen and nitrogen, which do not act as GHGs. CO_2 is a by-product of the burning of fossil fuels and deforestation, while methane is largely a result of solid wastes, coal mining, oil and gas production, wet rice agriculture, and livestock. Nitrous oxide is partly derived from the use of fertilizers and energy production. Of the GHGs, CFCs trap twenty thousand times as much heat as an equivalent amount of carbon dioxide, while methane traps twenty to thirty times as much as CO_2. In the mid-1980s, the *immediate effects* on global warming from the four GHGs were as follows: 53.2%, CO_2; 21.4%, CFCs; 17.3%, methane; and 8.1%, nitrous oxide. CFCs' contribution to global warming is far less than CO_2 despite the former's efficiency as a GHG, because the concentration of CFCs in the atmosphere is so much less than that of CO_2 (see Table 4.5, p. 104). If, however, the long-term residency of the pollutants in the atmosphere is also taken into account, then the overall contributions to global warming of the four GHGs are quite different: 80.3%, CO_2; 8.8%, CFCs; 2.2%, methane; and 8.7%, nitrous oxides.[24] Based on the immediate effects, any comprehensive policy to curb global warming would have to include the buildup of all GHGs. If longer-run aspects are stressed, then CO_2 accounts for more than 80% of the global-warming problem, but other GHGs still contribute. In consequence, ozone depletion, tropical deforestation, and global-warming problems cannot truly be investigated in isolation. Even sulfur dioxide, associated with acid rain, is believed to reflect energy back into outer space, thereby alleviating global warming. Because particulates (for example, sulfur oxides and nitrogen oxides) are jointly produced with CO_2 in power plants, there is

---

24. These numbers are reported in Nordhaus (1991), where additional sources are listed.

yet another ground for linking policies for two or more global concerns.

Unabated accumulation of GHGs can raise the mean temperature by as much as 2° to 5° C during the next century; estimates differ widely and much uncertainty remains. The *exact* relationship between the accumulation of GHGs in the atmosphere and the extent of global warming has not been quantified. The offsetting influences of other pollutants are just becoming recognized. Moreover, there is as yet no comprehensive model that indicates the influence that a warmer climate will have on the distribution of rainfall, the levels of the seas, and the distribution of the food-producing regions. Unlike most global difficulties where all nations are harmed, global warming may greatly benefit some nations by enhancing their agricultural productivity. Understandably, nations that may gain from a warmer climate and greater rainfall are not motivated to curb global warming. Even the potential losers are reluctant to institute carbon taxes and other measures that would slow down economic activity when the true costs of a warmer atmosphere are unknown. To achieve sought-after reductions in CO_2 emissions of 50%, the world may have to expend 2% or more of its gross national product (GNP) in perpetuity.[25] Is the world prepared for this kind of sacrifice to forestall a problem whose consequences are not well understood? Clearly, it is not.

Small amounts of CO_2 reductions can, however, be accomplished at little cost through greater efficiency and conservation, but significant reductions will require large outlays as the marginal costs of curbing CO_2 emissions rise rapidly with greater cutbacks.[26] In fact, a recent study has shown that energy is underpriced in the United States, so that a *small* carbon tax would limit CO_2 emissions and impose no true opportunity cost on the economy until an optimal price is reached.[27] This suggests that some (small) efforts to curb CO_2 emissions may be in a nation's interest independent of what other countries do to control emissions.

Beyond these limited cutbacks, roadblocks abound. The time pro-

25. Schelling (1992) has some interesting observations about the costs of global warming versus the costs of curbing global warming. Also see Intergovernmental Panel on Climate Change (1990).
26. Nordhaus (1991).
27. See Boyd, Krutilla, and Viscusi (1995) and Congressional Budget Office (1990).

files of costs and benefits inhibit actions, since the costs of abatement are experienced *immediately* and in the future, while the benefits are experienced only in the distant future as GHG levels in the atmosphere stabilize. Discounting these benefits, owing to the wait, means that less outlays are warranted than had the benefits been more immediate. Another roadblock involves the global public good aspects of curbing global warming. Cutbacks in GHG emissions yield benefits that are primarily nonrival among nations and nonexcludable globally. Apparently, a classic example of a Prisoners' Dilemma applies. Suppose that the developed nations and the LDCs form two separate coalitions to bargain over a treaty. Each coalition would benefit if the other curbed emissions, while it did nothing. Thus, both coalitions want to frame a global-warming treaty to achieve this lopsided result. The outcome in Rio and Berlin has thus far been a global-warming treaty that effectively does little to stem the rise in carbon emissions – a Prisoners' Dilemma dominant strategy of inactivity. The Convention of Climate Change requires a nonbinding commitment on the part of developed countries to stabilize CO_2 emissions at 1990 levels by the year 2000. Only CO_2 emissions have been included thus far. In contrast, the LDCs did not make any commitment, since past accumulations of GHGs have been blamed by them on the developed nations. In mid-1995, the treaty commitments of the developed countries have not been met and do not look as though they will be met in the near future.[28] These nations want tree planting, assistance to the LDCs, and reduced CFC emissions to substitute for some CO_2 reductions. LDCs want to hold out for favorable terms before making commitments. Thus, the bickering continues with another meeting held in Geneva during July 1996. A protocol is sought by 1997 if possible. A third stumbling block involves the large number of countries that must abide by an abatement agreement if their actions are not to be undone by free riders.

Global warming is not a problem contained to a few nations – it involves the myriad activities of all nations. Data reported by the World Resources Institute allow the problem to be put in perspective. In Table 4.3, I list the sixteen largest polluters of industrial-

---

28. *The Economist* (1995). Also see Fridtjof Nansen Institute (1996) for treaty participants and commitments.

Table 4.3. *Major polluters of industrial-based CO_2: 1991*

Country	Rank	CO_2 emissions (000 metric tons)	Percent of world total	Per-capita CO_2 emissions (metric tons)
United States	1	4,931,630	21.8	19.53
USSR	2	3,581,179	15.8	12.31
China	3	2,543,380	11.2	2.20
Japan	4	1,091,147	4.8	8.79
Germany[a]	5	969,630	4.3	12.13
India	6	703,550	3.1	0.81
United Kingdom	7	577,157	2.5	10.00
Iraq	8	520,281	2.3	27.86
Canada	9	410,629	1.8	15.21
Italy	10	402,516	1.8	6.96
France	11	374,113	1.7	6.56
Mexico	12	339,873	1.5	3.92
Poland	13	308,164	1.4	8.06
S. Africa	14	278,695	1.2	7.18
S. Korea	15	264,547	1.2	6.05
Australia	16	261,818	1.2	15.10
Total		17,558,309	77.4	—
World		22,672,832	100.0	4.21

[a] Includes West and East Germany.
Source: World Resources Institute (1994, table 23.1) and author's calculations.

based CO_2, which derives from the burning of fossil fuels and cement production.[29] The table depicts CO_2 emissions (middle column), percent of world total emissions (fourth column), and per capita CO_2 emissions for 1991 (rightmost column). Emissions are concentrated: the top three emitters accounted for over 48% of the world's industrial emissions, while the top sixteen accounted for over 77%. But this is not the whole story. The effects of land-use changes in equivalent CO_2 emissions are given in Table 4.2. Except for Mexico, there is no overlap between countries in Tables 4.2 and 4.3, so that thirty-four significant GHGs polluters have now been identified and many others exist. The eighteen largest methane polluters are listed

29. Recently released emission figures for 1992 show much the same pattern, except that a few rankings change, because the Soviet Union is now broken up into its republics. The Russian Federation is ranked third, behind China. Ukraine is ranked seventh, and Kazakhstan is ranked fourteenth. Iraq's rank is much reduced. Otherwise, the rankings and emission levels are similar to those reported for 1991.

Table 4.4. *Major polluters of methane from anthropogenic sources: 1991*

Country	Rank	Methane emissions (000 metric tons)	Percent of world total
China	1	40,000	16.0
India	2	35,000	14.0
United States	3	29,000	11.6
USSR	4	28,000	11.2
Brazil	5	9,800	3.9
Bulgaria	6	8,700	3.5
Indonesia	7	7,100	2.8
Bangladesh	8	6,200	2.5
Thailand	9	6,000	2.4
Australia	10	4,500	1.8
Vietnam	11	3,900	1.6
United Kingdom	12	3,800	1.5
Argentina	13	3,600	1.4
Japan	14	3,600	1.4
Myanmar	15	3,600	1.4
Canada	16	3,300	1.3
Pakistan	17	3,200	1.3
Germany[a]	18	3,000	1.2
Total	—	202,300	80.9
World	—	250,000	100.0

[a] Includes East and West Germany.
Source: World Resources Institute (1994, table 23.2) and author's calculations.

in Table 4.4, which indicates that some major methane polluters – Bulgaria, Bangladesh, Argentina, Pakistan – are not included in either Table 4.2 or Table 4.3. Thus, there are a lot of significant contributors to global warming, and an effective treaty must include the major contributors, now and into the future.

Suppose that a treaty is drawn up that includes *just* the five major polluters from Table 4.3, so that the participants account for over 50% of industrial CO_2 emissions. Such a treaty will be ineffective for at least two reasons. First, the fastest growth in CO_2 emissions is expected from LDCs, and, except for China, these countries' emissions would not be constrained by the proposed treaty. Some predictions indicate that CO_2 emissions of the LDCs will probably exceed those of the developed countries by 2010.[30] Second, nations

30. *The Economist* (1995).

Table 4.5. *Atmosphere concentrations of selected greenhouse gases: 1980–94*

Year	CO_2 (ppm)	CFC-11 (ppt)	CFC-12 (ppt)	N_2O (ppb)	CH_4 (ppb)	CO (ppb)
1980	338.5	158	289	299	NA	NA
1981	339.8	166	305	299	NA	71.7
1982	341.0	175	325	301	NA	72.5
1983	342.6	182	341	302	NA	70.2
1984	344.3	190	355	303	NA	73.1
1985	345.7	200	376	304	NA	75.5
1986	347.0	209	394	305	1,600	75.5
1987	348.8	219	411	306	1,611	76.9
1988	351.3	231	433	306	1,619	74.4
1989	352.7	240	452	306	1,641	71.5
1990	354.0	249	469	307	1,645	69.4
1991	355.5	254	483	307	1,657	67.2
1992	356.3	260	496	308	1,673	68.8
1993	357.0	260	502	308	1,671	NA
1994	358.8	261	509	309	1,666	NA

Notes: ppm denotes parts per million, ppb is parts per billion, and ppt indicates parts per trillion. N_2O is nitrous oxide, CH_4 is methane, and CO is carbon monoxide. NA indicates not available. Only the CO statistics come from the World Resources Institute (1994, table 23.3).
Sources: World Resources Institute (1994, table 23.3; 1996, table 14.3).

not party to the treaty may increase their GHG emissions as emission levels decrease in the treaty-bound countries. Free riding will take place that can undo the good acts of others. Industrial activities would be expected to move to these free-riding countries.

Tables 4.5 and 4.6 provide a picture of the accumulation of GHGs in the recent past. In Table 4.5, atmospheric concentration of CO_2, CFCs, nitrous oxide, methane, and carbon monoxide (CO) are given annually for 1980–94. With the notable exception of CO and methane, the atmospheric concentrations of GHGs have increased each year. Notably, the rate of increase of CFCs has slowed considerably in recent years owing to the Montreal Protocol. The world's emission of CFCs decreased between 1989 and 1991 and will continue to decrease (see Table 4.7, p. 112). In Table 4.6, industrial emissions of CO_2 are indicated for selected years; an upward trend is clear. Per-capita emissions are indicated in the rightmost column.

Global warming has little in its favor to encourage national and transnational action in the near term. Until the uncertainty sur-

Table 4.6. *World CO₂ emissions from fossil fuel consumption and cement manufacture: Selected years*

Year	CO_2 emissions (millions of metric tons)	Per-capita emissions (metric tons)
1955	7,511	2.71
1960	9,475	3.15
1965	11,556	3.48
1970	14,964	4.03
1975	16,935	4.14
1980	19,390	4.36
1985	19,833	4.10
1990	22,343	4.21
1991	22,673	4.21

Source: World Resources Institute (1994, table 23.4).

rounding benefits and costs from global warming is resolved, nations will be, understandably, reluctant to invest in abatement efforts. Unlike most other global crises, there are few localized benefits recognized that are *specific* to the nation undertaking the CO_2 cutback. The closest example of a localized benefit from reduced global warming would be to nations with large portions of their population living at or near sea level, such as Australia and Bangladesh. Such nations may have to relocate coastal populations or erect sea barriers as the seas slowly rise as a warmer atmosphere melts portions of the polar icecaps. Individual actions by these nations, which are generally small CO_2 emitters, to reduce emissions will have a tiny overall impact on stemming global warming. Hence, why bother? The once-dire forecasts of polar ice melting have been toned down considerably in recent years, thus limiting localized benefits still further.

More recently, some potential localized benefits from curbing CO_2 have been identified, because CO_2 is produced along with particulates (for example, sulfur oxides). These particulates tend to fall close to the source, so that cutting CO_2, if it limits the particulates, might provide localized benefits. In many cases (for example, coal-fired power plants), however, these particulates can be controlled without necessarily reducing CO_2 emissions. Because these pollutants can be unjoined, CO_2 must still be viewed as adding to global pollution with few localized influences.

Another barrier to action involves the adverse net benefits perceived by some of the major polluters. The US case is instructive. Although estimates of the costs of curbing CO_2 emissions in the United States vary greatly, a reduction of CO_2 emissions on the order of 10% to 20% may result in as much as a 4% fall in GNP. William Nordhaus estimated that a 3° C warming of the climate may cost the United States about one-quarter of 1% of its GNP.[31] For the United States, the net gain from unilateral action of a sizable magnitude to reduce CO_2 emissions is perceived to be negative. If the major polluters do not perceive gains from curbing CO_2 emissions, the other countries will be hampered in their efforts to achieve meaningful overall reductions. The free-riding potential is great. Given emission projections, a large number of nations must abide by an agreement to limit CO_2 emissions if their efforts are not to be undone by nonparticipants. Myriad activities add to GHG emissions; hence, real economic sacrifice would have to be made by almost everyone in every nation if progress is to be achieved. Even if abatement occurs, it will take decades for atmospheric concentration of GHGs to begin to decrease. The global-warming problem is, indeed, besieged by roadblocks that do not motivate nations to act.

Until the major polluters can be convinced that global warming represents a real threat, I would anticipate that progress on a protocol to the Convention of Climate Change, which would mandate explicit CO_2 emission reductions, will be very slow. This progress hinges on a demonstration that benefits associated with curbing GHGs outweigh the associated costs. If important localized effects from curbing GHGs can be established, then this realization will support such a protocol.

OZONE SHIELD DEPLETION

The depletion of the stratospheric ozone shield shares some similarities with global warming, but, most notable, there are subtle differences that have united countries to take decisive actions in recent years to curb CFC emissions. When one is warned that the UV (ultraviolet) index is high and to stay out of the sun without the

31. Nordhaus (1991).

proper protection, the consequences of ozone shield thinning are behind the warning. UV radiation is absorbed into the skin of animals and can damage essential molecules, such as DNA, thereby leading to harmful effects including tumors. Of all of the current global concerns, the thinning of the ozone layer could cause the greatest cataclysmal effects, resulting in the mass extinction of species (for example, amphibians), the disruption to the food chain, the inducement of skin cancers, impairment of the immune system, and other ailments (for example, cataracts). Despite its minute concentrations in the earth's atmosphere, representing less than one part per million (see Table 4.5), the ozone shield stretches from ten to twenty-five miles overhead and absorbs much of the earth's short-wave UV radiation and, in doing so, protects plants and animals. When compressed, the ozone layer is just three millimeters thick.[32] Any dissolution of this shield would not only enhance the risk of skin cancers to humans, but would also endanger food supplies by adversely affecting phytoplankton at the base of the marine food chain. Phytoplankton is influenced because increased UV radiation can disrupt the photosynthesis process, whereby CO_2 and water are converted into sugars. If phytoplankton is reduced, the nutrient stock in the ocean ecosystem is limited and, consequently, the population of other marine species will be reduced worldwide. The global house analogy is apparent. The Environmental Protection Agency (EPA) estimated that a 50% cutback in CFC emissions from 1986 levels could save the United States $6.4 trillion by 2075 in reduced costs associated with skin cancers.[33] Without these reductions, skin cancer incidence was based on annual growth of CFC use at 2.5% through 2050. The long-run costs from cutting CFC use was estimated to be between $20 and $40 billion during the 1989–2075 period, given these projected growth rates.

As early as 1974, Mario Molina and Sherwood Rowland theorized that released CFCs could migrate upward to the stratosphere where they could be broken down by sunlight, thus giving up chlorine, which would combine with ozone. In the process, the protective ozone layer would be thinned. CFCs are used in air conditioning, refrigerators, aerosols, insulating foam, and the cleansing of circuit

32. de Gruijl (1995).
33. EPA (1987a, 1987b) and Morrisette et al. (1990, 16).

boards. With each application, CFCs can escape into the atmosphere. Concern was heightened because CFCs remain in the atmosphere for upward of a hundred years; hence, the impact of earlier releases is not fully experienced until a considerable delay. Even a complete ban on CFCs today would not end the depletion of the ozone layer for years. Thereafter, it will take a half century for ozone levels to return to 1970 concentrations. Subsequent findings, provided by scientists with the Department of Transportation, the Federal Task Force on Inadvertent Modification of the Stratosphere, and the National Academy of Science, convinced the EPA to prohibit the nonessential use of CFCs as aerosol propellants in 1978.[34] Most other countries did not immediately follow the US ban,[35] because there existed disagreement in the scientific community over whether CFCs really depleted the ozone layer and, if so, how the process took place. This disagreement ended after further monitoring of the ozone layer and more scientifically acceptable explanations were formulated.

In 1985, the British Antarctic Survey presented evidence that an alarming 40% drop (from 1964 levels) in the springtime atmospheric concentration of ozone took place over Halley Bay, Antarctica, between 1977 and 1984. This so-called hole in the ozone layer of the stratosphere then drifts northward during the summer and mixes with other air masses, thus allowing the depletion to be shared worldwide on a more or less equal basis as the layer thins. The uniform thinning during the summertime makes the problem purely public in nature. One nation's increased exposure to enhanced UV radiation does not lessen the risks to people in other nations; a nonrivalry is clearly present. Also, the thinning has consequences for nations worldwide once summertime mixing takes place, so that the harm caused is nonexcludable. During 1990, scientific evidence indicated that the thinning of the ozone layer had worsened and that a large springtime hole had opened over the North Pole.

Recent scientific theorizing has formed the following picture of the depletion process: Once released into the atmosphere, CFCs are broken down by sunlight into chlorine, which, in turn, combines with

---

34. Morrisette et al. (1990, 10–12).
35. Canada banned aerosol use of CFCs in 1978, Sweden in 1979, and Norway in 1981. Others sat on the fence waiting for more convincing evidence.

nitrogen dioxide, methane, and ozone to form stable reservoirs of chlorine nitrate and hydrochloric acid. Throughout this initial lower atmosphere process, ozone depletion is modest. The real destruction takes place over the polar regions in the upper atmosphere during the long cold winters when stratospheric clouds of nacreous acid and nitric acid trihydrate trigger a chemical reaction that causes the stable reservoirs of chlorine to release molecular chlorine.[36] When sunlight returns in the spring, the free chlorine along with ozone combine to form chlorine monoxide and oxygen. In the chemical process, stratospheric ozone is destroyed. Stable chlorine reservoirs do not form under these frigid conditions, because the nitrogen compound, required for reservoir formation, precipitates.

A better picture of the extent of stratospheric ozone losses also emerged. Since the late 1960s, ozone thinning averaged about 5% worldwide, with slight variations according to latitudes. Every 1% loss in ozone leads to a 2% increase in harmful UV radiation exposure, so that increased UV radiation exposure is now approximately 10% higher than in that late 1960s.[37] This increased exposure is of great concern as documented by the 1987 EPA report.

The gathering of scientific information on the extent of the depletion, its process, and consequences had a profound influence on ozone diplomacy.[38] Just prior to the discovery of the Antarctic ozone hole, nations negotiated the Convention for the Protection of the Ozone Layer in Vienna on 22 March 1985. This precursor to the Montreal Protocol mandated the ratifiers to study the harmful effects of CFC emissions on the ozone layer. Nations were committed to monitor the ozone layer, to exchange scientific findings, and to develop domestic programs for limiting ozone-depleting substances. By 1989, twenty-seven countries had signed the Vienna Convention or had approved legislation to accomplish its ends.

On 16 September 1987, the Montreal Protocol extended the Vienna Convention by setting explicit limits to the emission of ozone-depleting substances, particularly CFC-11 and CFC-12. Other depleting substances (for example, methyl chloroform, carbon tetrachloride) were to be taken up in later protocols. The Montreal

---

36. See Toon and Turco (1991).
37. This information is contained in de Gruijl (1995).
38. See Benedick (1991) on ozone diplomacy and issues raised.

Protocol entered into force on 1 January 1989, following the required signatures of more than eleven ratifiers, and included the following primary features:

1. From their commitment date to 1 July 1993, ratifiers must reduce their *annual* consumption and production of CFCs to 1986 levels.
2. From 1 July 1993 to 30 June 1994 and during each year thereafter until 1 July 1998, ratifiers' annual production and consumption of CFCs cannot exceed 80% of their 1986 levels.
3. From 1 July 1998 and thereafter, ratifiers' annual production and consumption of CFCs cannot exceed 50% of their 1986 levels.
4. To meet obligations, emission transfers between Protocol parties are permitted.
5. To induce ratification worldwide, Protocol parties must ban the import of controlled substances from nonratifiers starting in 1990. Beginning on 1 January 1993, ratifiers cannot export ozone-depleting substances to nonratifiers.
6. For developing countries whose annual consumption is less than 0.3 kilograms (kg) per capita on their entry date, a ten-year delay in terms of compliance was granted. A promise of technical and financial assistance to developing countries was made.

Ratifiers of the Montreal Protocol were automatically considered to be parties to the Vienna Convention. Developing nations had a great inducement to ratify the Montreal Protocol, because they could delay compliance by ten years, gain technical and financial assistance, and escape trade sanctions. As of 31 October 1995, 149 countries have ratified the Protocol.

On 29 June 1990, the Montreal Protocol was strengthened with a set of amendments put forward in London. Most notable, ratifiers accelerated their responsibilities by promising to reduce production and consumption levels of CFCs during 1995 to 50% of the 1986 levels. For 1997 and the following two years, these levels of CFCs could not exceed 15% of 1986 levels. By 1 January 2000, CFC production and consumption must be zero, except for the recycling of previously produced CFCs. Amendments also strengthened and better defined trade restrictions, and they established the Multilateral

Fund to assist developing countries. The London Amendment also added twelve chemicals to the list of ozone-depleting substances to be controlled. An additional thirty-four chemicals were placed under observation for possible future actions. The amended Protocol entered into force on 10 August 1992, following the required signatures. Still further amendments were put forward in Copenhagen on 25 November 1992 and primarily involved emission limits and eventual phasing out of hydrochlorofluorocarbons (HCFCs), which are CFC substitutes that also deplete the ozone layer. Other CFC substitutes, hydrobromofluorocarbons, were eliminated along with three halons. The elimination date for carbon tetrachloride and methyl chloroform was moved up to 1996 by the Copenhagen Amendment, which entered into force on 14 June 1994.[39]

So why did the global community put forces into motion to meet this contingency, and can these forces be harnessed for other global crises? There are many factors that promoted action in the case of ozone. A crucial one was the reduction in uncertainty concerning CFCs as an ozone-reducing substance that came with the discovery of the ozone hole in 1985 and the subsequent explanation of why stable CFCs would deplete ozone under the frigid conditions of the polar winters. As the case against ozone mounted, the major emitters were more willing to consider increasingly drastic measures. The EPA studies also limited uncertainty by documenting that the benefits from reducing the release of CFCs would outweigh the associated costs.

Another factor that fostered international collective action involved the concentration of interests affected adversely by the curbing of CFC use. In 1986 prior to the Montreal Protocol, just three nations – the United States, Japan, and the former Soviet Union – accounted for 46% of CFC emissions. If these and other major industrial countries were to curb production and consumption of CFCs, significant progress in stemming the ozone-depletion problem would be achieved. Given the concentration of users and producers, free riding among the nonparticipants was less of a concern than global warming, provided that the main producers and consumers joined the agreement. In Table 4.7, the major emitters of CFCs for 1989 and 1991 are listed along with their percent of world emissions.

39. Fridtjof Nansen Institute (1996, 105).

Table 4.7. *Major emitters of CFCs: 1989, 1991*

Country	1989 CFCs emissions (000 metric tons)	1989 percent of world total	1991 CFCs emissions (000 metric tons)	1991 percent of world total
United States	130	22.4	90	22.5
Japan	95	16.4	64	16.0
USSR	67	11.6	44	11.0
Germany[a]	34	5.7	23	5.8
United Kingdom	25	4.3	17	4.3
Italy	25	4.3	17	4.3
France	24	4.1	17	4.3
Spain	17	2.9	11	2.8
China	12	2.1	8	2.0
Canada	11	1.9	8	2.0
Australia	8	1.4	5	1.3
S. Africa	7	1.2	5	1.3
Total	455	78.4	309	77.3
World	580	100.0	400	100.0

[a] Includes West and East Germany.
Source: World Resources Institute (1992, table 24.2; 1994, table 23.2) and author's calculations for percent.

Twelve countries accounted for over 78% of the emissions. Table 4.7 also shows that the major polluters have reduced emissions from 1989 to 1991 to begin to meet treaty obligations. In this short time span, worldwide emissions of CFCs decreased by more than 30%.

Interests were also concentrated in terms of production: There were only sixteen producers of CFCs at the time of the Montreal Protocol. In 1985, the United States accounted for 30% of world production.[40] A mere five firms accounted for 100% of US production: Du Pont, 49%; Allied Signal, 25%; Pennwalt Corporation, 13%; Kaiser Chemicals, 9%; and Racon, 4%.[41] For the United States, this concentration of production interests meant that those affected by a curtailment in production and an eventual ban would not be too widespread. This is particularly true because the major producers were large diversified firms, whose CFC production did not account for an appreciable portion of sales – for Du Pont, less

40. Benedick (1991, 270).
41. Morrisette et al. (1990, table 1, 57).

than 2% of its sales was CFCs in 1986.[42] Thus, the political pressures to ignore the mounting scientific case against CFCs and other halocarbons were limited. These constrained political pressures were aided by a public in some of the primary producer nations that became aware of the health costs associated from a thinned ozone layer. This same public was much less informed of the costs that they would bear from a curtailment and eventual ban on CFC production. Much of this ignorance still holds today. In short, the political climate was conducive to action.

Good fortune also played a role in promoting the ratification and subsequent strengthening of the Montreal Protocol. Faced with the mounting evidence against CFCs, the major producers began to search for substitutes that would have universal applications and a benign impact on stratospheric ozone. Two important substitutes were found: HCFC and hydrofluorocarbon (HFC). Each could substitute for a wide range of applications of CFCs with little loss in efficiency. HCFCs pose 90% less risk to the ozone layer than CFCs, but some danger still remains owing to the presence of chlorine in HCFC that leads to the same process of ozone depletion described earlier. Thus, HCFCs will be eliminated by the year 2030 under the Copenhagen Amendment. HFC possesses no chlorine and, hence, poses no ozone threat. Both HFC and HCFC are GHGs and will add to global warming, as did the CFCs. The rapid development of acceptable substitutes meant that producers had much to gain from a CFC ban and, therefore, did not put up any political opposition to the global diplomacy concerning the Montreal Protocol.

Arguably, the most important factor that facilitated the Montreal Protocol was the leadership role played by the United States as the world's largest producer and consumer of CFCs. In 1987, the EPA report convinced US policy makers that the net gains from curbing CFC emissions were positive even if no other countries joined the United States. These gains would be even greater if the United States could induce the other major producers and consumers to sign a treaty reducing CFC emissions. From an economic standpoint, the economic consequences of limiting CFC emissions were far less than those associated with reducing CO_2 emissions. And this too worked in favor of transnational collective action, since the short-run sacri-

42. Morrisette et al. (1990, 15).

fice was relatively small. To date, US leadership has been conspic-
uously absent in global-warming negotiations. Given its pessimistic
view of net gains from curbing GHGs and the considerable uncertainty still surrounding global warming, the United States has opposed agreements that would tie its hands.

Can the Montreal Protocol serve as a blueprint for other global
crises? The answer is mixed. Surely the framing of conventions, such
as the Vienna Convention to monitor the problem and to gain
greater scientific certainty, is a crucial initial step that applies to a
host of global crises, including global warming and acid rain. However, the special circumstances associated with the ozone-depletion
problem do not necessarily apply to other global crises. A contrast
between global warming and ozone depletion is instructive. Both
problems are public bads in a global sense, but crucial differences
abound between the problems. GHGs are emitted from a much
wider range of activities than those that emit CFCs; curbing GHG
emissions will have more drastic economic ramifications than those
for CFCs. Substitutes for a wide range of GHGs are unlikely to be
developed; hence, some of the cutbacks in GHG emissions will
surely have to come from reduced economic activity. Currently,
there are a far greater number of significant GHG-emitting countries
than CFC-emitting countries, so that collective action is much more
difficult to achieve for global warming; that is, agreements must include more ratifiers. With time, the number of major emitters will
grow as LDCs expand their economies and bring up the standard of
living of their people. Free-riding opportunities by treaty nonparticipants or cheaters are much greater for global warming, both now
and into the future. Unlike ozone depletion, more uncertainty sur-
rounds the global-warming problem. The possibility that some
nations may gain from global warming differs from ozone depletion,
in which every nation loses. Potential gainers will resist any international treaty on global warming. Once costs and benefits from
reducing GHG emissions are weighed, the major polluters will not
want to assume a leadership role since they have much to lose. When
these and other factors are taken into account, we see that global
crises may differ fundamentally from one another, so that one successful treaty instrument or diplomatic process is not necessarily ap-
plicable to another problem.

Despite the success of the Montreal Protocol, the world still confront challenges to the ozone layer. Perhaps the greatest challenge will be policing the illegal trade in CFCs. High taxes on CFCs mean that significant profits can be made by unscrupulous individuals, who illegally trade CFCs at lower prices that do not include the tax. Large seizures in New York ports in 1995 suggest that this illegal trade is a problem to be reckoned with. Some estimates put the black market in CFCs at five to ten kilotons in the United States and 2.5 kilotons in the Economic Community.[43] These supplies are believed manufactured legally in the Russian Federation and Article 5 countries and then traded illegally. As the phase-out of CFCs continues, this illegal trade will increase owing to greater profits as taxes on legally traded CFCs increase. Another challenge involves ozone thinning from other halocarbons and even from CFC substitutes such as HCFC, which are now controlled by recent amendments to the Montreal Protocol. More benign substitutes for the substitutes will have to be found. Yet another challenge concerns how the ratifiers assist the Article 5 nations financially to afford CFC substitutes and to adopt alternative technologies. The size of the Multilateral Fund intended to accomplish these ends is woefully inadequate and funded by a few countries. A final challenge involves what will ultimately come of the CFCs produced prior to the upcoming ban.

ACID RAIN

Unlike global warming and stratospheric ozone depletion, acid rain is a more localized problem that affects nations regionally. Within North America and Europe, countries have made progress toward limiting just *some* of the emissions that lead to acid rain. Why the mixed results? In particular, why has more progress been achieved with respect to limiting sulfur emissions than has been made on curbing nitrogen oxides (NO_x)? Are the protocols curtailing these emissions a significant achievement in transnational cooperation? These questions are addressed here.

When sulfur and NO_x emissions from the generation of electricity, transportation, vehicles, and other sources combine in the lower atmo-

43. Fridtjof Nansen Institute (1996, 26).

sphere with water vapor and tropospheric ozone, sulfuric acid and nitric acid can form. These acids can later fall with the rain and degrade lakes, rivers, coastal waters, forests, and man-made structures. This degradation can also stem from dry depositions of sulfur and NO_x that lead to increased acidity of soils and watersheds. In 1980, sources of sulfur emissions were: 47.8% from power plants; 37.4%, industry; 10%, residential and commercial; 3.7%, mobile (for example, cars and trucks); and 1%, miscellaneous. In 1980, sources of NO_x emissions were: 53.6% from mobile polluters; 23.5%, power plants; 15.4%, industry; 6.1%, residential and commercial; and 1.3%, miscellaneous.[44]

In addition to acid rain depositions, sulfur and NO_x emissions lead to reductions in ambient air quality that may cause serious human health impairments to susceptible populations – particularly, the young and old. NO_x and volatile organic compounds (VOCs) are the primary precursors to tropospheric ozone in cities. Tropospheric ozone is created when UV radiation breaks down sulfur dioxide, water vapor, VOCs, NO_x, and other substances into their constituent parts. It is instructive to distinguish tropospheric ozone, which is harmful, from stratospheric ozone, which is helpful. The essential physical difference between the two ozones is merely location – low versus high atmosphere. Thinning of the stratospheric ozone lets more UV radiation through to the troposphere, which, in turn, creates more tropospheric ozone. Thus, less "good" ozone in the upper atmosphere means more "bad" ozone in the lower atmosphere, so that there exists some relationship between the two ozone problems. Ambient levels of particulate matter, which are potentially more damaging than tropospheric ozone, are also influenced by sulfur and NO_x emissions. Although a relatively small percentage of these emissions add to ambient degradation, human health is adversely affected.[45] Thus, ambient and depositional aspects of these pollutants must be recognized.

A variety of strategies are available for the control of sulfur and NO_x emissions. Both emissions can be limited through improved

44. The figures in this paragraph come from the Organization for Economic Cooperation and Development (OECD) (1990).
45. See Schwartz (1991). Approximately 10% of emitted SO_2 is converted to airborne sulfate aerosol, and up to 20% of total particulate matter mass is attributable to sulfates. A fraction of NO_x is converted to nitrates which constitute up to 5% of particulates.

efficiency, especially in the case of residential and commercial uses, and increased conservation. Sulfur pollution can also be controlled through the use of low-sulfur coal and oil as well as flue-gas desulfurization for power plants. In the case of NO_x, emissions can be reduced in power plants by installing low-NO_x burners. Pollution from mobile sources can be curtailed by setting emission standards on vehicles and by the rate of turnover of the vehicle fleet. New vehicles can incorporate improved emissions control technologies.

Both sulfur and NO_x emissions pose a transnational pollution concern, because once released into the atmosphere these pollutants can remain aloft for days and travel from their emission source to be deposited on the territory of a downwind country. Sulfur emissions can remain in the atmosphere for 0.01 to seven days, while NO_x can remain aloft from two to eight days.[46] On average, sulfur pollutants travel shorter distances than NO_x pollutants and land nearer to home.

The publicness character of sulfur and NO_x pollutants differs from other global contingencies and can be illustrated as follows: Suppose that a group of first graders are playing in a large sandbox on a blustery day. Each student marks out his or her territory in the sand. At various times, a child grabs a handful of sand and throws it directly overhead. Some of the tossed sand will land on the thrower or on his or her territory, while the rest will fall either on another's territory or else beyond the sandbox. Any grain deposited on one child's plot cannot be simultaneously dropped on another's territory. In terms of deposition, the sand is completely rival in consumption among the plots. As the sand is airborne, some nonrivalry of consumption is present, since the same grains can blow past more than one child. The grains are nonexcludable for those children in the sand's wind-driven path. The analogy is particularly apt for sulfur and NO_x emissions, in which acid rain depositions are completely rival, while ambient influences are nonrival for downwind countries.

To illustrate the transport and deposition of these two pollutants, I present data, collected by the Cooperative Programme for Monitoring and Evaluation of the Long-Range Transmission of Air Pollutants in Europe (EMEP), in map form.[47] Because depositions do

46. Alcamo and Runca (1986, 3).
47. The data used for these maps come from Sandnes (1993) and World Resources Institute (1992).

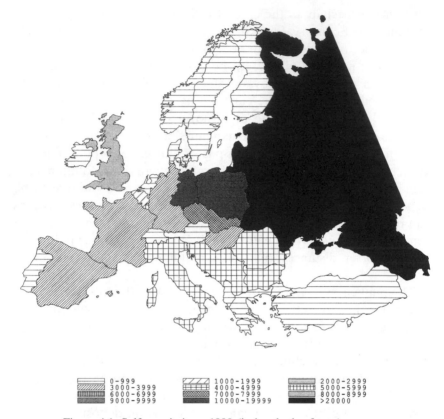

0-999   1000-1999   2000-2999
3000-3999   4000-4999   5000-5999
6000-6999   7000-7999   8000-8999
9000-9999   10000-19999   >20000

Figure 4.1. Sulfur emissions: 1990 (in hundreds of tons).

not differ much from year to year in terms of transport percentages,
I present maps for just a single year – 1990. In Figure 4.1, sulfur
emissions are displayed in hundreds of metric tons, in which increased shading indicates greater emissions. The largest polluters
were the former Soviet Union, Poland, the former East Germany,
and the United Kingdom. Although all European nations emit sulfur
pollutants, there is a wide variation among European nations. Of
greater interest for treaty formation is Figure 4.2, which displays the
percentage of a country's own sulfur emissions that landed on itself.
This self-pollution is a strong motivation, in terms of localized benefits, to do something about the problem, regardless of the actions
of others. As shown in Figure 4.2, the majority of nations received

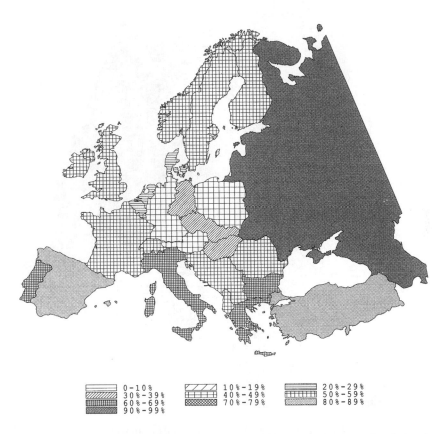

Figure 4.2. Own depositions of sulfur: 1990 (as a percentage of emissions).

over 50% of their *own* sulfur emissions as depositions. Localized benefits from reducing these sulfur emissions are, consequently, great. Figure 4.3 displays the amount of sulfur depositions in hundreds of metric tons that the countries received as pollution "spillins" (or spill-ins) from nearby states. Those nations – the former Soviet Union, Poland, West Germany – that received the most spillins had the most to gain from a treaty restricting sulfur emissions. Because of wind direction, countries to the east and center experienced, on average, the greatest spillins of pollutants from other countries. Figure 4.4 illustrates how sulfur depositions disperse from their source of emissions in West Germany. Neighboring states

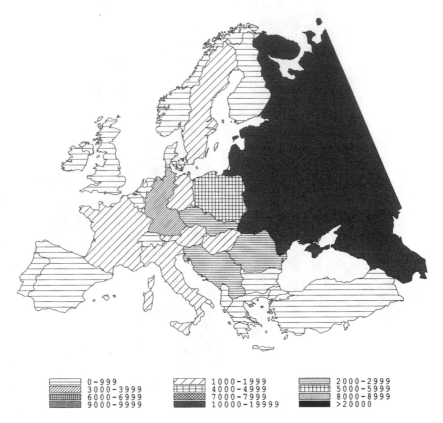

	0-999		1000-1999		2000-2999
	3000-3999		4000-4999		5000-5999
	6000-6999		7000-7999		8000-8999
	9000-9999		10000-19999		>20000

Figure 4.3. Sulfur spillins: 1990 (in hundreds of tons).

downwind and to the east received a greater share of West German emissions as depositions. The greatest percentage (44%) of West German emissions fell on West German soil. Dispersion from other countries followed similar patterns and is not shown.

Table 4.8 also displays some of this same information. For sulfur emissions, the second column lists the country's emissions in 100 metric tons for 1990, the third column displays the spillins from each country, and the fourth column indicates the portion of own emissions deposited on the emitter. Some countries – Albania, Austria, the Netherlands, Norway, Sweden, Switzerland, Turkey – were net importers of sulfur emissions, since their emissions were less than

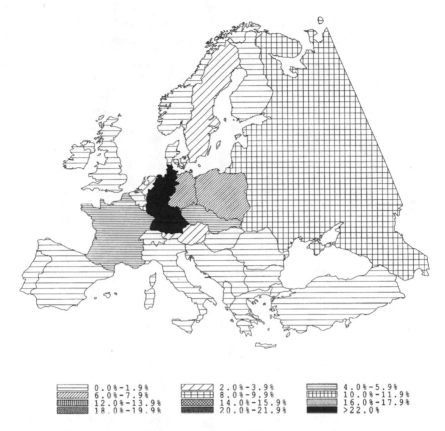

Figure 4.4. Depositions of sulfur from West Germany: 1990 (as a percentage of West German emissions).

their imported depositions.[48] These countries had much to gain from an agreement restricting emissions even if such restrictions also tied their hands. Not surprisingly, these countries (except for Albania and Turkey) were among the first to meet agreed-upon emission reductions.

Figures 4.5–4.8 display similar maps for NO_x emissions, while the three right-hand columns of Table 4.8 indicate emissions, spillins, and the percentage of own depositions. The largest emitters included

48. West Germany was almost a net importer.

Table 4.8. *Sulfur and nitrogen oxides emissions for Protocol countries: 1990*

Countries	Sulfur			Nitrogen oxides		
	Emissions[a]	Spillins[a]	Depositions[b]	Emissions[c]	Spillins[c]	Depositions[b]
Albania	76	172	53.9	4	70	25.0
Austria	256	1,311	44.9	275	677	16.7
Belgium	1,465	404	28.4	615	216	4.4
Bulgaria	4,099	904	61.3	263	276	29.7
Czechoslovakia	7,861	2,573	39.6	1,632	834	13.9
Denmark	419	341	24.1	440	222	4.5
Finland	735	830	52.6	442	443	26.7
France	3,956	1,941	52.1	2,803	1,065	30.8
E. Germany	16,030	1,260	36.8	1,127	801	9.1
W. Germany	3,239	3,174	44.2	4,615	1,363	19.2
Greece	560	786	67.3	361	180	36.0
Hungary	3,505	1,140	37.5	428	416	14.7
Ireland	333	127	53.5	126	79	14.3
Italy	4,325	1,285	64.4	1,593	708	38.7
Luxembourg	60	26	21.7	38	15	0
Netherlands	574	615	26.8	951	280	5.7
Norway	104	900	57.7	206	718	28.8
Poland	10,529	5,555	49.4	2,244	1,795	22.8
Portugal	359	147	63.0	101	57	30.7
Romania	4,674	2,176	58.0	442	616	30.5
Spain	3,805	485	80.4	621	389	59.7
Sweden	414	1,413	55.6	568	971	27.6
Switzerland	167	480	50.3	185	304	18.4
Turkey	541	847	83.2	97	339	62.9
USSR	22,309	10,724	92.1	5,043	4,888	88.6
United Kingdom	8,189	320	57.4	2,984	232	19.9
Yugoslavia	4,096	2,189	58.7	501	909	32.9

[a] In 100 metric tons of sulfur.
[b] In percentage of own emissions.
[c] In 100 metric tons of nitrogen.
Source: Sandnes (1993, tables C6, C13).

the Soviet Union, West Germany, the United Kingdom, France, Poland, Czechoslovakia, Italy, and East Germany (see Figure 4.5 and
Table 4.8). Except for the Soviet Union, Turkey, and Spain, own
depositions were not greater than 40% and in many cases were less
than 20% (Figure 4.6 and Table 4.8). By comparing Figures 4.2 and
4.6, there appear to be more localized benefits from limiting sulfur

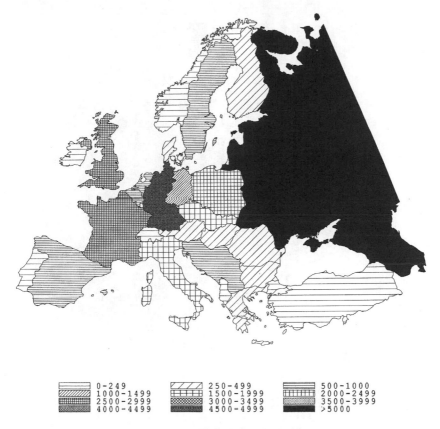

Figure 4.5. NO_x emissions: 1990 (in hundreds of tons).

emissions as compared with reducing NO_x emissions in terms of acid rain depositions. Another interesting contrast concerns the percentage of overall European emissions of sulfur and NO_x that fall within the countries depicted. For sulfur, the majority of emissions is deposited in the countries shown, while for NO_x, a smaller percent of these emissions is deposited in these countries. Figure 4.7 indicates the NO_x spillin or imported pollution pattern. The largest "importers" were the Soviet Union, Poland, France, Sweden, and the former Yugoslavia, Czechoslovakia, and East Germany. These countries had much to gain from an agreement that reduces pollution. Finally, Figure 4.8 shows that the dispersion of West German NO_x pollution

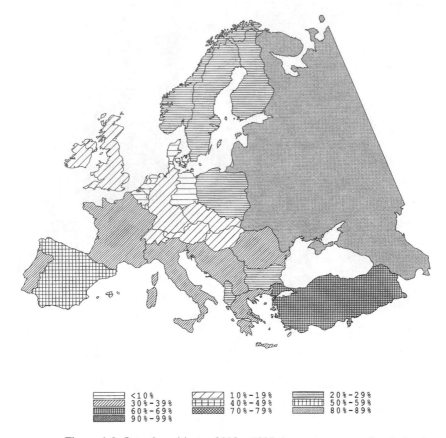

	<10%		10%-19%		20%-29%
	30%-39%		40%-49%		50%-59%
	60%-69%		70%-79%		80%-89%
	90%-99%				

Figure 4.6. Own depositions of NO_x: 1990 (as a percentage of emissions).

had the greatest impact on West Germany, its immediate neighbors, and eastward nations.

One international convention and four subsequent protocols are relevant to the acid rain problem in Europe. On 13 November 1979, the Long-Range Transboundary Air Pollution (LRTAP) Convention was drafted at a high-level meeting of the UN Economic Commission for Europe on the Protection of the Environment. This treaty mandated scientific investigation and evaluation of the problem by establishing a system of monitoring stations throughout Eu-

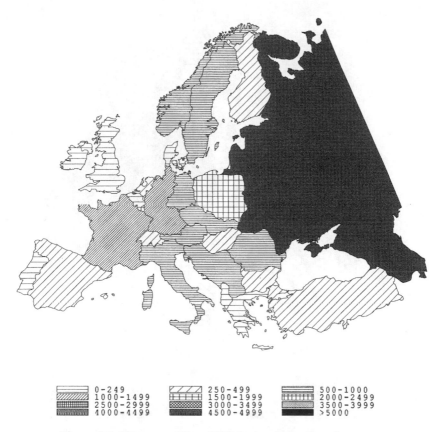

0-249
1000-1499
2500-2999
4000-4499

250-499
1500-1999
3000-3499
4500-4999

500-1000
2000-2499
3500-3999
>5000

Figure 4.7. Nitrogen spillins: 1990 (in hundreds of tons).

rope.[49] Data from these stations were used to derive the weights for determining transnational deposition of sulfur. The LRTAP Convention was ratified on 16 March 1983 after the required sixteen nations signed. Signatories included Austria, Belgium, Bulgaria, Canada, Czechoslovakia, Denmark, Finland, France, East Germany, West Germany, Greece, Hungary, Iceland, Ireland, Italy, Liechtenstein, Luxembourg, the Netherlands, Norway, Poland, Portugal, Romania, the Soviet Union, Spain, Sweden, Switzerland, Turkey,

49. UN Environment Programme (1991) contains the treaty text.

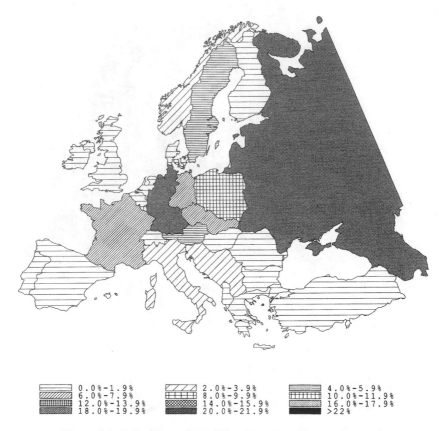

0.0%-1.9%	2.0%-3.9%	4.0%-5.9%
6.0%-7.9%	8.0%-9.9%	10.0%-11.9%
12.0%-13.9%	14.0%-15.9%	16.0%-17.9%
18.0%-19.9%	20.0%-21.9%	>22%

Figure 4.8. Depositions of NO$_x$ from West Germany: 1990 (as a percentage of West German emissions).

United Kingdom, United States, and Yugoslavia. On 8 July 1985, the Helsinki Protocol to the LRTAP Convention was adopted and committed ratifiers to reduce sulfur emissions by at least 30%, based on 1980 levels, as soon as possible or by 1993. This Protocol entered into force on 2 September 1987. In the case of NO$_x$ emissions, a protocol was much slower. On 31 October 1988, the Sofia Protocol was signed, requiring reductions in NO$_x$ to return to 1987 levels by 31 December 1994. This Protocol entered into force on 14 February 1991.

More recently, the Oslo Protocol of 14 June 1994 (not yet in force) mandated future cutbacks in sulfur emissions beyond those of the Helsinki Protocol for most nations. Unlike earlier protocols, the Oslo Protocol was based on minimizing control costs for achieving carrying capacity limits. As such, assigned percentage reductions from 1980 levels differ by country.[50] A fourth protocol, the Geneva Protocol of 11 November 1995, sets emission reduction to selected Volatile Organic Compounds (VOCs) to ameliorate surface ozone pollution.[51] These protocols are discussed in Chapter 5; the Helsinki and Sofia Protocols are analyzed later in this chapter.

As in the case of the Montreal Protocol limiting ozone, a convention mandating scientific monitoring and evaluation preceded the protocols that actually limited behavior. This pattern is now the norm when transnational cooperation is contemplated. Uncertainty surrounding a transnational crisis must be curtailed prior to nations being willing to act. For sulfur, nations were, especially, motivated to act, because of the high degree of self-pollution. It is interesting to note that prior to the formulation of the Helsinki Protocol, ten of the subsequent signatories had already achieved the targeted reductions.[52] Another six nations had achieved at least a reduction of 23% by the end of 1985. The overwhelming number of Protocol participants had met the treaty's mandate or were well on their way to meeting it by the time of adoption. *Mean reductions from 1980 levels were 20.59% prior to the treaty.*

A different pattern of voluntary cutbacks for NO_x emerged prior to the Sofia Protocol. Reductions in NO_x emissions between 1980 and 1987 as a percentage of 1980 emissions were positive for only eight participants to the Sofia Protocol. Prior to the Protocol, the average reduction of NO_x emissions was negative, so that emissions increased by almost 3% from 1980 to the end of 1987. This failure to make much progress in curbing NO_x pollution influenced the modest goals set forth in the Sofia Protocol. Both the Helsinki and Sofia Protocols reflected the cutbacks that many nations had already achieved. As such, these treaties were not milestones of international cooperation. Nations that had already achieved reductions framed the treaty in such a way that did not limit their actions, while

50. United Nations (1994) and Fridtjof Nansen Institute (1996, 96–7).
51. United Nations (1992b).
52. Information in this and the next paragraph come from Murdoch et al. (1994, 1997), based on data from Sandnes (1993).

they pressured other nations to achieve similar reductions. A similar pattern characterized the subsequent Oslo Protocol on further limits to sulfur emissions (see Chapter 5).

Nations were more prepared to do something about sulfur than NO_x because a much greater share of these nations' sulfur emissions befouled their own air and soil than that associated with NO_x. Another consideration involved the pollution sources – sulfur sources are more concentrated and include public utilities that are easy for a democratic country to control. NO_x comes primarily from vehicles and requires that citizens do their part rather than rely on government fiat. Political and civil liberties had an opposite influence on the two problems. Freer countries had a better track record in controlling sulfur than NO_x as compared with the more autocratic regimes in Europe.[53] Apparently, democratic governments were more reluctant to enact laws that could lose political support by limiting the use of private vehicles. Given their eastern location, the autocratic countries experienced greater NO_x spillins and, thus, had much to gain from a treaty that controlled NO_x emissions. Yet another difference concerned the effect of larger GNP on the two problems. Increased GNP was positively related to curtailing sulfur, while no clear relationship characterized income and NO_x. This latter finding might be due to opposing forces: Higher income increases the demand for a cleaner environment, but it also increases the need and use of vehicles. A final difference involved the extent of spillovers for sulfur and NO_x emissions. A much greater portion of NO_x emissions was never deposited on the parties to the Protocol but either was absorbed in a sink or else was deposited outside of the treaty region. This meant that treaty participants perceived more limited benefits from an agreement in the case of NO_x. Some action needed to be taken because tropospheric ozone, produced in part by NO_x, reduced ambient air quality and adversely affected health. Regardless of where NO_x emissions ultimately come to rest, their transport has potential health risks to everyone in their path.

For sulfur, the collective action is needed at the transnational level as nations limit emissions from public utilities. NO_x requires more complex collective action, since cooperation is needed among private citizens *within* each nation as well as among nations. The

53. See Murdoch et al. (1997) and the statistical analysis that supports this statement.

differences between the two acid rain problems imply that the LRTAP Convention was properly designed when it provided for subsequent protocols to focus on separate pollutants. If all pollutants had to be treated identically by the Convention, then the most difficult substance to control would have determined the pace at which a treaty was adopted to limit acid rain inducers. To underscore this insight, we note that more limited and slower progress has been made to date in reducing the larger number of VOCs that also cause acid rain and health problems.

TRANSNATIONAL TERRORISM

Lest the reader think that global crises are only environmentally based, I now consider the threat posed by transnational terrorism and what is likely to be done about this threat. Terrorism is the premeditated use, or threat of use, of extra-normal violence or brutality to gain a political objective through intimidation or fear. Terrorism is an activity that has characterized modern civilization from its inception. Many nations, including the United States, relied on terrorism to gain their independence. To qualify as terrorism, an act must be politically motivated; that is, the act must attempt to influence government policy at home or abroad. Acts that are solely motivated for profit and do not directly or indirectly support a political objective are not considered to be terrorism. Although the political objectives of terrorists differ and may include nationalism, separatism, anti-capitalism, Marxism, religious freedoms, or other goals, terrorists resort to common modes of attacks (for example, bombings, kidnappings, skyjackings) to pressure a government to alter its policies.

To manufacture an atmosphere of fear, terrorists make their attacks appear to be random so that large numbers of people feel at risk. Also, this violence is often unleashed at a vulnerable target group, such as foreign tourists, business interests, or pedestrians, not immediately involved in the political decision-making process that the terrorists seek to influence. Thus, terrorists may open fire on passengers attempting to check in at an airline ticket counter, or they may explode a car bomb on a city street. Even though the risks of becoming a statistic are small, it is human nature to overreact to

these low-probability terrorist events with catastrophic consequences to anyone in the way. Terrorists may employ tactics that
result in particularly gruesome outcomes in the hope of promoting
this over-reaction. Also, such acts capture media attention and publicize "the cause." As a society becomes numb to the carnage, terrorists may resort to even more deadly attacks to capture headlines.

Terrorists attack the innocent because they are undefended and,
thus, easy prey. If terrorists can attack with impunity, then the government, which is expected to protect life and property, will appear
ineffective and weak. This weakness may lead to a crisis in governing, whereby the government either seeks an accommodation with
the terrorists or else faces defeat in an election. Although terrorism
has, at times, led to political change, terrorist campaigns more often
than not do not bring about a government capitulation.

When a terrorist act in one country involves victims, targets, institutions, governments, or citizens of another country, terrorism assumes a transnational character. It is these acts that pose a global
and regional challenge to the modern world. The kidnappings of
Americans and other Westerners from the streets of Beirut in the
1980s by groups such as the Hezbollah and the Revolutionary Justice
Organization are examples of transnational terrorism. Another
transnational incident is the truck bombing that killed nineteen US
airmen and maimed hundreds at a housing complex in Dhahran,
Saudi Arabia, on 25 June 1996. The downing of Air India Flight 182,
over the Atlantic Ocean on 23 June 1985, and the downing of Pan
American Flight 103, over Lockerbie, Scotland, on 21 December
1988, are transnational events with great loss of life.[54] Three hundred
and twenty-nine people died in the 1985 crash, and two hundred and
seventy died in the 1988 tragedy. A skyjacking that originates in
country A but that terminates in country B is transnational, as is a
threat of a bombing campaign in country A that places demands on
individuals or institutions in another country. If a terrorist group
launches its operation from a second country, then the incident is a
transnational terrorist event. Transnational terrorist incidents are
examples of a *transboundary externality*, since the actions conducted
in one country may impose uncompensated costs or benefits on the

54. For a description of specific incidents, consult Mickolus et al. (1989).

people or property of another nation. Some kind of international collective response might be required to address this externality.

Recent terrorist incidents, such as the sarin attack in the Tokyo subway, underscore the vulnerabilities of modern societies whose dependency on advanced technologies may provide the terrorists with targets that can be attacked, with catastrophic consequences. The ultimate fear is that nuclear weapons from the former Soviet Union may land in the hands of a terrorist group that uses them to blackmail the world community to concede to a set of demands. Although it is in every country's interest to keep this from happening, it is less clear that one of these former Soviet republics will deploy sufficient security measures to account for the risks that these weapons' existence impose on the world community. The willingness of the United States to subsidize the dismantling and destruction of these weapons is an indication that US policy makers doubt whether sufficient safeguards are in place.

The emergence of transnational terrorist acts at a heightened level can be traced back to 1967 and the aftermath of the Arab-Israeli wars. Since 1967, transnational terrorism appears to follow a cyclical pattern with peaks and troughs. According to the US Department of State, the number of such attacks in recent years are as follows: 665 in 1987, 605 in 1988, 375 in 1989, 437 in 1990, 565 in 1991, 363 in 1992, 431 in 1993, and 321 in 1994.[55] Overall attacks have been down since the end of the Cold War, thus suggesting that terrorism had been used as a tool during these earlier years by the superpowers. Sometimes a new mode of attack leads to copycats, thus creating a spate of attacks. This scenario is best illustrated by the skyjacking of Northwest Airlines Flight 305 on 24 November 1971 by a man who identified himself as D. B. Cooper. The hijacker demanded and received $200,000 in $20 bills and four parachutes, two of which he used to jump from the rear door of the B-727 aircraft while it cruised at 197 miles per hour at 10,000 feet altitude. Although the hijacker was never seen again and presumed killed in the jump, there were seventeen subsequent copycat incidents.[56] Things became so bad

55. These figures come from the US Department of State (1995).
56. For a description of this event see Mickolus (1980, 287–8) and Landes (1978). None of the copycats were successful – they were captured either before or after their planned parachute jump.

that the rear doors of B-727s and DC-9s had to be redesigned so that they could not be opened in flight. The dispersion of successful tactics through such a demonstration effect supports the transmission of terrorism worldwide. By publicizing such events and their tactics, the news media unintentionally fosters the diffusion of successful tactics. A ban on the reporting of these events would curtail the dispersion, but at the price of freedom of the press. Most people would not want to limit these rights.

Transnational terrorism raises many policy issues that we encountered before. Although it is in the interests of all nations that each takes a tough stance on terrorism (for example, to keep its promise never to concede to terrorist demands), nations often renege on this promise when faced with an incident that could end in a costly fashion if an accommodation is not reached. To illustrate the dilemma, I put forward a hypothetical scenario where five nations are confronted with a common terrorist threat from a nation that sponsors terrorism. Suppose that the five target nations are contemplating a treaty that pledges to punish state sponsors of terrorism with retaliation. Once the treaty is signed, each nation has two strategies or choices: to abide or not to abide by the agreement. These choices are exercised when a state-sponsored incident occurs that requires a response. Suppose further that each nation that abides by the treaty confers benefits of 5 to itself *and* to the other nations in the pact, but at costs of 8 to itself. The costs arise from engaging in the retaliation, while the benefits stem from the deterrence accomplished and the destruction of terrorists' resources. Benefits from the retaliation have the properties of a pure public good in that they are nonrival and nonexcludable. A classic *n*-person Prisoners' Dilemma results when the resulting payoffs are analyzed.

In Figure 4.9, the game matrix is displayed from the viewpoint of a representative nation. If nation i abides by the treaty and the other four nations follow suit, then the ith nation receives net benefits of 17 equal to gross benefits of 25 (5 times the number of abiders) minus the nation's costs of 8. If, however, nation i does not abide while the others do, then it receives 20 or the free-rider payoff of 5 times the 4 abiders. Next suppose that nation i and three others abide, then nation i receives a net benefit of $12 = (4 \times 5 - 8)$, or the difference in total benefits minus its costs of 8. The other payoffs are computed in a similar fashion. When the payoffs in the two rows

Number of treaty-abiding nations other than nation *i*

	0	1	2	3	4
Nation *i* abides by treaty	−3	2	7	12	17
Nation *i* does not abide by treaty	0	5	10	15	20

Figure 4.9. Prisoners' Dilemma and terrorism treaty.

are compared, it is clear that nation *i* is always better off from not abiding, because the payoffs in the bottom row are always greater than the corresponding payoffs in the top row regardless of the other nations' actions. Not abiding is a dominant strategy (see Chapter 2). Because all nations view the game as does nation *i*, none abide when needed, so that the treaty may not amount to much. As with other *n*-person Prisoners' Dilemmas, the cooperative outcome, where each nation abides and provides net payoffs of 17 to every nation party to the agreement, is not attained as each participant does what appears to be best for it. Ironically, the resulting noncooperative outcome is to everyone's disadvantage.

The standard objection to this simplistic analysis of the *n*-person Prisoners' Dilemma comes from the notion that the game may be played repeatedly. For repeated game scenarios, nations may adopt punishment-based strategies – for example, tit-for-tat – that make a participant compare the short-run gain from not abiding by the treaty to the associated longer-run losses resulting from the sanctions imposed. Such a calculus could induce the nation to adopt a cooperative outcome, provided that it values the future sufficiently high. In the international political arena, however, this standard "fix" for the Prisoners' Dilemma is unlikely to work, because the elected official who decides the country's response may discount greatly or apply small weights to longer-run losses, owing to a short decision horizon associated with the length of officeholding. This desire to win reelection is apt to focus a decision maker's calculations on immediate gains. A second fix, based on reputation costs, is also unlikely to be influential, because one administration may be unworried about the negative reputation effect that its actions impose on subsequent administrations.[57] These future administrations may not share the same party affiliation. Authoritarian regimes are apt to have more concern about their reputations and, thus, be more consistent with respect to their tough stance against terrorists.

To underscore this reputation problem, consider the Reagan administration's stance toward terrorist negotiations. Publicly, this administration called on *all* countries never to negotiate with terrorists, since it was believed that if terrorists came to realize that hostage taking would *never* result in a ransom, there would then be fewer incentives, outside of publicity and martyrdom, for capturing and maintaining a hostage. If all nations were to stand united on such a policy, hostage-taking events could fall greatly in number. This view is sensible, provided that the targeted nations do not put the entire weight on the short-run gains from defecting so as to obtain the release of a particularly valuable hostage. A lame-duck administration is especially vulnerable to the lure of defecting from a no-negotiation commitment, since it will not suffer the longer-run reputation costs as hostage taking increases. This may have been behind the Reagan administration's willingness to barter arms for the release of hostages – Rev. Benjamin Weir, Rev. Lawrence Jenco, David Jacobsen – during 1985–6.

Almost every nation that confronts terrorism has, at times, violated its pledge never to negotiate with terrorists. Even Israel, the staunchest supporter of the no-negotiation strategy, has made noteworthy exceptions in the case of the school children taken hostage at Maalot in May 1974, and during the hijacking of TWA Flight 847 in June 1985.[58] The effectiveness of the conventional policy never to negotiate with terrorists rests on a number of crucial implicit assumptions. First, the government's pledge is completely credible to would-be hostage takers. Second, there is no uncertainty concerning payoffs. Third, the terrorists' gains from hostage taking only derive from ransoms received. Fourth, the government's expenditures on deterrence are sufficient to deter most attacks. Each of these assumptions may not hold in practice.

If, for example, the terrorist group realizes a net gain from a negotiation failure, as it may if it values media exposure or martyrdom,

---

57. On reputation and terrorism policy, see Lapan and Sandler (1988).
58. These events are described in Mickolus (1980, 453–4) and Mickolus et al. (1989, 2: 219–25).

then the government's proclamations and its level of deterrence cannot necessarily forestall an attack. Consequently, hostages may still be abducted. Once hostages are taken, the government must weigh the expected costs of not capitulating against those of capitulating. Situations may arise where a government views the cost of not capitulating as too high, even when accounting for lost reputation, and, hence, reneges on its pledge. If would-be hostage takers believe that they can impose costs sufficient for a targeted government to renege on its stated policy, then they will abduct hostages, because the credibility of the government's pledge depends on an uncertain outcome. Each time a government caves in, the terrorists will update or raise their beliefs about future capitulations. That is, learning based on past actions allows terrorists (and the government) to update their beliefs in an interactive fashion. When a government reneges and negotiates, it emboldens terrorists to take additional hostages. In doing so, a capitulating government imposes a public bad on future domestic governments and on governments worldwide. Constitutional constraints or congressional hearings, which impose huge costs on those officeholders who capitulate, may be the only means of raising the cost of capitulation sufficiently to make a precommitment never to negotiate a policy without regrets, once a hostage is taken. Such action would severely restrict discretionary actions for the good of the world community. Most governments are not so benevolent or farsighted and are, therefore, not predisposed to have their hands tied.

Strategic interactions may lead to undesirable outcomes with respect to deterrence expenditures when two or more nations are targeted by the same terrorist group. This situation is a classic example of a transferable externality in which the action taken by one agent to displace the external effect elsewhere may lead to ever-spiraling increases in displacement efforts without any noticeable improvement as everyone takes the same strategy. If each nation decides its deterrence expenditures independently, then each may allocate too many resources to inducing terrorists to switch their venue. Over-deterrence may result because the nations do not take into account the negative influence (by inducing the terrorists to operate on another nation's soil) that their deterrence choices create for others. If, moreover, the terrorists are sufficiently fanatical that they will attack one of their intended targets regardless of the deterrence level, then the overdeterrence is particularly wasteful, because targeted nations have not really increased their security. International cooperation seems to be the only solution; but nations are extremely reticent to limit their autonomy over internal security matters. This reticence is beneficial to the terrorists, since a united effort would be more difficult to circumvent.

Over the years, nations have formed international conventions and resolutions to thwart terrorist acts. Two early instances include the 1971 Montreal Convention on the Suppression of Unlawful Acts against the Safety of Civil Aviation (Sabotage) and the 1977 UN General Assembly Resolution 3218 on the Safety of International Civil Aviation.[59] Although well-intended, neither of these treaties appeared to have much effect on aviation's safety from terrorism. Other significant antiterrorism treaties include the following: the UN Convention on the Prevention and Punishment of Crimes against Internationally Protected Persons, Including Diplomatic Agents (adopted by the United Nations on 14 December 1973), the UN Security Council Resolution against Taking Hostages (adopted by a 15–0 vote on 18 December 1985), the UN General Assembly Resolution 2551 on the Forcible Diversion of Civil Aircraft in Flight (12 December 1969), the Hague Convention on the Suppression of Unlawful Seizure of Aircraft (16 December 1970), and the UN General Assembly Resolution 2645 on Aerial Hijacking (25 November 1970). Conventions are more binding than resolutions, since resolutions are merely agreements in principle and do not imply any real commitment on the part of the adopters. Conventions, in contrast, require that the nations rely on their *own* judicial system to implement and enforce the agreement. But in neither case is there a central enforcement agency that can force the nations to comply. Without such an enforcement mechanism, signatories will do what is convenient from their viewpoints – a Prisoners' Dilemma is apt to underlie the pattern of payoffs, as shown earlier.

When the average number of attacks is examined both before and after the adoption of these conventions and resolutions, there is *no* statistically significant reduction in the posttreaty number of attacks for the relevant attack modes (crimes against protected persons or skyjackings).[60] This is convincing evidence that these UN conven-

59. See Alexander, Browne, and Nanes (1979) for the text of the treaties on the suppression of terrorist acts.
60. This statistical analysis is presented in Enders et al. (1990).

tions and resolutions really had no impact. To acquire the requisite support from the world community, these antiterrorism treaties were drafted so as to permit too many loopholes and too much autonomy on the part of the signatories. A more effective treaty-making process involved neighboring nations agreeing to control a common terrorism problem that possessed localized effects. Thus, Spain and France have made progress in concerted efforts to control Basque terrorism. Even the United States and Cuba entered into a treaty on 15 February 1973 that pledged the nations to extradite or punish hijackers who divert planes to either country. This treaty became a much more effective deterrent when Fidel Castro announced on 6 July 1983 that skyjackers would receive forty-year jail sentences.

If multilateral treaties involving large numbers of nations have been ineffective in thwarting terrorism, then what procedures seem to work best? To thwart a *particular* type of event, the application of technology appears to be especially effective. The installation of metal detectors to screen airline passengers is, perhaps, the best instance of this application. These metal detectors were installed in US airports beginning on 5 January 1973. Shortly thereafter these devices were placed in airports worldwide to screen domestic and international flights. Prior to January 1973, skyjackings worldwide averaged over sixteen per quarter. Shortly after metal detectors were installed, there was an immediate and permanent drop of almost eleven skyjackings per quarter.[61] This is pretty dramatic. A similar effectiveness was experienced following the fortification of US embassies and missions in October 1976; a dramatic fall in embassy attacks has followed.

But this is not the whole story. When one mode of attack is made more difficult or expensive to conduct, terrorists have substituted other relatively cheaper events.[62] If, for example, skyjackings are more difficult due to metal detectors, then other hostage-taking events (kidnappings and barricade and hostage taking) are now relatively cheaper. For the effectiveness of an antiterrorism policy to be analyzed properly, then its influence on other related modes of attacks must be investigated. When the impact of metal detectors is examined more closely, these detectors are seen to decrease sky-

61. These means are computed in Enders et al. (1990). The statistical significance of this drop is also analyzed in that article.
62. The statistical analysis that backs up the statements in this paragraph can be found in Enders and Sandler (1993).

jackings *and* threats, but to increase other kinds of hostage incidents and assassinations, not protected by the detectors. Since many threats of future attacks involved planes and embassies, which had been made more secure by metal detectors, these threats may have declined as they became less credible. Enhanced embassy security, while effective at reducing embassy attacks, had the unintended consequence of increasing assassinations of diplomatic and military personnel when they left secured compounds. This substitution is toward events that are more costly to society than those being protected. This outcome suggests that piecemeal policy, in which a single attack mode is considered when designing antiterrorism action, is inadequate. Terrorist substitution among attack modes must be anticipated. Policies that decrease terrorist resources are particularly effective, because they should result in an across-the-board decrease in attacks. Another effective policy is group infiltration.

Although transnational terrorism poses a potential crisis to the world community, there has been no escalation in the number or lethality of attacks in the last two decades. At times, a newsworthy event has caught the public's attention, but the occasional spectacular event does not mean that transnational terrorism is on the rise. To date, nations have shared intelligence regarding terrorist activities, but have been unwilling to coordinate logistics, deterrence, and other activities. Moreover, global treaties have been ineffective owing to vague language and the absence of an enforcement mechanism. The threat of transnational terrorism is ever present and may escalate into the use of more lethal means of attacks – for example, nuclear weapons and exotic pollutants. If and when this occurs, nations may perceive greater benefits from coordinated efforts and, in consequence, may form tighter linkages with other nations. It is interesting to note that, when terrorist groups in Europe and the Middle East faced greater challenges from authorities in the late 1970s and early 1980s, these groups forged ties to one another to share resources, intelligence, and training facilities.[63] No less should be expected from governments. Benefits from increased government linkage must outweigh the cost in terms of lost autonomy if closer ties among governments are to be achieved.

63. See Alexander and Puchinsky (1992).

PEACEKEEPING MISSIONS

Maintaining peace in the post–Cold War era represents another global concern. In the past five years, conflicts in Kuwait, Bosnia, Somalia, and Haiti have threatened to escalate. Consider the case of the Iraqi invasion of Kuwait at the beginning of August 1990, which met with worldwide condemnation. The collective response was swift and surprising. Fearing further aggression on the part of Iraq, Saudi Arabia agreed to the stationing of multinational forces on its soil, thus starting Operation Desert Shield. Over the ensuing months, the Bush administration cemented together an impressive alliance that would grow still further during the subsequent warfare stage of Operation Desert Storm. Allies included the United Kingdom, Egypt, Syria, France, the United Arab Emirates (UAE), Oman, Canada, Australia, the Netherlands, and Turkey. Some allies needed to be given significant incentives or private benefits for participating – for example, the United States forgave billions of dollars of Egyptian debt.

During the Desert Storm stage, nearly $10 billion was pledged by Saudi Arabia, Kuwait, the UAE, Germany, Japan, and South Korea to support US expenses.[64] Saudi Arabia, Kuwait, and the UAE had much to gain from an end to the Iraqi aggression. Since Japan and Germany relied on oil from the Persian Gulf, these nations also had much to gain from stability in the region. Arms exporters – France and Britain – could showcase their weapons' capabilities to obtain future sales. Syria could win favor with the West by its token support of the alliance. Other participants could obtain lucrative postwar contracts from Kuwait to rebuild the country. Yes, the allies could gain from their participation. Localized and ally-specific gains were crucial to cementing together the alliance. When Operation Desert Storm began on the morning of 16 January 1991 with the bombing of Baghdad and other Iraqi targets, the alliance grew still further until it included over thirty allies. An additional $43 billion was pledged by the allies to support the war efforts. The Gulf War seemed to have little problem in uniting a group of allies to deal with an aggressor. The disruption

---

64. The information about Desert Shield and Desert Storm comes from Congressional Budget Office (1991a, 1991b).

to oil flows, which instability in the Gulf posed, meant that oil-dependent industrial countries had much to gain from an Iraqi defeat.

Next consider the Bosnia situation where action has been much slower to materialize. The Bosnian civil war represented little threat to the United States, which played the leadership role in the Gulf War. As long as the conflict remained within the borders of Bosnia, the Europeans saw few localized benefits from putting their armies at risk to maintain peace in Bosnia. Hence, world efforts had been minimal until the NATO air strikes in the latter part of 1995 after the war appeared ready to spread to neighboring states.

For the Haitian problem, the United States had the most localized benefits to gain. Despite its efforts to assemble a large number of allies, the US efforts received little but token support from other nations. This was also true of nations within the region that viewed the Haitian problem as confined to Haiti.

In general, keeping world peace is a classic example of a pure public good for which benefits are not excludable to nonparticipants. Moreover, world peace provides nonrival benefits. Unless maintaining peace is coupled with country-specific benefits to the would-be participants in a police force, as was clearly the case in the Gulf War, efforts will be undersupplied. Large, rich nations or collectives (for example, the United States or NATO) will provide the policing for the rest of the world. These policing nations may get tired of this role if their constituencies voice displeasure with the one-sidedness of peacekeeping. If this happens, and it is likely to occur, then local conflicts might have to escalate beyond national borders before the global community acts. If smaller, unstable nations were to obtain nuclear weapons or other weapons of mass destruction, then the need for collective peace enforcement would become a matter of great concern. By keeping nuclear weapons from proliferating, the world community can limit the need for peacekeeping, except in situations in which crucial resource supplies are disrupted as in the Gulf War. Arguably, the greatest threat to world peace derives from arms-selling nations and private arms dealers that supply aggressive regimes with advanced weapon systems or technologies that can be applied to modern warfare.

CONCLUDING REMARKS

By examining a number of specific global crises, I have tried to show that factors may exist to motivate nations to act. Regional problems that affect a relatively small number of nations are likely to be addressed successfully through supranational cooperation as was the case for sulfur emissions in Europe. For more global concerns, scientific evidence must be gathered first so as to convince nations that the status quo is unacceptable in terms of the costs imposed on each nation and on the world community. Supranational actions can often be speeded up if an important nation assumes a leadership role to foster action. In the case of the Montreal Protocol, the US role was crucial, especially since the United States was the major producer and consumer of the CFCs. A leadership void is evident in the global-warming problem. Even for the small list of challenges presented in this chapter, it is clear that the recipe for success for one problem may not serve as a recipe for solving a different problem, because the pattern of incentives may differ drastically among problems. Finally, there is cause to doubt the dire forecasts that paint a future world as an environmental wasteland. For most exigencies, nations are motivated to act either alone or in concert with others as the costs of doing nothing rise. The main concern arises if the associated costs of inactivity rise precipitously once a problem surpasses a threshold. In this case, delayed action may come too late, so that catastrophic consequences are experienced that may be difficult or impossible to reverse. The gathering of information can uncover these dire consequences from inactivity. Once these consequences are known, nations are motivated to act.

5   Architecture of institutions

Some global contingencies may require nations to consider institutional initiatives and forms of governances that extend beyond the traditional nation-state. In select cases, current global challenges could eventually result in institutional changes greater than any experienced since the creation of the nation-state. The nation-state ushered in an era of nationalism in which a sense of citizenship flourished. In contrast, the establishment of supranational linkages could promote a blurring of nationalism in which an identity of world inhabitant takes root. In Chapter 4, I argued that not all global challenges require federations or explicit linkages, where nations sacrifice their authority to a higher supranational authority. Many challenges possess the appropriate incentives to motivate nations to bargain among themselves or else to form loose ad hoc agreements without the need for elaborative structures. Although the world is besieged by transnational problems, there is as yet no need for a world government where nationalism is cast aside. Given general trends for the breakup of nations, it is naive to expect a reversal in which smaller nations combine into larger units. The sole exception to this trend – the European Union (EU) – remains far from being a single nation-state. Even more unrealistic is the possibility that nations will join a single world federation that oversees their affairs. The nation-state will remain an important player in world affairs for the foreseeable future.

There are a number of reasons to anticipate that ad hoc supranational agreements and structures will be sufficient to address many

142

of the crises challenging the world today. When the efforts of one or two nations are sufficient to avert a bad event, no formal structure is needed if these cooperating nations perceive a net gain from their actions. Nation-specific gains can motivate nations to undertake actions that may have the consequences of benefiting others in the process. In other situations, the pattern of payoffs can be supportive of collective action without much formal apparatus.[1] In still other situations, the configuration of payoffs can be made to be more conducive through inducements (for example, debt-for-nature trades) to foster collective action without a formal linkage. Most problems facing nations are quite localized and can be adequately handled at the national or regional level. Supranational structures should be reserved for those challenges for which the payoffs from cooperation are large, and for which nations have little incentive to act alone or in conjunction with neighboring nations. These linkages may also be needed when the actions of the whole are required if any headway is to be made, as in the case of global warming. For the design of supranational linkages, simplicity is best in the light of complexity; that is, complex interactions among nations may be best fostered with the help of very simple structures that respect the nation-state as a crucial player.

The purpose of this chapter is to investigate the need for supranational linkages. I begin by identifying what mechanisms in the form of infrastructure are required to support these linkages. Design principles for supranational structures are then considered. Throughout the presentation, I try to be pragmatic by accounting for countries' reluctance to surrender their autonomy. The focus is therefore on linkages that are flexible and that preserve nations' rights to direct most of their own affairs. No utopian view is advocated; instead, I am interested in identifying what can be expected and how this relates to what has been experienced to date. Nongovernmental alternatives – clubs – are also presented. The Long-Range Transboundary Air Pollution (LRTAP) Convention and its subsequent protocols are analyzed as a case study to show the likely structure for some future treaties on transnational contingencies.

1. Patterns of payoffs conducive to collective action without a formal institution tying together the agents are examined by Hardin (1982), Lichbach (1996), and Sandler (1992).

THE NEED FOR SUPRANATIONAL
INFRASTRUCTURE

Infrastructure provides the underlying foundation to support a larger activity. For example, roads, communication networks, airports, and waste-treatment facilities constitute some of the infrastructure that allow communities to function. The assignment and enforcement of property rights provide the requisite infrastructure for markets to operate when goods and services are voluntarily exchanged. Within a nation, a system of tax collection and enforcement provides revenue to finance government expenditures on public goods and the correction of externalities. This tax system is an example of infrastructure. These taxes are also used to redistribute income in an attempt to engineer a "more desirable" distribution of income. For international interactions, infrastructure is also required to promote the exchange of goods and services, enforce contracts, finance global public goods, and limit access to common property.

  If a supranational linkage is required, two contrasting scenarios may be envisaged. Nations can form loose linkages of a temporary nature, or else they can form tighter federations.   If recent behavior is any indication, then looser linkages are the likely response when coordinated actions on behalf of two or more nations are needed. In fact, linkages tend to start off very loose, requiring little more than a willingness to acknowledge a potential problem that warrants further study. Cooperation initially assumes the form of gathering and sharing information. If the information supports action, then explicit mandates on nations' future behavior can be embodied in treaties and subsequent linkages. This scenario characterized the Vienna Convention on ozone depletion. As information was obtained about ozone depletion and the case against CFCs and other halocarbons mounted, subsequent actions (for example, the Montreal Protocol) set limits on CFC consumption and production.

  If externalities are to be corrected by assigning taxes or subsidies to adjust for uncompensated costs imposed or benefits received by one nation from the activities of another (for example, downwind depositions of acid rain), then a taxing or subsidizing authority is a prerequisite. The alternative is to rely on the nation's own taxing authority, but this often leads to problems when some nations do not want to pay the taxes. In the case of liability assignments, an international court is needed that has the muscle to adjudicate cases that it wishes to hear. Currently, both parties must consent to have the case heard and to abide by the Court's ruling if the World Court is to accomplish anything by listening to the case.[2] The enforcement of property rights and contracts internationally relies on the laws of the participating nations. This, too, can present difficulties if the nation's laws with respect to contracts are weak or ambiguous. Consider China and its failure to recognize intellectual property rights as embodied in compact disks, computer software, movies, and books. Although in early 1996 China publicly showed its willingness to protect these property rights by steamrolling over thousands of unauthorized copies, the problem remained despite this publicity stunt. A threatened trade war with the United States over this issue induced the Chinese to pledge protection of intellectual property rights in June 1996. Whether or not their pledge will be carried out remains to be seen.

If well-intentioned treaties are to make headway on global difficulties, then an enforcement mechanism may be needed to execute the treaty's mandate. This is particularly true when payoff patterns are not conducive to carrying out pledges. North Korea's violation of the Nuclear Nonproliferation Treaty in the mid-1990s highlights the enforcement problem. Another case involves controlling the illegal trade in CFCs. Even though most nations have voluntarily abided by the Montreal Protocol's provisions curtailing CFC production and consumption, private individuals have seized upon a profitable opportunity to traffic in CFCs. By not paying the required CFC taxes, these illegal traders limit the treaty's intention to make more-benign CFC substitutes relatively cheaper and undermine the cutbacks in CFC emissions. Nations with insufficient resources to control the elicit trade in CFCs may have to rely on an international police force or on the efforts of a more powerful nation. These halocarbon profiteers will quickly spot where law enforcement is the weakest and gravitate to these venues. A worldwide effort is needed to stem this trade. Consequently, a more capable international police force represents another infrastructural requirement if some supranational actions are to work more fully.

---

2. See Dubner (1980) on the powers of the World Court and its evolution into its current form.

The assignment to open-access common property rights is yet another crucial infrastructural concern in the years to come. Mining the deep seabeds is a case in point. Manganese nodules are rich in manganese, nickel, cobalt, copper, and other substances and lie at the bottom of the sea. Since these nodules lie well outside territorial waters, countries like the United States that possess the know-how to mine this wealth will do so. Their action will cause even greater skewness to the income distribution among nations (see Chapter 7). It is easy to envision a few technologically advanced nations racing to recover these nodules despite the costs that their mining activities might cause to the ocean ecosystem. The failure of the United Kingdom and the United States to sign or ratify the UN Law of the Seas treaty with its restrictions on deep-seabed mining foreshadows that this exploitation is inevitable. Satellite orbital bands, airsheds, the stratosphere, the troposphere, and the electromagnetic spectrum are just a few of the world's resources where open access can cause a problem. As a consequence, the world may have to consider alternatives to "squatter's rights" for some of these assets, especially when income distribution concerns are considered. If these property right problems are addressed at an early stage, then there may be less need to resort to supranational linkages.

Although nations have cooperated on some important issues, it is crucial to remember that more adequate infrastructure is a prerequisite for these treaties to succeed. Supranational linkages cannot always depend on the infrastructure of nations to enforce commitments that the nation may be later uninterested in implementing. More thought needs to be given to providing some of this infrastructure before more effort is expended on designing supranational structures for addressing some global concerns. Financing these structures is another crucial concern. In recent years, the United Nations has been poignantly aware of its dependence on nations to pay their dues, since major contributors, such as the United States, which pays a quarter of the UN budget, are behind in their payments.

At times, a supranational agreement can mandate its own financing mechanism, as in the implementation of the Montreal Protocol and its amendments. The Multilateral Fund underwrites the Protocol. The administrative budget of the Multilateral Fund ran

$3,048,735 in 1994, $3,699,050 in 1995, and $2,818,215 in 1996.[3] For 1991–4, the primary contributors were the United States, Japan, Germany, the United Kingdom, Spain, and Canada. Much greater funds that could run in the billions will be needed to assist the Article 5 nations to implement control measures and to adopt CFC substitutes. Problems will surely arise when raising these funds.

DESIGN PRINCIPLES

Once the required infrastructure is in place at the supranational level, there are a number of factors supportive for designing supranational linkages. First, it is imperative to try to start with a small set of crucial participants. As the number of nations increases, more alternatives and viewpoints must be considered, so that any agreements achieved are apt to be weak in order to obtain a consensus. Consider the UN General Assembly resolution condemning terrorism on 9 December 1985. This resolution allows for "the inalienable right to self-determination and independence of all peoples under the colonial and racist regimes and other forms of alien domination, and upholding the legitimacy of their struggle, in particular the struggle of national liberation movements."[4] This provision of the resolution calls into question whether terrorism may be justified under some extenuating circumstances. Self-determination can be broadly interpreted to justify a wide range of grievances. On 18 December 1985, the fifteen nations of the Security Council took a much less equivocal position in condemning *all* acts of hostage-taking.[5]

Second, the resolution of uncertainty is a necessary precondition to convincing nations to take actions.[6] To date, this information for environmental problems has come from one or more concerned nations commissioning the studies. A permanent body of qualified

3. Fridtjof Nansen Institute (1996, 105–6).
4. Murphy (1990, 386).
5. See Murphy (1990) for a fuller discussion of UN resolutions and conventions on terrorism. The text of the early resolutions and conventions can be found in Alexander et al. (1979).
6. In the 1996 movie *Independence Day*, the destruction of the world's major cities convinces the world's peoples to unite against the aliens.

scientists and social scientists, funded by the international community to learn routinely about global contingencies, would be supportive of collective action. Currently, too much time elapses before a problem is recognized, after which nations still have to agree to meet and act on the commissioned study. Surely, this process could be streamlined, so that actions can be taken more quickly, thus avoiding greater deterioration. Since research discoveries depend on the greatest or best-shot effort, the pooling of resources across the international community is likely to increase the effectiveness of gathering information.

Third, it is very conducive to international responses if one or more nations can assume a leadership role as the United States did for the Montreal Protocol. If the leader nations are crucial players in the underlying problem, then their leadership activity is particularly important. For a time, Australia tried to assume a leadership role in the global-warming treaty, but its efforts were ineffective due, in part, to its status as a relatively small emitter of greenhouse gases (GHGs). A leadership role by the United States or the EU on global warming would be more supportive of transnational action. The United States has, however, not assumed such a role with respect to GHGs. Potential leadership nations must perceive a net benefit from addressing the crises before taking on such a role.

Once the leadship nations have assembled a critical number of participants, a bandwagon effect may take over as nonparticipating nations worry about being out-of-step with others.[7] Large groups of treaty participants can apply pressure to induce holdout nations to join. This has been true for the Montreal Protocol after enough participants ratified the treaty.

Fourth, the presence of nation-specific or localized benefits is also supportive of transnational cooperation, as shown for acid rain and other problems in Chapter 4. In arranging the summit on terrorism on 13 March 1996 at Sharm el-Sheikh, Egypt, Israel and the United States assumed a leadership role. This is not surprising insofar as these two nations had the most nation-specific benefits to gain from international action to curb such acts, which have jeopardized the peace process in the Middle East. The summit led to an Israeli-American security agreement but, unfortunately, did not produce

7. The presence of bandwagon effects is explored in Weiss and Jacobson (1996).

any specific actions on the part of most of the other twenty-seven delegations.[8] Those nations that reap the greatest localized benefits should be motivators for actions. The presence of localized benefits can promote the trading of support among diverse global contingencies, so that nations engage in logrolling owing to vested interests. When, therefore, the solution to a global challenge possesses a wide range of localized benefits, transnational action should be easier to achieve. These selective incentives can be drafted into the treaty or linkage rules, as was the case where developing nations were promised technical assistance, financial help, and delayed implementation in the Montreal Protocol on ozone depletion.

Fifth, the media can serve an essential function in forging linkages. With their ability to communicate with the world's billions, the media can alert the world's people to the need for collective action for some problems even when this action can limit national autonomy. As people become aware of the required transnational cooperation, they can pressure their leaders in a democracy to join efforts with other nations. This chain is more tenuous in an authoritarian regime, since the dictator may be deaf to the wishes of the people. The Olympic Games in Atlanta, Georgia, during the summer of 1996 were viewed by nearly half of humankind, while "Baywatch" is viewed by even greater numbers. With this kind of communication potential, the media can educate people worldwide on the need to take transnational actions on some issues, even if adjustments to lifestyles are required.[9] When linkages are forged, the media could facilitate referendums on policy initiatives. The potential here is great, provided that the media exercise restraint and do not take up too many causes.

Sixth, the formation of supranational linkages is enhanced if they are started loose with the autonomy of the participating nations preserved and then tightened over time if warranted. It is better to forge some link than to set one's sights too high and achieve nothing. If initial agreements are made too complex and require potential participants to surrender a great amount of sovereignty, then negotiations are apt to drag on for a long time without a linkage being culminated. If, instead, a simple structure can be established, the

8. For an article on the conference, see *The Economist* (1996a).
9. I owe this insight to Norman Myers.

A's strategy \ B's strategy	Don't Contribute	Contribute
Don't Contribute	* 0, 0 a	5, –2 b
Contribute	–2, 5 c	3, 3 d

Figure 5.1. Public good Prisoners' Dilemma.

potential participants can better judge with experience the likely net gain from greater cooperation. Once these structures are established, nations acquire communication channels with other nations affected by a contingency. Meetings can be set up quickly, and information can be disseminated rapidly. Learning is nurtured in such an environment.

Seventh, supranational pacts can be better promoted if the international community does not blindly apply what works for one crisis resolution on another. What worked for curbing CFC emissions is probably not suited to global warming, where the major players are far greater in numbers and have much less to gain from an agreement. There is no single blueprint to success.

LINKAGE BENEFITS AND COSTS

To more fully consider the net gains from cooperation, I return to the two-player Prisoners' Dilemma. In Figure 5.1, the payoffs for the two nations are based on a public good (for example, curbing pollution, deterring international terrorism), where each unit confers 5 in benefits to both nations at a cost of 7 to just the provider. Each nation has two strategic choices: contribute one unit or don't contribute. If neither contributes, the status quo gives no benefits, so that the payoffs are 0 in cell *a*. If, however, only player 1 contributes, then player 2 receives a free-rider payoff of 5, while player 1 receives −2 as costs of 7 are deducted from the gain of 5. A similar scenario with players' roles and payoffs reversed applies to cell *c*. When both nations contribute, each receives 3 as the costs of 7 are deducted from total benefits of 10 (= 5 × 2). For each player, the dominant strategy is to not contribute, thus leading to the Nash equilibrium in cell *a*. When compared with the cooperative outcome of cell *d* where both nations contribute, each can gain up to 3 from striking a deal. Obviously, the greater the difference between the noncooperative and cooperative payoffs, the greater the inducement to cooperate. This increase in benefits from cooperation is the *efficiency gain* from forging a linkage to provide the public good. But this is not the whole story.

Cooperation may bring additional benefits and costs, not captured by the efficiency gains in moving from cell *a* to cell *d* through a supranational link. Unless all of these costs and benefits are identified, the feasibility of such a link cannot be judged adequately. Consider two nations that want to coordinate pollution control activities on a shared lake, so as to move from cell *a* to cell *d* in Figure 5.1. In addition to efficiency gains, linkage or coordination benefits may arise from scale economies that lower per-unit costs of public good provision when provision is at a larger output level.[10] For instance, the operation by two nations of a single water treatment plant, which serves to purify the water for the lake, may be less expensive per unit of operation than is the construction of two separate plants, where the capacity of the two plants together is equivalent to that of the large plant. In calculating the payoffs in Figure 5.1, I did not allow unit cost to fall with increased output. Another linkage benefit can arise from the increased information and communication possibilities that the increased cooperation produces. Information gains and communication ties are jointly produced when nations become linked to address a common concern. Sometimes existing links come in handy when other contingencies arise.

But these linkage benefits come at a cost. Linkage costs are associated with the operation and establishment of the linkage and must be distinguished from the production costs of the public good. Three primary linkage costs, associated with a supranational linkage, are decision-making costs, interdependency costs, and enforcement costs. Only those linkage costs that are incurred by the supranational link and *would not be experienced by independent nation provision*

---

10. On transaction costs, see Arrow (1970). On linkage costs and benefits, see Auster and Silver (1973), Cauley, Sandler, and Cornes (1986), Sandler and Cauley (1977), and Sandler, Cauley, and Tschirhart (1983).

are included. Provision, financing, and timing decisions represent some of the issues that must be answered when a supranational structure attempts to coordinate public good provision among participating nations. Increased coordination necessitates information, administrative, and planning costs that would not be incurred under national provision of the public good. Decision-making costs may also take the form of bargaining expense as the parties attempt to reach a voluntary agreement.

These additional decision-making costs have, for example, characterized joint ventures by allies to develop and to procure new weapons. Examples include the French-British *Jaguar* strike aircraft, the British-German-Italian *Tornado* combat aircraft, the American-British *Harrier* vertical-takeoff-and-landing jet plane, and the British-German-Italian-Spanish *Eurofighter* aircraft. According to Keith Hartley, "Collaboration also involves substantial transaction costs reflecting duplicate organizations, management by consensus, excessive bureaucracy, and delays in decision-making."[11] Even though administrative costs are higher on these joint ventures, linkage benefits arise because R & D does not have to be duplicated among countries and scale economies stem from higher production runs. Overall net savings of 10–15% have been estimated for two-nation ventures, despite the greater transaction costs.[12]

As nations join a supranational structure, a loss of autonomy and flexibility may result unless unanimity is the decision rule, since sometimes a nation may have to go along with majority decisions that the nation opposes. These costs are termed *interdependency costs*. In cases of disagreement where dissenters must be made to go along with a decision, *enforcement costs* in terms of military force or economic sanctions may have to be expended by the supranational structure. Just to keep nations in line may require some enforcement infrastructure even if for deterrence purposes alone.

Net linkage benefits, or the difference between total linkage benefits and total linkage costs, figure prominently into the two key design issues: (1) linkage formation and (2) linkage structure. Total linkage benefits or costs include the *sum* of the various categories of benefits and costs identified above.

11. Sandler and Hartley (1995, 235).
12. Hartley (1991, chapter 9) contains an extensive discussion on these joint ventures.

LINKAGE FORMATION

At least two conditions must be satisfied if a linkage is to be viable so that it should be instituted. First, there must be some linkage form in which net linkage benefits are positive for the entire set of potential participants; that is, there must be some linkage structure where efficiency gains and the other linkage benefits outweigh the associated linkage costs. As the extent of integration goes up so that linked nations must act more like a single nation, both linkage benefits and linkage costs are anticipated to rise. Insofar as incremental benefits are expected to level out rapidly with increased integration, while incremental costs may accelerate with greater integration, less complex, "loose" structures appear to stand a better chance of initial formation. With greater integration, linkage benefits rise at a decreasing rate owing to diminishing returns. Consider the number of meetings, which is a measure of the extent of linkage integration. The gains from the first few meetings each year are surely greater than those associated with the fifth or twentieth meeting. Linkage costs may go up at a rapid rate especially because of the unwillingness of nations to sacrifice their autonomy – that is, incremental interdependency costs may rise rapidly as integration increases. For example, the EU has achieved far less than hoped, due, in large part, to members' resistance to give the European Parliament much governing authority. As a consequence, it is still a loose federation. Had the framers of the EU attempted to form a tighter structure from the outset, it might not exist today.

Second, the net linkage gains from cooperating must be distributed in such a way that each nation perceives a net gain from the link. To accomplish this second requirement, some participants may have to be given side payments or concessions, as in the case of the "Article 5" countries in the Montreal Protocol on controlling CFC emissions. For the Oslo Protocol to the Long-Range Transboundary Air Pollution Treaty (LRTAP) drafted on 14 June 1994, mandated cutbacks of sulfur emissions from a 1980 baseline vary greatly among treaty participants for the year 2000 and beyond. A couple of nations are required to make little or no cutbacks (see discussion later in the chapter). As a prospective linkage includes more heterogeneous nations, there may be a greater need to institute side payments if each nation is to view the linkage as giving it more than what it must sacrifice to join.

LINKAGE STRUCTURE

Once a supranational link is established, the extent of integration can be ascertained in an effort to achieve the greatest difference between linkage benefits and linkage costs. Since both linkage benefits and costs depend on the extent of integration, net linkage benefits also depend on the level of integration. Simply put, the linkage-structure decision requires choosing among the proposed linkage forms (or extent of integration) the one with the greatest net benefits. In some cases, integration can be measured along a continuum, as in the case when linked nations must decide the level of common funding provided. Increased common funding implies greater integration, in which the optimal level of common funding is the one that maximizes net linkage benefits. Alternatively, the integration choice might involve the choice of a host of integration parameters – for example, the number of annual meetings, common-funding levels, the decision rule, and decision bindingness. When this is the case, the parameters must be chosen to maximize net linkage benefits, while accounting for interdependencies among the parameters.

The most likely scenario involves a discrete choice where a finite number of alternative linkage structures are put forward, each containing a different combination of form parameters. The optimal choice involves two decisions. First, an estimate of the total net linkage benefits of each alternative form must be ascertained, and the structure with the largest net benefits chosen. Second, the distribution of the gains must be decided, so as to continue to fulfill the sufficiency requirement that every participant gains something. A specific distribution of the gains may be needed to maintain sufficiency. The distribution decision will often be contentious as participants maneuver for the greatest possible payoff. This bickering is a daily event in the EU whenever policy measures imply disbursements or contributions. As technology, leadership, tastes, and other changes occur, the optimal linkage structure must be reevaluated over time to maintain its viability and optimality. Links that remain viable may need to have their forms adjusted periodically based on the current configuration of linkage benefits and costs. For example, amendments to protocols are structural changes that may be necessitated by new information or an increased desire of the member states to do more to address a common problem.

If more than one linkage involves some participants, then inter-linkage effects must be identified when determining linkage viability and structure. Sometimes *economies of scope* in linkage costs exist when cost savings arise when two or more linkages share the same facilities, which then implies *common or joint costs*.[13] Once established, the bureaucratic structure of the United Nations can be and has been used for collective activities other than promoting world peace owing to these scope economies. Common costs can stem, for example, from a communication network or meeting facilities that can serve a host of purposes. If these economies of scope are sufficient, then multiple linkages on a variety of problems may be best handled by the same supranational structure. The United Nations and NATO embrace a wide range of activities with myriad links. The United Nations is anticipated to serve an important role in promoting supranational links that involve a large number of nations, while smaller regional supranational linkages (for example, the EU) are believed to serve a similar role for more localized problems. The use of existing structures will economize on linkage costs, thus increasing the viability of future linkages.

NONGOVERNMENTAL ALTERNATIVES

Public goods whose benefits can be excluded at a relatively small cost are shown to be able to be provided by a *club*, even with multiple generations of members (see Chapters 2 and 3). In a club, members form a nongovernmental collective that provides a club good (for example, a park or a canal). These club goods are financed by tolls or visiting fees levied against members when they use the club.[14] Although each visit costs the same toll, a member's total tolls

---

13. On economies of scope, see Baumol, Panzar, and Willig (1988) and Sandler and Tschirhart (1997).
14. Clubs are analyzed in detail by Buchanan (1965), Sandler and Tschirhart (1980), and Cornes and Sandler (1996).

vary according to tastes as revealed by the number of visits made. Members with a greater need for the club good pay more in total tolls by visiting more frequently than those with a smaller interest. A properly designed toll attempts to make the user compensate for the crowding and related costs that his or her visit creates.

Clubs can provide a low-cost alternative to formal supranational structures, provided that the shared good possesses benefits that can be excluded from nonpayers. In a transnational setting, clubs represent a viable means for allocating resources to a transnational public good without having to resort to a costly structure to coordinate nations' actions. For transnational clubs, the members can be multinational firms, states within a nation, or nation-states. Nations can, for instance, share a commando squad whose purpose is to manage terrorist incidents.[15] Each deployment of the squad would result in a toll charge to the nation requesting the assistance to crisis manage an incident. Cost allocation may be decided based on which nations use the commando squad rather than by negotiations, but the size and makeup of the force would still require negotiations. Clubs economize on linkage costs because the distribution decision regarding each nation's net gains can be made through the use patterns dictated by circumstances and preferences. Provision costs are limited as each nation does not have to provide its own commando force, which would lead to a duplication of efforts.

Since access to many forms of infrastructure can be monitored and charged a toll, some of the infrastructure requirements for greater transnational interactions can be provided through a club arrangement. Technology can be expected to create new and inexpensive means for limiting access, thus augmenting the number of goods that can be allocated by clubs. Communication links, information links, police protection, and stock markets are examples of club goods. Even peacekeeping forces could be financed on a user basis, where fees or tolls are assigned to nations according to their proximity to troubled regions requiring the deployment of crisis-management efforts.

Clubs illustrate that nations can form a collective that preserves much of their autonomy, so that nations do not have to look toward supranational governments to address their common public good

15. On this application of club theory, see Sandler et al. (1983).

needs. These clubs can include a wide range of participants as illustrated by INTELSAT, which links much of the world in an external communication network carrying the majority of transoceanic messages.[16] The system consists of nineteen geostationary satellites positioned some 22,300 miles above the equator. At that altitude, the satellites orbit the earth in the same time interval that the earth rotates about its axis, and hence each satellite remains stationary over a point on the earth's surface. Only three satellites are required to provide point-to-multipoint service throughout the earth, except at the poles. Ten satellites are positioned over the Atlantic, four each are positioned over the Pacific and Indian Oceans, and one is positioned over the Asia-Pacific region. Because the largest message flow is across the Atlantic Ocean, this region requires more communication satellites than elsewhere to provide sufficient capacity. Of the nineteen satellites, some serve as spares, increasing the system's reliability to better than a 99.9% effectiveness rate. An INTELSAT satellite receives weak radio signals in the megahertz frequency band from earth-station transmitters. The satellite then amplifies and retransmits the signals in the gigahertz band to earth-station receivers, between which signals travel via microwave links and cables.

The INTELSAT communication system represents a club good since access to the network can be restricted by coding or scrambling signals, and the network can be simultaneously used by its members. Additionally, this use can be monitored and tolls charged according to the amount of utilization. As utilization of the system increases, the benefits per signal transmitted diminish, owing to congestion (for example, interference or "noise") as an increased volume of signals shares the same frequency band. A club arrangement can allocate utilization rates efficiently on the basis of congestion-based toll charges. The current structure of INTELSAT conforms closely to that of an economic club with firms *and* governments as members. These members pay fees according to their utilization on a per-unit basis, and voting at meetings of the Board of Governors is weighted based on the members' utilization rates and investment shares. Although the other bodies of INTELSAT (for example, the Assembly

16. This write-up on INTELSAT is taken from Cornes and Sandler (1996, 412–13). Also see Sandler and Schulze (1981, 1985) and INTELSAT (1995).

of Parties, the Meeting of Signatories, and the manager) make policy recommendations, the Board of Governors is the ultimate decision-making body of INTELSAT.[17] A weighted voting scheme based on utilization is consistent with efficient allocative decisions for the network, because heavier users will be serving more individuals whose interests must be reflected, and consequently these heavier users will support a greater share of the costs resulting from policy changes. INTELSAT is operated like a corporation. Toll revenues support the system and underwrite investment in upgrades and increased capacity. It is not a supranational link that requires nations to sacrifice their political autonomy to the wishes of the majority. Members determine their own levels of utilization and can choose to leave the system if they wish. Other private allocation alternatives can be explored for a host of transnational public goods (for example, satellite-based remote sensing) provided that use can be monitored and charged accordingly.

A SUPRANATIONAL LINK CASE STUDY: LRTAP

In Chapter 4, the sulfur and NO_x acid rain problem has already been discussed along with the LRTAP Convention and two of the subsequent protocols – the Helsinki and Sofia Protocols. The progress made in establishing and structuring this supranational linkage is now put into perspective using the design principles presented in this chapter.

Progress on the acid rain problem began with a very loose linkage, since the LRTAP Convention only asked that its ratifiers recognize that the emissions of sulfur and NO_x posed a problem. To assess this problem, the Convention required that data on these emissions be collected and evaluated. The Convention established the Cooperative Programme for Monitoring and Evaluation (EMEP) of these emissions.[18] Under this program, monitoring stations were set up throughout Europe to track the emission, dispersion, and deposition of sulfur and NO_x. Volatile organic compounds (VOCs), which add to tropospheric ozone and include methane, propane, ethane, bu-

17. See Edelson (1977) and INTELSAT (1973) on the organization of INTELSAT.
18. The treaty text can be found in UN Environment Programme (1991).

tanol, and many others, would be monitored by EMEP at a later date as technology permits. EMEP was also assigned the tasks of modeling atmospheric pollution dispersion and monitoring air and precipitation quality. On 28 September 1984, the Geneva Protocol established assessments for financing EMEP. Each of the European ratifiers of the LRTAP Convention was assigned an individualized share of the annual costs of EMEP. These EMEP cost shares amounted to very modest obligations when compared with these governments' overall budgets; hence, the financial burden associated with the Geneva Protocol was modest and spread over a large number of nations. The Geneva Protocol entered into force on 28 January 1988; thirty parties had ratified it by 11 November 1995.[19]

It was only after these nations understood the pattern of dispersion, acknowledged the harm of these pollutants, and curtailed their own pollution levels that they were willing to participate in framing a tighter agreement. For sulfur emissions, this tighter treaty mandated a 30% *across-the-board* cutback from 1980 levels for ratifiers of the 1985 Helsinki Protocol. For NO_x, the Sofia Protocol entailed more modest percentage reductions since, as mentioned in Chapter 4, nations had a more difficult time in achieving emission reductions. These two protocols are noteworthy because they imposed explicit constraints on the behavior of the ratifiers. Nations that were having a difficult time in achieving the protocols' provisions failed to ratify them,[20] so that nations still had a way out of these binding constraints. Nevertheless, many European nations perceived sufficient net gains from the treaties to go along with their provisions even though this placed some constraints on their sovereignty.

As the EU nations achieved further progress on cutting sulfur and NO_x emissions, they framed even stricter requirements in the Large Combustion Plant Directive (LCPD) of 24 November 1988.[21] The LCPD restricted emissions for most EU nations beyond the limits of the earlier protocols. These new restrictions took effect in 1993 following ratification. In Table 5.1, LCPD-mandated sulfur and NO_x

19. Fridtjof Nansen Institute (1996, 96).
20. For the end of 1990, ratifiers are listed in Murdoch et al. (1994, table 2A). Notable nonratifiers of the Helsinki Protocol included Greece, Ireland, Poland, Spain, Turkey, the United Kingdom, and others. By 1996, all but Turkey had signed the Helsinki Protocol, but none of the six countries had yet ratified it (Fridjhof Nansen Institute 1996, 194–209).
21. The text of this treaty is in Council of the European Communities (1988).

Table 5.1. *Large combustion plant directive: Voluntary and mandated reductions in sulfur and NO$_x$ emissions*

Country	Sulfur		Nitrogen oxides	
	%Sul88	Mandated %[a]	%NO$_x$88	Mandated %[b]
Belgium	49	40	29	20
Denmark	46	34	− 7	3
France	63	40	11	20
W. Germany	61	40	4	20
Greece	−25	− 6	0	− 94
Ireland	32	− 25	−67	− 79
Italy	37	27	−19	2
Luxembourg	33	40	17	20
Netherlands	41	40	− 1	20
Portugal	23	−102	27	−157
Spain	32	0	12	− 1
United Kingdom	22	20	−14	15

Notes: %Sul88: Percentage reductions in total sulfur emissions from 1980 to the end of 1988 as a percent of 1980 emissions.
%NO$_x$88: Percentage reductions in total NO$_x$ emissions from 1980 to the end of 1988 as a percent of 1980 emissions.
Calculations of %Sul88 and %NO$_x$88 use Sandnes (1993) data on emissions.
[a] Only includes sulfur reductions for large combusion plants.
[b] Only includes NO$_x$ emission reductions for large combustion plants.

emission reductions from 1980 levels are given in the third and fifth columns, respectively. The second and fourth columns list the percentage of *overall* sulfur and NO$_x$ reductions, respectively, actually achieved by the end of 1988. For sulfur, large combustion plant emissions represent about half of overall emissions; for NO$_x$, these emissions constitute about a quarter of overall emissions. When columns 2 and 3 of Table 5.1 are compared, ten of twelve nations had met the mandated limits on total sulfur emissions at the time that the treaty was framed. An eleventh nation (Luxembourg) was close to the target; only Greece was some distance away. A pattern similar to the Helsinki Protocol applied to the LCPD: Nations achieved emission reduction levels and then drafted the treaty with these levels as targets. This pattern means that constraints to their autonomy, as implied by the linkage, would be small. For NO$_x$, inference is more problematic, insofar as combustion plants only accounted for 20–25% of emissions. Thus, it is difficult to compare the stricter requirements of the LCPD to the cutbacks of the Sofia Protocol.

Table 5.2. *Mandated sulfur emission cutbacks from 1980 levels: Oslo Protocol*

Country	Mandated cutbacks from 1980 levels (percentage)		
	2000	2005	2010
Austria	80		
Belarus	38	46	50
Belgium	70	72	74
Bulgaria	33	40	45
Croatia	11	17	22
Czech Republic	50	60	72
Denmark	80		
Finland	80		
France	74	77	78
Germany	83	87	
Greece	0	3	4
Hungary	45	50	60
Ireland	30		
Italy	65	73	
Liechtenstein	75		
Luxembourg	58		
Netherlands	77		
Norway	76		
Poland	37	47	66
Portugal	0	3	
Russian Federation	38	40	40
Slovakia	60	65	72
Slovenia	45	60	70
Spain	35		
Sweden	80		
Switzerland	52		
Ukraine	40		
United Kingdom	50	70	80
European Community	62		

Source: United Nations (1994, Annex II, pp. 15–16).

Nevertheless, it is noteworthy that half of the EU nations met or almost met the percentage reductions for *overall* NO_x as those mandated by the LCPD for *just* combustion plants at the time of the treaty drafting (see Table 5.1). This suggests that the NO_x restrictions of the LCPD encoded reductions that nations had already achieved.

On 14 June 1994, a still stronger protocol on sulfur emissions was framed in Oslo.[22] As of November 1996, the Oslo Protocol was un-

22. The text of the Oslo Protocol is in United Nations (1994).

ratified, but was expected to be ratified soon. In Table 5.2, the mandated cuts for the years 2000, 2005, and 2010 are given by country. A blank entry means that no additional reductions beyond the ones listed are required. Thus, for Austria, the 80% reduction from 1980 levels mandated for the year 2000 is not increased in either 2005 or 2010. Both the LCPD and the Oslo Protocol differ in a fundamental way from their predecessors. Namely, *reductions are tailored for the treaty parties* based on their costs of emission cutbacks, so that across-the-board cuts are no longer applied to each nation. This tailoring practice allows the treaty instrument greater flexibility in ensuring that each party perceives a net gain from the linkage, despite their different dependencies on fossil fuels and their diverse abilities to curb emissions. Consequently, the sufficient condition for feasibility should be easier to reach, and the number of ratifiers should be larger. Moving away from across-the-board cuts is a sensible step to facilitating wider ratification of the treaties. Future treaties are anticipated to incorporate this innovation.

In the case of VOCs, the Geneva Protocol of 18 November 1991 required ratifiers to reduce annual emissions by at least 30% by 1999, using 1988 levels as the baseline.[23] As of early 1996, the Protocol has not entered into force. This Protocol, which has been very slow in coming, again imposed across-the-board cutbacks with a small degree of variation among countries. Some flexibility was allowed because ratifiers could specify a different baseline year within the 1984–90 period as well as the area of the country for which the reductions apply. Thus, a ratifier could limit its obligation greatly by choosing a higher than normal emission year as its basis of cutbacks. The Geneva Protocol on VOCs was particularly difficult to formulate because it involved so many different substances, and this made the agreement complex. In addition, it took longer to obtain measurements on VOC emissions and dispersions. Negotiations would have achieved quicker success had the VOCs been unbundled in a number of different protocols.

The protocols that followed the LRTAP Convention illustrate another important insight regarding these transnational linkages. By initially establishing a linkage, a convention allows the nations to acquire the infrastructure, in the form of treaty rules and procedures,

23. The text of the Geneva Protocol is in United Nations (1992b).

to facilitate future updates and fine-tuning. A repeated game framework then applies, and, thus, participants may be willing to become more cooperative with time, since interactions are not viewed as one-shot affairs. Moreover, failure to adhere to an earlier protocol can then mean losses in terms of future cooperative benefits as nations retaliate against the treaty buster. Even if conventions do not immediately accomplish much in terms of explicit commitments, they still play a crucial role in promoting more cooperative behavior at a later stage.

OTHER DESIGN-PROMOTING FACTORS

There are a few additional considerations that can foster a transnational linkage. First, agreements among few nations are typically easier to achieve than those among larger groups, since the viability condition, requiring that each nation achieve a net gain, is easier to satisfy. Second, nations that share the same tastes and have similar national income levels should be easier to link, insofar as a net gain for one should translate into a net gain for all. Thus, linkages should be easier to achieve if one starts with more homogeneous nations. Once a linkage among reasonably homogeneous nations is established, it can be expanded to include more heterogeneous nations. In some ways, this is the approach taken by NATO and the EU. Third, cost-sharing arrangements can facilitate linkage, since the choice as to whether to contribute or not is made less of a burden for the contributor as everyone shares the costs. Fourth, private inducers can support nations' actions to cooperate. These selective incentives can be positive (inducements) or negative (sanctions). The Montreal Protocol on ozone protection threatened sanctions in terms of trade restrictions on nations that did abide by the Protocol.

CONCLUDING REMARKS

This chapter has identified some useful principles that facilitate supranational linkages. Just because there are gains that can be achieved through cooperation does not mean that a supranational linkage is warranted. Linkage costs must be considered along with linkage benefits in order to ascertain whether the link is viable. To be viable, net linkage benefits must be positive for the group as a whole *and* for each participant. Also, nongovernmental alternatives must be examined to determine whether linkage costs can be economized through clubs or similar arrangements. If a transnational link is warranted, however, then its form can be decided by comparing the net linkage benefits among alternative viable structures and choosing the one with the greatest net benefits. Structures that begin loose are more apt to form. Modest initial goals for the linkage may be most conducive to long-run gains as the initial structure provides infrastructure for achieving larger cooperative gains as warranted over time. The LRTAP Convention illustrates that loose initial linkage can be tightened as needed.

6 Change we must: Evolutionary concerns

This chapter takes a long-term view on global challenges by considering whether or not cooperation can develop through repeated interactions among nation-states. For acid rain, nations within a region confront the same pollution problem period after period, in which uncoordinated actions can create considerable costs to the pollution recipients. A cooperative outcome to limit these acid rain emissions would greatly benefit the nations involved. If cooperation were to develop for a particular problem, is it likely to occur at the regional or global level? When, say, cooperation initiates at the regional level, is it anticipated to diffuse to other countries and regions? These are important questions. Faced with significant regional and global challenges, successful nations may, like successful species, be those that develop strategies that maximize their fitness in terms of high payoffs. Behavioral patterns of successful nations are expected to be copied by other nations, thereby spreading throughout a region and, at times, beyond. If the diffusion is sufficient, then cooperators can "colonize" the population of nations and take over. For cooperators to last, they must be immune from invasion by opportunistic "mutants" who employ another strategy.

Consider the Prisoners' Dilemma where playing the dominant strategy would give the participants low payoffs. Subsets of nations that cooperate may capture greater payoffs and, with them, increase their long-run survival possibility. Concepts from repeated games and evolutionary games can be fruitfully applied to the study of global challenges.[1] For example, one may inquire whether *altruistic* behavior applied to neighboring nations will be reciprocated. Will the same reciprocation occur for far-distant countries, where cultures and economies differ? Moreover, will nations that display altruism stand a better chance of survival, as has been shown for some animals by sociobiologists?[2]

This chapter is primarily interested in addressing these questions so as to explain how cooperation may evolve with time and space, even for situations where short-term cooperative responses are not anticipated. I therefore investigate how evolutionary factors may facilitate successful resolutions to global challenges without the need for a formal supranational structure. In doing so, evolutionary considerations are distinguished at the regional and global levels. I argue that supportive evolutionary factors may assist nations to meet regional and global challenges. Efficacious strategies, as identified with nations, are self-selected over time through survival and may take over a regional group. For a particularly threatening global challenge, successful regional strategies should diffuse to other regions and eventually to the entire globe. As a secondary purpose, evolutionary considerations are related to the distribution of income among nations. Great differences in income distribution may, at times, inhibit the diffusion of successful cooperative strategies. At a regional level, income distributions may be more equal and, thus, more conducive to the spread of cooperation.

My intention is also to introduce the reader briefly to some ideas of repeated and evolutionary games. In doing so, I only mention a few key concepts and ideas, since the analysis is meant to be informal and nontechnical. Experimental evidence on the way people play games in laboratory settings is indicated in a number of places in this chapter. This evidence indicates that subjects play in a more cooperative fashion than typically predicted by game theory.[3] By

1. On repeated games, consult Binmore (1992); on repeated games and collective action, see Sandler (1992, chapter 3). Evolutionary game theory is a rapidly growing area of research. Important contributions include Axelrod (1984), Bergstrom (1995), Bergstrom and Stark (1993), Friedman (1996), Maynard Smith (1982), and Tesfatsion (1996). Much recent interest in the evolution of cooperation was generated by Axelrod's (1984) seminal study.
2. On altruism and evolutionary equilibrium, see Bergstrom (1995), Bergstrom and Stark (1993), and Dawkins (1976, 1995).
3. See Roth (1995) and references cited therein on this experimental literature and findings.

A's strategy \ B's strategy	Defect	Cooperate
Defect	P, P	T, S
Cooperate	S, T	R, R

$T > R > P > S$
$S + T < 2R$

Figure 6.1. Prisoners' Dilemma.

analogy, this suggests that nations confronted by contingencies may likewise adopt strategies more cooperative than those predicted by standard game solution concepts. When this is true, the need for intervention is reduced.

ON REPEATED GAMES

A repeated game is a particular game, complete with its strategies, players, and payoffs, that is played over and over again. In its standard form, the game is unchanged in terms of its three key ingredients from one play to another. Consider the two-person Prisoners' Dilemma depicted in Figure 6.1, where the payoffs are ordered as follows: $T > R > P > S$. The letters are used to denote payoff scenarios in which P is punishment for mutual defection, R is reward for mutual cooperation, T is temptation (the highest payoff) for unilateral defection, and S is sucker (the lowest payoff) for unilateral cooperation. Sometimes an additional requirement is attached to the Prisoners' Dilemma payoff matrix that $S + T < 2R$ or the sum of the off-diagonal payoffs is less than the sum of the mutual-cooperation payoffs. This last requirement means that the players cannot in total improve upon the aggregate cooperative payoff by agreeing for one to cooperate and for the other to defect and then split the total payoff.

Suppose that players A and B know that they are to play this game exactly twice. If the players were to look ahead, the dominant strategy in the final period is to defect as $P > S$ and $T > R$. Given that each player can anticipate that his or her counterpart will defect on the last round, the dominant strategy in the first round is also to defect. Each player views the strategic choice in period 1, *given the anticipated mutual defection in period 2 with payoffs of P*, as having the payoff matrix depicted in Figure 6.2. Each payoff displayed is the two-period payoff, conditioned on the second-period defections. Once again, mutual defection pays each player more regardless of the other player's strategy. In theory, defection is expected in every period when the endpoint of the game or repeated interactions are known. Thus, for example, a ten-period Prisoners' Dilemma would have the players defecting in the last period. Given that they defect in the last period, the dominant strategy in the next-to-last period is to defect. And so it goes for all ten periods. Thus, cooperation is not, *in theory*, anticipated to characterize a Prisoners' Dilemma that lasts a fixed (known in advance) number of periods. This result, however, does not agree with intuition because players that know they will interact for, say, five periods have much to gain by forming a cooperative agreement and sticking to it. When such an agreement can be achieved and enforced, each player stands to gain a great deal. This is particularly true as the number of periods increases.[4] In experimental situations, subjects tend to perform somewhere in between the noncooperative equilibrium and the cooperative outcome behavior for Prisoners' Dilemma repeated games, despite the theoretical prediction of noncooperation. The number of cooperators does tend to fall as the endpoint of the experimental trials is approached, but most subjects do not display the noncooperative behavior on all trials.

When communication among players is allowed, a greater degree of cooperation is observed.[5] This is a significant observation for regional and global public good problems that possess the Prisoners' Dilemma payoff structure, since, in the world of diplomacy, nations do communicate and attempt to address common concerns. Communications allow nations to signal their intentions to cooperate no matter how many times the interaction is repeated. Sending a false signal can be costly in terms of reputation. Nations that lie risk not being believed in the future when being believed may be crucial to

4. See Ledyard (1995), Roth (1995), Sandler (1992), and Young (1993).
5. Ledyard (1995, 156–60) reviews the literature on communication and games in an experimental setting.

A's strategy \ B's strategy	Defect	Cooperate
Defect	$2P, 2P$	$T + P, S + P$
Cooperate	$S + P, T + P$	$R + P, R + P$

Figure 6.2. Prisoners' Dilemma, viewed from first of two periods.

their interests. Common pollution problems are not one-time or even fixed-number-of-times affairs. The same is true about security and health threats. For instance, a terrorist threat against nations in a given region is unlikely to vanish in the next period unless the threat is explicitly neutralized or a political concession is granted. And the latter may encourage a new terrorist threat to materialize, because the government has revealed its vulnerability. Another example of repeated interactions concerns the diffusion of revolutions. When political instability in one country threatens to spill over to neighboring countries, the threat remains from period to period. Even if it is eliminated, the threat may surface at any time.

Cooperation is more likely if either the interaction is never ending or else the endpoint is unknown. For the former, the game is said to be infinitely lived. When the game's endpoint is unknown, a player must compare the temptation payoff with the likely consequences or retribution on the defector in the future periods. The same type of calculation is relevant when a player contemplates defection in an infinitely lived repeated game.

To better illustrate the basic principles behind these calculations, I must first explain the nature of a strategy in a repeated game. Essentially, a repeated-game strategy is a *program* that indicates, at the outset, the play in each ensuing period. Often the programmed response in a given period depends on the other players' actions in preceding periods. A well-known two-person dynamic strategy is *tit-for-tat*, in which a player begins by cooperating and then matches the opponents' previous-period play. If, therefore, the opponent defects in the first period, then the other player will defect in the sec-

170 Evolutionary concerns

ond period and will continue to do so until the opponent cooperates. With a tit-for-tat strategy, defection is immediately punished; this punishment is applied until a cooperative response is evoked. Tit-for-tat is not very forgiving, since it will never hold out an olive branch until the opponent alters his or her behavior. For tit-for-tat, a cooperative response that is misinterpreted can plunge the game into repeated periods of defection until a new mistake is made.[6] With a 50–50 chance of an error of interpretation, two players using tit-for-tat would cooperate only half of the time on average. Misinterpretation is a particular concern for international interactions where different languages and customs can be easily misperceived. The lack of forgiveness associated with tit-for-tat can have a real drawback as feuds among neighbors, ethnic groups, and nations aptly demonstrate. Once relations get off track, it is difficult with unforgiving strategies to get things back on track. Nevertheless, tit-for-tat has performed very well in tournaments and can lead to a great deal of cooperation owing to the automatic punishment that it metes out to a defector.[7]

An even less forgiving strategy is "Grim," where the player starts by cooperating and switches permanently to defection following the opponent's *first* defection. Grim gets its name because its punishment phase never ends. Grim is programmed to be completely unforgiving. More forgiving strategies may punish a defection with two or more "tit" for each tat. The most forgiving strategy is the always-cooperate strategy, in which a player cooperates in every period no matter the choice of the other player. Players employing such a strategy could be easily exploited so that the opponent receives the temptation payoff period after period in a Prisoners' Dilemma situation.

For a "tit-for-two-tats" strategy, a player begins with cooperation and defects only after the other player defects twice. Thereafter, the player alters his or her strategy only after the opponent changes to a different strategy for two consecutive periods. Tit-for-two-tats is more immune to misinterpretations, since two mistakes in a row must happen before cooperation is thrown off. Although this strategy ensures against errors, it will perform poorly against opportunistic strategies that take advantage of its forgiving nature. One such

6. Dixit and Nalebuff (1991) presents this example.
7. The seminal study is that of Axelrod (1984).

strategy would be to defect in the first round and every *other* round thereafter. This opportunistic strategy would receive T in the odd-numbered rounds and R in the even-numbered rounds.

Recent work has examined a "Pavlov" strategy where a player repeats a strategy that gives a high payoff and switches from a strategy that gives a low payoff.[8] Again consider a Prisoners' Dilemma game. A Pavlov player repeats cooperation after receiving R for a mutual-cooperation outcome. If the player receives T after getting away with a unilateral defection, the player then repeats defection. In contrast, the player switches to defection (cooperation) when receiving S (P). Experimental work at the Santa Fe Institute has shown that a group of Pavlov strategists respond quickly to correct errors unlike the tit-for-tat–type strategists. If, for example, a mistaken defection occurs in a two-player Prisoners' Dilemma, then after one round of mutual defection with payoffs of P, both players switch to cooperation. This suggests that a society of Pavlov strategists is very stable against errors. Such strategies can give interesting results when evolutionary equilibria are investigated.

For an infinitely repeated game, there can be many so-called Nash equilibria, where neither player would unilaterally change strategy. An equilibrium can, for example, result when each player uses a tit-for-tat strategy if he or she does not discount the future too greatly. For mutual tit-for-tat, each player would cooperate in the first period and every period thereafter, since no player would have cause, given the opponent's programmed strategic choice, to defect, provided that no mistakes are made. The multiperiod payoff would then be equal to the present value of a perpetual income stream of R. Suppose that a player decides, instead, to use an always-defect strategy against a tit-for-tat strategy. In the first period, the defector would receive T, but thereafter he would receive P. The defect strategy is only better over the long run if T plus the present value of the punishment income stream exceeds the present value of the reward income stream.[9] This also means that the first-period gain from defecting ($T - R$) must exceed the long-run loss from being punished from then on.[10] Often, the always-defect strategy will *not* give a

8. Nowak, May, and Sigmund (1995) summarizes recent simulations done with a Pavlov strategy at the Santa Fe Institute. This paragraph is based on their article.
9. The comparison requires that $T + (rP/1 - r) > R/(1 - r)$ where r is the discount factor or $1/(1 + i)$.
10. This means that the following inequality holds: $(T - R) > (R - P)/i$. This inequality

higher payoff than tit-for-tat when the opponent uses tit-for-tat. When this is the case, mutual tit-for-tat constitutes an equilibrium, illustrating that cooperative outcomes can occur in a repeated Prisoners' Dilemma. Other equilibria may involve each player always defecting. In fact, many strategy combinations may represent equilibria.

Even for games repeated only a finite number of times, equilibria may, in theory, involve mutual cooperation when the endpoint is unknown, so that players must estimate the long-run losses that would result from defecting and compare these losses to the anticipated gain; that is, a defection may mean a number of additional periods of punishment. In political situations, the last term of office may not be known in advance if term limits do not exist. For regional and global challenges, nations may view some interactions as continual or with an uncertain endpoint, so that the anticipated equilibria may indeed involve some form of cooperation. This provides further hope that nations can rise to the occasion for some challenges and cooperate. Thus far, I have only conceptualized the two-player Prisoners' Dilemma. For n-player repeated games, the principles remain the same as elucidated above. Mutual tit-for-tat can constitute an equilibrium, and players must compare defection gains with long-run consequences as players dish out punishments.

Differences may also distinguish the behavior between two-player and n-player repeated games. For example, a sole defector is more difficult to detect when a large number of players are involved. This can increase the anticipated short-run gains from defecting, thus making the defection a more attractive strategy. In a cartel, for example, individual firms have an incentive to increase profits by secretly undercutting other cartel members. If the cartel membership is large, it might take a while to uncover a sole defector, because the reduced sales of the other firms, if sufficiently small, may either go unnoticed or be attributed to reduced market demand. With n players, opposing coalitions can form where one coalition cooperates and the other does not. Communication is more demanding and costly as the number of participants increases. As explained in Chapter 5, linkage costs are greater for larger rather than smaller num-

---

is likely to hold if T is high relative to R, P is high relative to R, and i is high. A high i indicates a time impatience and, thus, a low discount rate. In simple words, the player wants gratification now rather than later.

bers of nations. In addition, the existence of n players means that some strategies may *evolve* over time toward equilibrium by garnering high payoffs, which increase their ability to produce offsprings that imitate the "winning" strategy. This brings up the notion of evolutionary games.

EVOLUTIONARY GAMES

Evolutionary game theory studies the population dynamics of a repeated game. Unlike standard repeated games, the number and type of players are allowed to change over time in evolutionary games. If each player type is identified with a strategy (for example, tit-for-tat), then evolutionary game theory predicts that the "fittest" players will survive, multiply, and eventually take over a population. A population of a single type of players is known as a *monomorphic* population.[11] Fitness is determined by the payoffs that a player receives through its strategy. The likelihood that an agent survives to reproduce is positively related to its payoff received through its interactions. Often, evolutionary game analysis is concerned with *kin selection*, where offsprings interact with siblings in the subsequent period. Strategic choices are programmed by the player's genetic code and are not a conscious choice.

A question of considerable interest concerns whether monomorphic populations can be invaded or taken over by "mutants," or the appearance of an individual type, programmed with a different strategic response. *Stable* monomorphic populations are able to resist invasion, because their payoffs are higher, and, thus, they have greater numbers of their offsprings surviving. Consider a population of Pavlov strategists. While their population is resistant to invasions by tit-for-tat players owing to the Pavlovian forgiveness, a Pavlov population is not stable to an invasion by mutant defectors. This follows because the Pavlov strategists try every other round to resume cooperation. This forgiveness leads to their exploitation (that is, low payoffs) and eventual takeover. In simulations, strategies that

---

11. Monomorphic population is analyzed by Bergstrom (1995), Bergstrom and Bergstrom (1996), Bergstrom and Stark (1993), Hamilton (1964), and Maynard Smith (1982). Also see the interesting work on partner selection in evolutionary games by Ashlock et al. (1996) and Tesfatsion (1996).

are more forgiving and cooperative have been shown to be easier to maintain in equilibrium for homogeneous populations. Essentially, defection is able to go unnoticed for a longer time in a large heterogeneous crowd,[12] so that defectors can accumulate high payoffs and make population inroads. Neighbors with similar characteristics and strategies, however, tend to gravitate toward cooperation. Insights such as these have implications for the effective response of nation groups to global challenges. Homogeneous regional groups of nations should be better equipped to develop cooperative interfaces.

An *evolutionary equilibrium* is a resting point of a dynamic process among diverse types of players where successful strategies or types are able to gain a dominant position by replicating themselves more frequently. Interest has focused recently on how partner selection, altruism, and cultural considerations can influence these evolutionary equilibria. For example, work concerning evolutionary Prisoners' Dilemmas indicates that players can reduce their risks associated with cooperation through preferential partner selection, based on expected payoffs.[13] When the number of players is large, defectors can avoid punishment by switching partners. If, however, the number of players is small, defectors are easier to spot and then ostracized. Preferential partner selection tends to promote cooperation among players, particularly in small groups. Other possibilities are "wallflower" ecologies where players are socially isolated. It is fair to emphasize that experimental findings and simulations in evolutionary games have explored only a few kinds of games under fairly stylized assumptions. Thus, these results are just suggestive, but not conclusive, as to how real-world interactions, which involve many different game forms (for example, Assurance or Chicken games), may play out.

Another line of inquiry for evolutionary games concerns whether altruistic behavior can promote survival even though such action costs the player some immediate gain. In *The Selfish Gene*, Richard Dawkins points out that the gene is the replicating agent that is apt to appear in its relatives.[14] A gene programmed to help its kin may

12. The diffusion of cooperation is explored in work by Nowak et al. (1995). Spatial and other considerations are also investigated.
13. See, especially, Ashlock et al. (1996).
14. Dawkins (1976).

promote replication and fitness if the immediate cost of doing so is not too great. To appreciate why an individual may be better off by cooperating or demonstrating altruism, I return to the Prisoners' Dilemma of Figure 6.1. In an evolutionary game, an offspring is anticipated to interact with a sibling or a neighbor. In the sibling case, there is a high probability that the sibling will share the same genetic code or strategic program.[15] Suppose that the population consists of cooperators who receive a payoff of R. If an offspring inherits a defector strategy by mutation, then in the next period the mutant's payoff will be $T > R$. This looks promising, but it is not. The problem arises in the ensuing period when the mutant offsprings interact *with other mutant offsprings* and again defect owing to their programmed response, but end up with only P. Over time, mutant defectors will reproduce less rapidly due to the lower payoffs and will eventually vanish from the population. For the Prisoners' Dilemma scenario, a cooperative population can, thus, be stable against invasions by some forms of mutants.

For the study of global and regional crises, *cultural evolutionary games* provide a more relevant analogy, developed from the study of evolutionary games.[16] Strategies are programmed or hardwired in the case of evolutionary games; but for cultural evolution, behavior toward one's neighbor is acquired by imitation. Closeness in space or time means that there is a greater likelihood that a player or nation will interact with another that uses the same strategy. Once again, it can be shown that cooperative behavior in a population may be stable and able to resist infiltration by mutant defectors, because players are more apt to interact with others who are imitating the same role model of cooperation.

Cultural evolutionary games for some kinds of strategic situations – for example, Prisoners' Dilemma – have some interesting conclusions that could be applied with care to understanding possible responses to regional and global contingencies. Imitation, which can promote altruism and cooperation, depends on nearness. This nearness can refer to spatial proximity, such as countries in a well-defined geographical area that copy a neighbor's response that has

---

15. Of course, this probability depends on simple Mendelian combinatorics as to the genetic code of one's relatives. See Bergstrom (1995).
16. See Bergstrom (1995) and Bergstrom and Stark (1993).

a high payoff. Nearness can also refer to similar political and economic systems, so that democracies may be more apt to cooperate with other democracies rather than with autocracies. Similarly, capitalistic systems may be more likely to replicate successful strategies of other capitalistic systems. Closeness may also depend on similar stages of development, implying, for example, that the Western European members of the European Union may be more likely to prosper from a cooperative response than more dissimilar nonmember nations. When nations are allied through common culture, migration, race, or history, they are more prone toward imitation. As such, these nations are likely to evolve to an equilibrium in which the most successful strategy is adopted, thereby abiding by the principles of evolutionary games.

Using an experimental framework, Daniel Friedman has examined a variety of game scenarios for which the game form is varied along with the number of players.[17] His findings show that evolutionary equilibria for games other than Prisoners' Dilemma, including games of Coordination, appear to characterize the experimental outcomes. Most important, small homogeneous communities tend to settle on cooperative outcomes that account for altruism. Heterogeneous populations tend to mix their strategies at random, thus implying less trust of the intention of the other players. These results imply that small regional collectives of nations with similar characteristics are more likely to evolve to a cooperative equilibrium than are large heterogeneous groups.

EVOLUTIONARY GAMES AND GLOBAL CHALLENGES

Insights from cultural evolutionary games suggest patterns of cooperation that should appear as nations confront common problems over time. The findings of the theoretical and experimental literature on cultural evolutionary games indicate that cooperation will begin at the local or regional level especially among nations at identical stages of development with similar economic and political systems.

17. Friedman (1996).

Regional proximity is also anticipated to increase the possibility of cooperation. Consider the European response to the sulfur-induced acid rain problem. The Scandinavian nations first pushed for an agreement to limit sulfur emissions. These nations were the nearest in terms of their cultural, economic, and political heritage. With time, other nations took an interest in limiting sulfur pollutants and began to curb their own emissions. At first, the richer capitalist nations joined with the Scandinavian nations to form an agreement curbing emissions. When there were a sufficient number of these nations to maintain a cooperative agreement, they reached out to neighboring autocratic nations to join them in their efforts. Cooperative intentions did start at the regional level where nations are homogeneous and then spread from this enclave to other national groupings that shared similarities with the Scandinavian nations. Co-operation regarding the control of sulfur and other acid rain inducers seemed to increase after the political changes of the early 1990s as more European nations became less autocratic and started their transition to capitalism.

Next consider a group of developed nations that are targeted by the same terrorist organization – for example, the Abu Nidal Organization's attacks on Western European soil during the 1980s. Given the relatively small number of neighboring countries with similar economic and political systems that faced the same terrorist threat, these countries understandably were prepared to cooperate so as to neutralize this terrorist threat. In fact, steps were taken to coordinate actions after a series of deadly attacks. The Abu Nidal Organization's activities have lessened somewhat in recent years for some unexplained reason. Attacks do persist: A Jordanian diplomat was assassinated in Lebanon in 1994.

Supportive cultural factors may allow nations to address successfully regional issues of desertification and tropical deforestation. Difficulty may arise when neighboring countries are dissimilar in their political systems or stages of development. For example, suggestions by the geographically distant developed countries that the tropical LDCs curb their deforestation have not been met with favor. It is likely that neighboring tropical nations evolve understandings among themselves, insofar as the forests of one nation have effects on erosion, watersheds, and the climate of neighboring nations.

Tropical nations that succeed in conserving their forests and pros-
pering from this act will have their behavior copied by other tropical
nations.

When it comes to widespread global challenges, such as global
warming, evolutionary game theory provides less hope or guidance
for an agreeable outcome, given the heterogeneity of the participants in terms of their cultural diversity. Simulations performed for
large groups indicate that enclaves of cooperators may start regionally and spread to other areas. At times, cooperative strategies may
colonize an entire population rather abruptly; but this is rare for
heterogeneous populations.[18] When a problem requires the cooperation of many nations, the ingredients for successful cultural evolution are missing; that is, a nation is not, in general, likely to
interact in the next period with other nations that copy successful
strategies of the nation's immediate neighbors. So-called leader
nations may be spatially and culturally separated from many of the
required cooperators. For global warming, China, Brazil, Russia,
Canada, Japan, and the United States are key required participants
but are culturally different from one another along many dimensions. Historically, many of the necessary participants have not cooperated with one another. Communications among these nations
are often troublesome. Moreover, altruism is not expected to be
displayed on such a global scale, owing to cultural and economic
diversity. Since almost all nations must be part of the cooperative
solution, partner selection, which can promote cooperative outcomes, is not really a consideration except for the initial groups that
are formed.

But not all global problems are plagued by the lack of cultural
similarities among the key participants. Curbing CFC emissions to
protect the stratospheric ozone shield represents an interesting
counterexample to global warming. As shown in Chapter 4, consumption and production of CFCs were highly concentrated in countries that were economically advanced and, hence, similar in some
key cultural attributes. Additionally, many of the producer countries
had similar political systems and high standards of living. Cooperation first formed small enclaves – the United States and Canada
banned the aerosol use of CFCs in the late 1970s, followed by Swe-

18. This paragraph is based on Nowak et al. (1995).

den and Norway. CFC producer nations became the "leader" nations, whose actions were imitated by neighbors and culturally similar nations, before spreading to more diverse nations.

The containment and the eradication of diseases also require universal participation. If a disease is almost eliminated but is allowed to maintain a presence in some isolated population, then it can mutate into a more harmful strain and resurface to threaten everyone. Cultural diversity works at odds for eliminating these disease footholds. Hygiene, living standards, health care, nutrition, and customs differ greatly among the world's people and inhibit the universal cooperative equilibrium from being attained. Even within the same country, there can be great differences in these factors.

When a cultural evolutionary equilibrium develops over time and nations adopt identical strategies to ward off challenges, a monomorphic population has developed in terms of the strategy employed. Whether or not this monomorphic population of nations can fend off "mutants" or nations identified with alternative strategies is a relevant concern. The answer follows the results developed in the cultural evolutionary game literature; it depends on the nature of the underlying game and the strategy associated with the equilibrium. The stability of a population of cooperators to a mutant invasion is relevant to international politics today. Consider the spread of religious fundamentalism in the Middle East and elsewhere. The fundamentalist attitude can be viewed as a mutant strategy that seeks a foothold in one or two nations, from which it can colonize a region. Based on the principles of cultural evolutionary games, nations in close proximity with similar demographic characteristics as the fundamentalist-based nations are most in danger of takeover. If existing regimes adopt a strategy that impoverishes their people, then these regimes may be unable to fend off the invasion by the fundamentalists, who appear to hold out the promise of higher payoffs.

A more-benign example involves foreign aid, which may have some altruistic component. Based on cultural evolutionary tenets, this altruism is more apt to be displayed toward neighboring nations, which, in turn, are more likely to interact with the donor on an ongoing basis. Efforts to improve the well-being of a neighbor could have paybacks as the neighbor becomes better equipped to imitate the successful strategies of the donor. Also, keeping one's neighbors strong means that these neighbors are better able to fend off mutants.

Is there a means for socially engineering greater cultural homogeneity, so that the principles that support culture-based evolutionary cooperation can apply to more regional or global challenges? Surely, the media promotes increased cultural homogeneity among nations, as do expanding communication linkages. The spread of democracy is also a force that, by increasing cultural similarities, may foster greater global cooperation in the long run. Educational exchanges further cultural homogeneity. Liberal migration policies can also augment cultural similarities among countries as they become "melting pots" like the United States and Australia. Restrictions to freer immigration are still largely practiced worldwide, especially when employment appears at risk. To a much lesser extent, liberal trade policies can also increase cultural similarities as people consume similar goods and services.

The study of evolutionary games may hold many insights into how nations may increase their fitness by adopting more cooperative strategies over time. In the real world, interactions are repetitive with many unknown factors. For example, political upheavals in a neighboring nation may drastically alter patterns of interactions and are difficult to predict. Evolutionary game theory can yield insights as to the stability of cooperative equilibria to adverse changes, as when a defector nation joins a cooperative group.

EVOLUTION AND THE EFFECTS OF INCOME DISTRIBUTION

In Chapter 7, worldwide income inequality is shown to be increasing in recent decades. Both wealth and income have become increasingly skewed in favor of the industrial countries. This increased inequality does not bode well for evolution-based support of addressing global challenges, such as global warming, because greater cultural and other differences will remain among nations. At the regional level, however, income is becoming more equal in *some* areas, and that can facilitate evolution-based cooperation. Some countries in East Asia and the Pacific Basin are, for example, emerging market economies (for example, Malaysia, Singapore, South Korea, Taiwan) that have maintained excellent economic growth records in recent years. Through their shared culture and growth experience, these nations may be better able to adopt cooperative strategies when dealing with common contingencies.

Another consideration that involves evolutionary cooperation and income distribution concerns the aggregation of public good benefits. If, for example, income is becoming more equal within a region, then nations are better equipped to provide a weakest-link or weaker-link technology public good. Both regional proximity and increased income equality will assist in the achievement of co-operation. In a best-shot scenario, regional income equality is not conducive for providing the needed public good. A wealthy nation, surrounded by culturally homogeneous poorer nations, may be in a better position to evolve toward a cooperative equilibrium for best-shot public goods. The stability of these weakest-link and best-shot equilibria against invasion is unknown at this point. Insofar as so much depends on the behavior of the single best-shot nation for this latter equilibrium, stability may be tenuous when mutants appear.

CONCLUDING REMARKS

This chapter has attempted to apply evolutionary game insights to the study of regional and global challenges. Cultural evolution, where neighboring nations imitate successful strategies, can create favorable forces for nations to address regional problems. The more homogeneous the region, the greater the chance that evolutionary factors will be supportive of a cooperative outcome even in a Prisoners' Dilemma scenario. Regional problems involving neighboring nations at similar stages of development are more prone to achieve cooperative behavior. For some global problems, cooperative enclaves can spread their behavior to other culturally similar enclaves and, in doing so, can diffuse cooperation on a wider basis. Dynamic considerations have been explored and hold promise for acquiring useful insights on how cooperative equilibria can be achieved by nations that interact repeatedly. More study is needed in the application of evolutionary principles to the manner in which nations address challenges.

7   Equity among nations?

This chapter, like the last, is speculative. Since 1960, income disparity among nations has increased worldwide: The richest nations have
experienced an increase in their share of world gross national product (GNP), while the poorest nations have experienced a decrease
in their share of world GNP. Between 1960 and 1991, the richest
fifth of all nations had its share of world income rise from 70% to
85%, while the poorest fifth of all nations had its share fall from
2.3% to 1.4%.[1] In a UN press release reported by CNN Interactive
(16 July 1996), income disparity was indicated to have widened both
within and among countries in the last few years. This trend toward
greater inequality gives every indication of continuing into the next
millennium as the underlying factors show no signs of abating. Will
increasing world inequality worsen or alleviate global conflicts? Furthermore, will increased inequality make these conflicts easier or
more difficult to address in the future? This chapter examines these
questions. At the outset, I must emphasize that there are no simple
answers. An increase in worldwide inequality may worsen some
problems through its impact on international trade and development, while it may lessen other problems through the underlying
incentives for the rich to provide crisis-averting public goods to the
world at large. Some global challenges are better handled with increased global inequality, while others are not. The number of sce-

---

1. See UN Development Programme (1994, 35). For even more detailed figures, see UN
   Development Programme (1992).

Table 7.1. *Worldwide income inequality measures: 1989*

Cohort of nations %	% Share of world GNP	% Share of world trade	% Share of world investment	% Share of world savings
Richest 20	82.7	81.23	80.56	80.51
Fourth 20	11.7	13.94	12.65	13.39
Third 20	2.3	2.53	2.92	2.59
Second 20	1.9	1.35	2.62	2.53
Poorest 20	1.4	0.95	1.25	0.98

Source: UN Development Programme (1992).

narios are great. Rather than enumerate all of these cases, my more-modest task is to address some important representative cases, so as to establish that increased inequality may be both a curse and a blessing.

Perhaps contrary to expectations, increased inequality can assist in averting some of the greatest threats to humankind. These are the global challenges where the greatest effort determines the level of consumption for all nations, contributors and noncontributors alike. A new form of foreign aid – *"free-rider aid"* – may come from the provision of transnational public goods and may increasingly replace traditionally tied and untied foreign aid of the post–World War II period. That is, free-riding behavior on the part of the poor may limit even greater worldwide inequality.

This chapter investigates the underlying causes of and prospects for worldwide inequality. The chapter then studies the impact that increased inequality among nations has on creating global exigencies. Next, the chapter examines how this increased inequality affects solutions to global challenges. Finally, the notion of free-rider aid is analyzed.

CAUSES OF INCREASED GLOBAL INCOME INEQUALITY

In Table 7.1, some share measures of global income inequality are listed for 1989. In the left-hand column, nations are grouped in terms of *quintiles* starting from the richest 20% of nations with the highest

Table 7.2. *Worldwide income disparity: 1960–91*

Year	Poorest 20% of nations[a]	Richest 20% of nations[a]	Richest to poorest ratio	Gini coefficient
1960	2.3	70.2	30 to 1	0.69
1970	2.3	73.9	32 to 1	0.71
1980	1.7	76.3	45 to 1	0.79
1989	1.4	82.7	59 to 1	0.87
1991	1.4	84.7	61 to 1	—

[a] Percentage of world GNP.
Sources: UN Development Programme (1992, 1994).

GNP levels and ending with the poorest 20%. The second column indicates the shares of world GNP earned by each quintile. For example, the richest quintile earned 82.7% of the world's GNP, while the next quintile (the fourth) earned 11.7% of the world's GNP. The top 40% of all countries earned 94.4% of world GNP in 1989, leaving just 5.6% earned by the remaining 60% of nations.[2] These shocking statistics indicate that income is very unequal among nations. A similar pattern of inequality is reflected by the share of world trade, the share of world investment, and the share of world savings, as shown in the remaining columns of Table 7.1. Insofar as investment determines the level of economic growth, the investment figures imply that growth among the richest 40% of nations is likely, on average, to surpass growth of the poorest 60%. As a consequence, income inequality should show no signs of abating in the near term. Since savings finance investment, it is not surprising that savings share displays a similar pattern to that of investment. When the investment share exceeds that of savings, as it has for the bottom three quintiles, the difference is usually financed by foreign savings in the form of capital inflows, such as foreign direct investment.

During 1960–91, the worsening inequality between the top and bottom quintiles is displayed in Table 7.2. The second column indicates the shares of world GNP earned by the poorest quintile, while the third column lists these shares earned by the richest quintile. The next column depicts the ratios of income shares of the

---

2. At the time of writing, the most current figures available for these measures are those reported in Tables 7.1 and 7.2.

richest quintile to the poorest quintile. All three columns indicate a pattern of equality that deteriorates with time. This worsening inequality may breed revolutions, especially if the poor view their situation as hopeless. An even greater pattern of inequality shows up when wealth (that is, the value of accumulated assets) inequality is measured.[3] Within countries, income distribution is typically highly unequal, thus exacerbating the potential threat of civil war and revolution.

In the last column of Table 7.2, the Gini coefficient is given for the sample years and is a measurement of the overall world inequality. A Gini coefficient of 0 indicates perfect equality, so that shares of GNP coincide with the corresponding percentage of nations – for example, 17% of the nations earn 17% of world GNP. In contrast, a Gini coefficient of 1 indicates perfect inequality – the single richest nation earns 100% of the world GNP, leaving the remainder with nothing. The increasing Gini coefficient supports my claim that the world had an increasingly more unequal income distribution since 1960.

Many factors contribute to this disturbing trend toward greater world inequality, and these factors, unfortunately, will persist to support this trend. Income growth is partly dependent on technological advances stemming from research and development (R & D). Less developed countries (LDCs) can engage in their own technology development or else rely on developed countries to transfer technological advancements to them. The lion's share of R & D is carried on by the advanced countries.[4] Even within this set of advanced countries, R & D is concentrated: In 1986, the United States spent more on R & D than Japan, West Germany, France, and the United Kingdom combined.[5] In 1989, the US government, its agencies, US firms, and US universities spent \$132 billion on R & D.[6] Not surprisingly, the developed countries own over 90% of the patents owing to their R & D efforts. By determining the pace and direction

3. According to the UN Development Programme, the wealthiest 1% of people owned 36% of the world's financial assets in 1990, up from 20% in 1975 (CNN Interactive, "UN Reports Wider Income Gap in US, World," 16 July 1996).
4. For an excellent treatment of technology and international relations, consult Walters and Blake (1992, chapter 6). Many of the stylized facts in this and the next paragraph of the text derive from this source.
5. Walters and Blake (1992, 179).
6. US National Science Board (1989, 264).

of technological advancements worldwide, the developed countries are able to maintain their grip on incomes.

LDCs must rely on the developed countries to transfer new technologies in the form of imported goods, direct foreign investment, license agreements, turnkey factories, educational exchanges, published scientific literature, scientific conferences, and other means. Until these LDCs manage to educate a more scientifically and technologically oriented workforce, the LDCs will not be able to take full advantage of technology that is transferred. Much of this technology is capital intensive and labor saving. A more-appropriate technology for these labor-rich, capital-poor nations would be labor intensive and capital saving. Unless the LDCs engage in their own R & D efforts, these more-appropriate technologies are unlikely to be developed.

Another contributing cause to the growing income inequality involves the composition of goods exported by the LDCs. A key concept behind understanding this problem is the notion of the *income elasticity of demand*, which indicates the percentage of change in the quantity demand that results from a percentage change in income. If, say, the income elasticity is 1, then a 10% increase in income will induce consumers to purchase 10% more of the good. If, however, the income elasticity is less than 1 in value but greater than 0, then a 10% increase in income will result in less than a 10% increase in the purchases of the good. Such goods are said to be normal but *income inelastic*. Negative income elasticities denote inferior goods for which purchases decline for a given percentage increase in income. Finally, an income elasticity above 1 denotes an *income elastic* good for which a percentage increase in income induces an even greater percentage increase in the good purchased.

The notion of income elasticity also applies to a nation's aggregate demand for exports. Because economic growth implies an increase in national income, nations that export goods for which world demand is income elastic are anticipated to experience an even greater percentage rise in exports over time. Unfortunately, nations in the lower quintiles typically export foods and low-technology goods whose income elasticity is inelastic. As a consequence, world income growth favors the demand for exports from the high-quintile nations over those from the low-quintile nations. This pattern bodes badly for closing the income gap.

Another contributing cause to the growing inequality in the world concerns the global distribution of wars and political violence. During 1993, forty-two nations were engaged in fifty-two major military conflicts, while another thirty-seven were attempting to quell political violence.[7] Of these seventy-nine nations, some 82% (sixty-five nations) were in the developing world. Political instability drives foreign direct investment to other countries where risks are lower, thus robbing LDCs of much-needed savings.[8] Since foreign direct investment is an important source of savings in these savings-poor countries, the resulting impact on investment and growth can be devastating. A war effort directs savings and investment into weapons that do not typically add to economic growth in the near term. Long-running conflicts divert resources into nonproductive activities. Casualties lead to the loss of manpower and capital as well as the destruction of infrastructure. Losses of infrastructure can be particularly destructive to national income as the overall productivity of the economy suffers. Nations at war also underinvest in their children, since they are sent to the battlefield at an early age; consequently, investment in human capital may have a smaller than usual expected return, thus leading to reduced human capital formation.

Debt burdens represent another cause for the growing gap between the rich and poor. According to the World Bank, developing countries' debt rose by 8% to just over $2 trillion in 1995.[9] The burden of this debt is measured by the debt-service ratio, which equals the ratio of the nation's payments of interest and principal (that is, its debt service) to its exports' value. The numerator indicates the nation's outgoing payments, while the denominator represents a potential source of funding from foreign exchange earnings. Although regional differences abound, the debt-service ratio for LDCs in general has been falling from 18.3% in 1990 to 16.3% in 1995. Paying back debt and interests limits a country's ability to save so as to support investments. The accumulation of debt is not necessarily bad if the money finances productive activities such as infrastructure, capital, or human capital. For many LDCs,

---

7. UN Development Programme (1994, 47).
8. A recent study by Enders and Sandler (1996) demonstrates that terrorism can drive away significant amounts of foreign direct investment. Spain and Greece are the sample countries in their study.
9. These figures are taken from *The Economist* (1996b). Other figures in this paragraph derive from the same source.

borrowed money supported corrupt officials, who spent it for personal gains.

Large population growth represents yet another underlying cause of the relative declining fortunes of the poor countries when compared with the richer countries. Since 1950, almost 90% of global population growth has taken place in the developing countries.[10] This trend is expected to continue or even worsen in the next millennium.[11] Current forecasts indicate that another billion people will be added to the world population every eleven years, with most of this increase concentrated in the tropical countries and LDCs. Population growth is a leading cause of desertification, tropical deforestation, global warming, and soil erosion.[12] As a country's population base expands, more resources are required to feed and clothe its people, which leaves less for growth-promoting activities. A related problem involves the trend toward urbanization, especially in the poorest countries. By the year 2000, urban population will be half of the world's total, with some three hundred cities of a million people or more in the LDCs alone.[13] This increased urbanization will place greater demands on urban infrastructure in the form of housing, sanitation, schools, police, and transportation. A large-scale investment in this infrastructure will be necessary in these LDCs, and this will initially divert funds from private investment.

Economic growth can be encouraged by an educated population. In fact, the acts of educating its people and investing in technology and R & D lead to growth-promoting outcomes, known as endogenous (or self-determining) growth.[14] If, however, a country stretches its means to provide subsistence to an expanding population base, then the country will be inhibited from making the choices that will lead to endogenous growth.

Population growth may perpetuate the difficulties that limit economic growth. Consider the influence of population growth on income per capita (GNP divided by population), which is a measure

10. Haub (1995).
11. Myers (1993).
12. According to Myers (1993, 208–9), population growth resulted in 72% of the desertification during 1961–85, 79% of the tropical deforestation during 1973–88, and 46% of the growth in CO_2 from fossil fuels during 1960–88.
13. UN Population Fund (1994).
14. On endogenous growth, see Barro (1991) and De Long and Summers (1991).

of the average standard of living for a country's residents. The growth of income per capita bears a simple relationship to income and population growth: Income per capita growth equals the difference between income growth and population growth. If, for example, income grows by 11% and population grows by 10%, then income per capita grows by only 1%. High population growth may lead to decreasing income per capita as the nation sinks deeper into poverty. A recent study found that economic growth degrades the environment at low per-capita income levels, but improves the environment at per-capita income levels above $7,500.[15] Inasmuch as most LDCs are nowhere near this threshold, an increase in income per capita is imperative for LDCs to attain sufficient well-being to demand increased environmental quality. With high population growth, it will take some time before income per capita increases sufficiently. In the meantime, deteriorating air, water, and environmental assets will further constrain poorer nations' growth.

A vicious cycle is apparent. High population growth implies low per-capita income, which, in turn, means a deteriorating environment, less support for education, less savings, and less investments. These latter consequences perpetuate low income per capita, which means less endogenous growth and continued poverty. Poverty, in turn, supports high population growth levels. The developed world has an interest in seeing this cycle broken, because environmental degradation in the LDCs transcends boundaries and harms everyone. For example, greenhouse gases released by the LDCs add to the global warming. Poverty also breeds discontentment that could erupt into civil wars and revolutions that could cause instability elsewhere. The potential export of fundamentalist revolutions has caused particular concern during the 1980s and 1990s. Revolution-inspired terrorism can also spill over boundaries. In short, a host of negative externalities can flow from the poor nations to the rest of the world.

Two other considerations that allow the income gap between rich and poor countries to widen are low savings rates and low investment rates in the poor countries. In Table 7.1, the world's poorest 60% of nations saved only about 6% of world savings. The factors

15. See Grossman and Krueger (1995).

presented earlier account for these low savings and investment rates. It is difficult for nations to save and invest for the future when their day-to-day subsistence is an all-consuming task.

TRADE AND THE ENVIRONMENT

Economists have typically looked toward free trade as improving living standards. If trade distortions (for example, tariffs, quotas) are absent, then a movement from no trade (autarky) to free trade is traditionally viewed as increasing the trading countries' well-being. In recent years, environmentalists have raised questions about whether or not trade liberalization truly improves trading countries' welfare. These environmentalists are concerned with two primary issues. First, trade-induced increases in income might also lead to greater domestic pollution that reduces the trading countries' true welfare. Second, free trade might provide incentives for polluting industries to relocate in nations where environmental standards are low or even nonexistent. If this relocation were sufficiently great, then many countries could suffer losses in well-being from trade-induced transboundary pollution. Conceivably, pollution-generated losses in well-being could swamp gains from freer trade if the pollution were especially harmful, thus leaving some countries impoverished by trade. How likely is this scenario? This outcome is more relevant when the resulting pollution is a global public bad, as in the case of CFCs or greenhouse gases. For more *localized pollution*, nations that attract "dirty" industries are unable to transport the problem abroad or to create losses for others, so that trade benefits must be sufficiently large to outweigh detrimental localized pollution.

The effect of free trade on the environment when income differs between two or more parts of the world is of considerable interest.[16] Suppose that the world is made up of two groups of nations – developed and less developed, denoted by "North" and "South," respectively. Further suppose that production activities yield pollution, in the form of a global public bad, along with output. By increasing

16. The Copeland and Taylor (1994, 1995) articles consider trade and transboundary pollution for various scenarios. A number of the insights presented here derive from their work.

income, free trade is sure to add to the pollution by-product. Since environmental quality is a normal good whose demand rises with income, this increased income will also heighten people's concern for the environment. But which influence dominates depends on a number of considerations: on how industry relocates between the North and South, on whether free trade equalizes the input prices among trading countries, and on whether the pollution is a local or global public bad. When pollution is globally public and the North and South differ in their income, "pollution havens" are likely to emerge in countries with weaker environmental standards, which are the poorer Southern countries. Thus, the North will have its trade gains offset, in part or in whole, by higher levels of pollution spillins from abroad. In fact, the South can exercise a strategic advantage by purposely keeping its environmental regulations weak to attract industry from the North.[17] The South gains from trade as it achieves a higher income level and receives reduced spillins of pollution from the North. In contrast, the North may gain or lose depending on trade-induced pollution increases.

When pollution is globally public and input prices are equalized worldwide through trade, overall production levels need not change but may merely shift from the North to the South.[18] If, however, pollution levels were controlled globally with each country receiving pollution permits entitling it to pollute up to a certain amount, then a permit market would be beneficial by eliminating pollution havens. Freely traded pollution permits would equalize pollution permit prices worldwide. If the South then attempts to be the pollution haven, it would have to purchase greater pollution permits, which, in turn, would raise its effective costs of polluting. Consequently, the South's strategic advantage is eliminated through trade in pollution permits. Since there is still no recognized global authority to set, issue, and oversee trading in these permits, a pollution permit market is not currently a feasible solution to pollution havens. Such a permit market has much to recommend it and should be explored further by the world community.

If, instead, the North and South had equal income and tastes, then there would be no pollution havens, because pollution would be

17. On these strategic policy choices, see Barrett (1994) and Ulph (1996).
18. This is the result found by Copeland and Taylor (1995) in a highly stylized model.

valued the same everywhere. In this case, free trade would raise both income *and* the global demand for a cleaner environment. Some of this increased income would be directed toward improving environmental quality. Despite the greater income, overall pollution might drop as no country has a strategic advantage to specialize in pollution-generating production activities.

Unfortunately, the trend toward greater inequality between the North and South means that potential pollution-haven effects should *worsen* with time. This is not good news since increased inequality will mean that global public pollutants will be particularly difficult to control, as pollution sources merely change venue from the North to the South. Given these income trends and the pessimistic forecasts of these emerging pollution havens, the North has much to gain from treaties and other supranational linkages that control transnational pollution. As the relative poverty of the South grows, its strategic advantage to produce pollution-intensive outputs will increase. With time, the LDCs will generate a much larger share of greenhouse gases and other global pollutants owing to their population growth, economic growth, and strategic advantage in acquiring pollution-intensive industries. The North will receive much greater spillins of pollutants as a consequence. Thus, there is a real downside to the increasing inequality among nations, stemming from the generation of global pollutants. A similar problem does not necessarily hold for local pollutants, in which generating nations have a strong motive to control their pollution. For these country-specific or local pollutants, pollution havens might be a problem *within* a country if states or provinces apply different pollution regulations. A strong central government that ensures that states enforce identical standards can eliminate any concerns.

At the global level, the role of foreign aid is an important consideration, since aid is a policy option that can lessen the growing gap between the North and South. For purely public global pollutants, redistributing income may be of limited value, because the income recipient's increased abatement efforts are anticipated to counterbalance the income donor's reduced abatement efforts.[19] Foreign aid may, however, be used to engineer income redistributions that in-

19. This is known as the neutrality theorem. In a pollution abatement context, see Copeland and Taylor (1995), Cornes and Sandler (1996), and Sandler (1997).

crease pollution abatement provided that the pollutant has some localized effects as in the case of acid rain. Aid recipients may then increase their pollution abatement effort substantially, because they cannot rely on others to provide these localized benefits. Additionally, the aid donors will receive smaller cutbacks in their pollution level from the efforts of the recipients, insofar as many of the benefits will be localized to the recipient.

WHEN IS INCOME INEQUALITY A GOOD THING?

Surprisingly, increased income inequality may actually be beneficial for some global challenges. In these important cases, a novel form of foreign aid may arise as the poor nations receive a free ride from actions of the rich nations to provide global public goods. The technology of public supply refers to the manner in which contributions to a public good combine to determine the overall provision amount. This technology of public supply is behind the cases where an increased income inequality is supportive for greater public good provision levels. Consider the best-shot technology where the largest contribution level determines the public good amount for everyone. Smaller contributions than the best-shot contribution add nothing to the public good level, so there is no incentive to provide the good unless the contributor is likely to be the best shooter. The best-shot contributor is often the richest, since the demand for most public goods is income normal, implying that the quantity demanded at each price increases with income. If a best-shot technology of public supply applies, then the quantity provided by the best-shot nation is anticipated to increase as income becomes more unbalanced with the rich gaining income. As such, the other nations can just sit back and enjoy a free ride.

Some of the world's most pressing challenges are associated with a best-shot or better-shot technology. Examples include finding a cure for deadly plagues, achieving research breakthroughs, and deterring a rogue state.[20] Finding new medicines (for example, a more effective antibiotic), neutralizing a terrorist group, or monitoring the

20. On these rogue states and policy options, see Klare (1995).

health of the planet also abides by these technologies. Yet another example would be recovering a nuclear-powered ballistic submarine from the ocean depths, where a worldwide contamination threat is posed as hull lifetimes are surpassed.[21] Containing the nuclear contaminants at the Chernobyl power plant in the wake of the explosion on 26 April 1986 is another best-shot example. Crisis management in the world's trouble spots can also correspond to a best-shot or better-shot technology, since the largest effort stands to determine the security achieved for everyone.

Even the summation technology of public supply, where total provision levels equal the sum of the nations' contribution amounts, implies that rich nations assume a greater burden for the public good.[22] As income becomes more skewed or unequal with time, the upper echelons of rich nations are anticipated to take on an increasing burden for providing global and regional public goods for the summation technology. Foreign aid may increasingly assume the form of providing a free ride for the poorer countries. In fact, there is a strategic advantage to being poor, because poverty facilitates free riding.[23] If, that is, a nation were to spend its income in earlier periods on goods other than the transnational public good, then, when needed later, the nation would have grounds for relying on the wealthier nations to provide the public good. Many global public goods abide by the summation technology, so that the burden-shifting influence of greater income disparity with time is an important consideration for the future. For many forms of pollution, abatement or cleanup results in a public good that corresponds to the summation technology. Examples include curbing CFC pollution, limiting lead emissions, and reducing greenhouse gas releases. Cleansing a common lake or waterway abides by a summation technology. Additionally, disengaging warring factions in a civil war corresponds to a summation technology, since it is the cumulative efforts that lead to the reduction in hostilities. The accumulation of

21. Examples include the *USS Thresher* (SSN-593), a nuclear-powered attack submarine lost in the Atlantic on 10 April 1963, and a Soviet nuclear-powered ballistic missile submarine with sixteen nuclear missiles lost six hundred miles northeast of Bermuda on 6 October 1986. Arkin and Handler (1989) document sinkings of nuclear submarines during the 1945–88 period.
22. See Andreoni (1988), Bergstrom, Blume, and Varian (1986), and Cornes and Sandler (1996) where public goods are assumed to be income normal.
23. See Konrad (1994) on this strategic advantage to poverty.

some forms of knowledge adheres to a summation technology: As the human genetic code is mapped, each part of the chartered region will eventually sum to an entire map.

WHEN IS INEQUALITY A BAD THING?

For trade-induced pollution havens, increased global income inequality was seen earlier to be a bad thing. The trend toward greater global inequality is also undesirable when a weakest-link or weaker-link technology of publicness applies. For these situations, the level of the public good is either determined by the smallest contribution or else more heavily influenced by the smaller contributions, respectively. When containing the spread of a disease or the dispersion of nuclear radiation, the least-effort levels may determine worldwide safety. If the operation of a network is involved, then the weakest points dictate the reliability and integrity of the entire network. If, therefore, nations are to rely on a network of monitoring stations to track the dispersion of pollutants or a pest, then the least-effective stations will gauge the network's effectiveness.

As global income inequality increases, the contribution of the weakest-link nation, which is usually the poorest nation, is expected to fall relative to the desired contributions of the richer countries. In consequence, the provision levels of these global public goods are anticipated to drop *unless* the rich countries either subsidize the poorer countries' contributions or else engage in an income redistribution program to bring up their provision levels. Another possibility is for the rich countries to step in and provide the public good for these poor countries. This is precisely what the United States has been doing to track and contain deadly viruses worldwide. Another instance of weakest link involves limiting the spread of religious fundamentalist revolutions. Those countries that do the least to check this spread determine the dispersion of these revolutions worldwide. Once again, the rich countries might choose to intervene to bolster the efforts of the weakest-link nations if the rich view this dispersion as a threat. Checking the spread of a civil war adheres to these same principles. This is why the United States has assumed the role of the world's policeman in places like Bosnia and Kuwait. Much to the consternation of many Americans, this policeman's role is anticipated to increase if income inequality worldwide continues to increase. If new plagues threaten to spread from the LDCs where populations are at greater risks owing to poor sanitation, education, and nutrition, then nations like the United States may have to assume the role of a health-care provider by financing inoculation and other programs in poorer nations. Even in the case of weakest link, heightened free riding may stem from the increasing inequality of world incomes.

IMPLICATIONS FOR INCOME POLICIES

Given the trend toward increased worldwide income disparity, a global income policy is a relevant option to redistribute income among nations. Based on the analysis here, income redistribution is not necessarily a desirable policy. For the best-shot scenario, inequality is conducive to greater provision levels of the public good on behalf of the best-endowed nation. If, in addition, a threshold level of the good must be achieved prior to any benefits being experienced, then improvements in the income of the richest are supportive of this threshold being attained. For the summation case, income redistribution is unlikely to have any effect except to redistribute public goods' burdens from the rich to the poor as the poor's income rises. For the weakest-link situations, however, income redistribution may be an effective policy alternative for increasing public goods provision, but these provision levels can be increased more directly by just providing the good.

At any point in time, the world faces a host of public good problems whose technology of publicness differs, so that a single income policy is unlikely to be useful for ameliorating the various shortfalls of the public goods. This suggests that if any income policy is used, then it must be based on trade considerations, strategic concerns, and equity grounds. In practice, nations will resist most rigorously any efforts to have them sacrifice their autonomy over their income earnings. Wars have been fought over less! While nations may be willing to cooperate in solving some global crises that threaten the collective well-being, they will still protect their autonomy over their income. A redistribution income policy may, however, be efficacious for cases where significant localized benefits accompany the global public benefits.[24] But even in these cases, directly subsidizing these activities is apt to have a greater influence with less opposition.

Another relevant consideration concerns whether the public good is local among a well-defined set of countries or whether it is global. For local or regional public goods, increased inequality may be conducive for nations to bargain toward a mutually acceptable agreement. Richer nations may consequently assume a leadership role or else be more willing to do something owing to their own anticipated gains. Redistribution may then create an *unfavorable* environment from which to culminate bargains among regional groupings of nations. As shown earlier, global prescriptions hinge on the underlying manner in which contributions add to the provision level. No simple statements are possible.

INTERGENERATIONAL PROBLEMS ONCE AGAIN

In Chapter 3, some global public good contingencies were identified as possessing an intergenerational dimension of publicness. For example, the containment of long-lived radioactive substances provides benefits to current and enumerable future generations. In an intergenerational context, incomes among generations will change in at least two ways: (1) future generations shall be richer than preceding generations, and (2) income disparity within future generations will be greater than within preceding generations. The increased income of future generations bodes well for these generations solving their public good challenges, insofar as public good provision tends to increase with overall income levels.[25] As environmental quality becomes scarcer, the willingness of nations to improve this quality should increase substantially. The greater disparity within future generations has more mixed results. For public goods abiding by best-shot, summation, or similar technologies, increased inequality should assist the achievement of effective collective action. Weakest-link problems will, however, be more difficult to solve without intervention on the part of a supranational authority. Stra-

24. See Sandler (1993, 1997) for an analysis.
25. Examples are presented in Murdoch and Sandler (1997) and Murdoch et al. (1997).

tegic maneuvering may characterize earlier generations if they make public good choices today in anticipation of what the future generations are likely to do. If, for example, the current generation is sanguine that the more well-to-do future generation will allocate more resources to preserving environmental quality, then the current generation may allocate less to this preservation. This is a particularly troublesome problem to address owing to the sequencing of generations. The current generation's strategy may fail when environmental quality decisions are irreversible.

CONCLUDING REMARKS

Increasing global disparity holds promise for providing global collective goods that require a best or a minimal effort. Most public goods may be provided at greater levels as income grows even if this income growth is distributed more unequally. Since successfully confronting many global challenges requires collective goods of this nature, increasing income disparity may assist the global community in averting many potential disasters. Increased global income disparity, however, works against solving those crises where everyone must contribute and where the smallest contribution fixes the safety level or well-being of everyone. These crises will require that the rich subsidize the efforts of the poor, or else disease, contaminants, and revolutions will disperse worldwide. For international trade, increased income disparity can augment the strategic incentives associated with pollution havens in the poor countries. On this score, increased inequality can portend worsening global environmental conflicts. When everything is considered, the increased disparity of income has its blessings and curses.

8 Near horizons

During the twentieth century, the world has become more interdependent in terms of its economics, politics, and environment. On a typical business day, about $1 trillion passes through the world's stock exchanges, while billions of dollars in goods and services are traded worldwide. People can communicate with one another globally via e-mail, fax, and the Internet. For example, a coauthor in Australia can work on an article during the day and transfer the file via the Internet, so that his or her US coauthor wakes in the morning to find the file on the computer. This enhanced interdependence is also reflected by political upheavals in one country having implications worldwide. Other examples abound. An innovative idea can be disseminated globally in a matter of days. A nuclear accident at Chernobyl dispersed a plume of radioactive material thousands of miles away, endangering much of Europe. As the carrying capacity of the planet is attained for a larger number of substances, pollutants will have a greater influence on deteriorating environmental quality at home and abroad. Now that multinational firms have become important participants in the world's economy, economic policies in one country have a greater impact on the economy of other countries. For example, more-restrictive pollution standards in a developed country can drive these multinational firms to a pollution haven in an LDC. Stock market crashes in one country create a loss of confidence in other countries' stock markets, owing to the greater economic interdependencies that arise from increased trade and capital flows.

199

We live in a "brave new world" where technologies, violence, economic activities, economic confidence, and pollutants transcend political borders. The whole notion of a nation-state loses part of its significance given the ease with which so many activities can pass through political borders. In modern times, economic borders, which delineate the extent to which an economic activity affects the well-being of others, have assumed an added importance to that of traditional political jurisdictions. This can be illustrated by sulfur and NO_x emissions from electricity-generating power plants. Once emitted into the air, these pollutants travel vast distances downwind to other countries, befouling their air and water. The emissions of CFCs and greenhouse gases are two further examples where activities within a country have impacts beyond the political jurisdiction where the activities originated. For these examples, the damages are worldwide as the protective ozone layer is depleted and the atmosphere is heated, respectively. Even though economic boundaries do not coincide with political boundaries and, in many instances, exceed these nation-state borders, the primary decision-making unit in the near term will remain the nation-state. As such, the nation-state typically unites people of common culture and ethnicity. Although supranational treaties may be framed and signed by these nation-states, they will jealously protect their autonomy. Only in the most dire circumstances will nations subordinate themselves to a higher authority. In wartime, this subordination has been accomplished through an alliance. If a threat or challenge is sufficiently great and if, moreover, the coordinated efforts of two or more nations are required, then nations will submit to a higher authority, whose mandate is specific to the crisis at hand.

Many factors determine whether these challenges are self-correcting, or whether outside intervention in the form of treaties or supranational structures are required. These factors include the number and nature of the participants, the pattern of associated costs and benefits among the participants, the extent of uncertainty, the presence of a leader nation, and the flow of benefits and costs over time. Given these differences among global challenges, no single prescription exists to address these problems. Some generalizations are still possible for particular *subgroupings* of challenges to the extent to which these global concerns share similar features. For many problems, a study period is needed during which uncertainties regarding the genesis of the crisis, its future trend, its remedy, and its prognosis are resolved. Once information has been gathered that establishes that a problem exists and that cooperators can achieve a net gain, then the form of the cooperation can be decided. Some simple rules of thumb are helpful. Since coordination looseness facilitates initial formation of a supranational link, it is best to begin with an unintegrated linkage that is tightened over time as warranted. These structures must possess positive net benefits for the collective as a whole and for each prospective participant if they are to be viable institutions. Additionally, it is advisable to look toward nongovernmental private alternatives, such as clubs, before turning to more integrated structures.

This chapter has four primary purposes. First, global challenges are assessed to ascertain whether they are myth or reality. Second, the outlook for global challenges in the near term is considered. In doing so, the ingredients for solvable problems are reviewed along with more problematic factors for less-solvable contingencies. Institutional aspects are also examined. Third, some important problems for the next millennium are identified, and, fourth, key conclusions are presented.

GLOBAL CRISES: MYTH OR REALITY?

This book is neither one of denial nor one of gloom and doom. There are some worrisome global challenges that, if not properly addressed by the world community, could spell widespread devastation. If, for example, global warming were to increase the frequency and severity of hurricanes as some meteorologists have predicted, then dire consequences could result. The same would be true if global warming were to lead to sufficient rises in sea level, owing to the melting of the polar ice caps. Similarly, the unchecked destruction of the ozone shield could disrupt the base of the food chain and result in large-scale extinction of species. Political violence and civil war in one part of the world could erupt into wars and instability elsewhere. The flying public could experience increased risks from bombs and even surface-to-air missiles if political grievances continue to result in transnational terrorism. The explosion that brought down TWA Flight 800 on 17 July 1996 may yet underscore this vulnerability. Urban centers could become the scenes of mass murder if deadly poisons are dispersed by terrorists. Reductions in the air quality in the major cities could lead to much-reduced life expectancies and increased incidences of asthma and other respiratory diseases.

Although this book acknowledges that challenges of major moment exist, it also recognizes that many of them are solvable, some through uncoordinated national actions and some through transnational collective action. Global crises are by no means a myth, but the exigencies that they present may not always be as great as the media would have us believe.[1] It is essential that the media exercise restraint in their assessment of these challenges, so that their credibility is maintained when the public must be informed about a real crisis. For some of the most-threatening problems, action may be swift simply because the richest nations have enough to gain from acting, even if most nations do not assist them in this effort. Reducing CFC emissions in the 1980s and 1990s is a case in point, since the primary-producer nations viewed a net positive benefit from finding substitutes for CFCs and acted quickly to stem this pollution threat. Once one or two key nations have assumed a leadership role, other less well-endowed nations often join in, especially if information is disseminated to show that these nations' help is crucial to the overall reduction in the threat. This is particularly true for public goods in which every nation's contribution bolsters the overall provision, as in the case of foreign aid where each nation's contribution adds to the total aid provided. After a number of nations are participating in the collective action, they can form a coalition to pressure others to join. This pressure can assume a number of forms, including trade sanctions, condemnation, severing diplomatic relations, positive side payments, and temporary compliance exemption. For severe problems, even an invasion might be necessary.

The truly worrisome crises are those that do not display warning signs of costly outcomes until it is too late to do much to alleviate the resulting disaster. If the consequences are irreversible, then the

1. In a recent book, Aaron Wildavsky (1995) argues that virtually all global challenges, except for ozone shield depletion, have been exaggerated by the media. While I agree that risks for many contingencies are either unknown or distorted by the media to attract readers, there are some real threats confronting the world. Wildavsky (1995) provides many interesting insights, but his ideology appears to drive what evidence is presented to support this thesis.

crisis is even more problematic, since collective action will not be able to return things to the way they were. Crises that require action by a large number of nations may also be difficult to avert, because many nations may free ride on the efforts of others. If enough nations take this free-rider strategy, efforts to address the challenge may be insufficient as actions of the free riders offset those of the activists. Global warming is particularly dangerous because a large number of participating nations are needed and its detrimental effects may be irreversible once an *unknown threshold* of the stock of greenhouse gases is accumulated in the atmosphere. For some problems, nations may actively undo the efforts of others as when nations provide a pollution haven or a sanctuary to terrorist groups.[2]

Other troublesome global challenges are those that require an effort on behalf of every nation, in which the smallest effort of the nations determines the security level for everyone. Examples include halting the spread of revolutions, containing nuclear contamination, and controlling the dispersion of epidemics.

GLOBAL CONFLICTS: THE OUTLOOK

By applying the modern theories of collective action and economics, this book shows that these theories can enlighten us as to why nations take actions willingly to address some contingencies but not others. If the world community can understand the factors that promote collective action when environmental or security concerns arise, then efforts can be directed at providing these preconditions so that nation-states will possess the proper incentives to act without the need for costly supranational linkages. Collective action concepts must be applied to identify cases where either nations will act automatically, or else coordinated actions are not worthwhile. For the global community, greater progress can be achieved to avert crises if nations can concentrate on only those problems in which some form of coordination is needed.

Global challenges that can be addressed by national actions with a minimum amount of international coordination possess a number

---

2. In contrast to free riding, this situation is known as paid riding. See Lee (1988) and Lee and Sandler (1989) on paid riders.

of characteristics. First, uncertainty has been resolved, so that the consequences of actions, in terms of costs and benefits, are reasonably well-known in advance. Moreover, the distribution of these costs and benefits among the countries is identified in advance. Second, those nations that add the most to the crisis are also the ones that have the most to gain from a solution, even after accounting for the cost of their efforts. Thus, these nations will assume a leadership role and serve as an important catalyst for change. Third, the presence of a large amount of nation-specific benefits, as in the case of acid rain reduction, also promotes action at the national level and may eliminate the need for explicit coordination among nation-states. Fourth, localized contingencies that affect a well-defined regional grouping are more apt to result in a negotiated solution without the need of a supranational linkage, especially if a small number of nations are involved that share common values, culture, and concerns. Such agreements are particularly promising if precedent has been achieved by earlier agreements as in the *Trail Smelter* case (1928–41), in which US citizens were compensated for damages emanating from a Canadian smelting factory.[3] Bilateral and multilateral agreements involving neighboring nations are easier to consummate than those involving more-distant nations. Fifth, global problems that rely on the largest or best-shot effort level are less difficult to address when income distribution is more unequal. Many of the most-worrisome and destructive challenges abide by a best-shot technology of publicness. At the *regional* level, however, incomes tend to be distributed more equally, and this bodes well for weakest-link kinds of problems, where the least effort determines the security level of everyone.

Global challenges are more apt to result in effective collective action when the gains from action are more in the present than in the future. If, however, associated costs must be expended immediately, while benefits are not experienced until the distant future, then nations may not be motivated to act alone or with others. This tendency toward inaction may be reinforced by elected officials or leaders who are concerned with pleasing the current constituency in order to win reelection. The prognosis for correcting global challenges worsens when a large number of countries are involved and

3. Dubner (1980, 246–7).

an agreement among a sizable number is needed to make any real headway on the problem. Another impediment to effective collective action arises if the crucial participants are anticipated to change and to increase in number over time. Problems occur because nations are understandably reluctant to limit their future flexibility. For example, LDCs do not want to constrain their development potential by agreeing to limits on CO_2 emissions when much of the stock of atmospheric CO_2, responsible for global warming, was emitted by the developed countries. By the same token, countries resent being told by the nuclear powers that nuclear weapons should not proliferate. Solutions to global crises stand a much better chance when a double standard is not applied. The developed countries must, therefore, be willing to set a good example and alleviate a number of problems if they want to bring the LDCs aboard. Furthermore, developed nations may have to provide significant positive inducements to these LDCs if they are to be part of the solution. In the case of weakest-link public goods, the developed countries may have to finance the required action if a sufficient fix to a challenge is to be achieved.

Although the outlook for the future is guardedly optimistic with respect to many of the global and regional contingencies on the horizon, the forecast would be even brighter if more efforts were made to establish a supranational infrastructure that would facilitate international cooperation. Some of the essential ingredients of this infrastructure are already in place. For example, the United Nations provides a meeting facility, while INTELSAT and other networks unite the world for communication purposes. As of yet, there is no permanent transnational peacekeeping force that is well-trained and that can be deployed at a moment's notice to a conflict in danger of spilling beyond national borders to embroil other nations. Currently, either the United States or the United Nations assumes the role of peacekeeper. NATO has recently developed a peacekeeping force that has been deployed to Bosnia. When a conflict needs management, often the United Nations must decide on an ad hoc basis whether or not a peacekeeping force should be deployed and, if deployed, what its composition should be. By the time these decisions are made, thousands can perish, as Bosnia aptly illustrates. At present, these peacekeeping forces are drawn on an as-needed basis from willing countries. Forces from different countries do not necessarily share common training, logistics, interoperable communications, standardized weapons, or other essential factors.

Another key ingredient for a supranational infrastructure would be a permanent research institute with scientists and social scientists drawn from many disciplines that would continually monitor and evaluate environmental, health, and security problems. This institute must be a prestigious one that attracts accomplished scholars and practitioners. Such an institute would require funding that must be above political and nationalistic pressures. Yet another aspect of this infrastructure is a taxing authority that could provide global public goods or that could facilitate their provision. This is the most drastic of my infrastructure proposals and will be the most challenging to institute, because nations will guard their sovereign rights to tax.

The world's judicial system also needs an overhaul so as to support supranational linkages when needed. Of the World Court's many faults, two are glaring. First, the Court needs the power to hear and decide cases that a majority of the international community agree should be adjudicated. There should be a "grand jury," drawn from the world community, that reviews evidence and determines if a trial is necessary. Most important, the verdict reached must then be imposed on the losing side, even without its consent to abide by the verdict. Second, an enforcement mechanism is required to carry out the judgment. This mechanism needs a military force that is permanent and of sufficient strength to be feared. The stronger this force is, the less it will be needed owing to deterrence. To achieve the proper reputation, it may have to be deployed a number of times. The earlier proposed peacekeeping force can serve this purpose.

Despite the need for a supranational infrastructure, I am *not* calling for a permanent supranational government that replaces the nation-states by usurping their powers. This is going too far! Lessons at Maastricht and beyond indicate the reluctance of nation-states to go very far in sacrificing their autonomy – myriad difficulties lie ahead for European integration in the EU.[4] In addition, nongovernmental alternatives in the form of clubs that have diverse members – for example, nation-states, multinational firms, provinces – should be used to address public good problems where exclusion is feasible.

4. For recent accounts of these problems, see *The Economist* (1996c, 1996d).

Multinational firms will continue to grow in importance as a world player and as a participant in collective action at the supranational level. For many environmental problems, these firms are the agents that created the problem in the first place and must be part of the solution. If the proper supranational infrastructure is deployed, then independent actions on the part of nations may alleviate many exigencies. Supranational linkages of an integrated nature should be employed only as a last resort when either serious consequences would follow if insufficient actions are taken, or else incentives for independent actions are not supported. Loose linkages in the form of treaties along the lines of the Montreal Protocol on ozone-depleting substances or the Helsinki Protocol on sulfur emissions provide a first means of defense.

PROBLEMS OF THE NEXT MILLENNIUM AND BEYOND

Since global contingencies are anticipated to grow in importance as exotic technologies are discovered, novel weaponry is developed, new hostilities are born, and the earth's carrying capacity for more substances is surpassed, the principles presented here will assume greater importance. Interest in these issues from a collective action viewpoint will, one hopes, spawn new insights. Although potential challenges abound, a few likely new crises are presented along with a more fanciful example.

Among the greatest pending global concerns is how to deal with China's rise as a superpower in the years to come. China poses a tremendous environmental risk to the world in terms of the emissions of sulfur, lead, cadmium, methane, nitrogen oxides, and other pollutants. Given its size, its carbon-dirty technologies, its breakneck pace of development, its population growth, and its fiercely independent attitude, China will without question be a major contributor to pollution during the next millennium. The problem is worrisome, because China has been more cautious than some nations to engage in binding environmental agreements. China also presents a threat to world peace as it continues its massive arms buildup. In 1996, not-so-veiled threats toward Taiwan underscore the potential concern. There is no question that China is a nation to reckon with.

Another threat is posed by "rogue states" that are willing to stop at nothing to achieve their goals,[5] which often involve territorial ambition. Recently, rogue nations have included Libya, Iraq, and North Korea. The real fear is that these nations will acquire nuclear weapons, biological agents, or chemical weapons that they are prepared to use for mass destruction. Disarming these nations would be a best-shot scenario as in the case of the Israeli raid on an Iraqi nuclear power plant, thought capable of producing weapon-grade plutonium, or the US stance against Iraq after the 1 August 1990 invasion of Kuwait. The possibility of nuclear weapons falling into the hands of rogue states is related to the nuclear proliferation issue and the disarming of the former Soviet republics. If nihilistic groups were to acquire nuclear weapons on the black market using materials from dismantled Soviet missiles, these groups could be prepared go so far as to kill millions to obtain some political concessions. For example, the religious cult leader suspected of the sarin attacks in the Tokyo subway was thought to be planning an air drop of the gas on Tokyo in an attempt to murder millions. His cult had even purchased an old Russian helicopter, allegedly to drop the gas. Currently, the Pentagon is considering how it can reconfigure its future defenses to defeat a rogue state or terrorist groups that may acquire weapons of mass destruction.[6]

Visions of future battlefields indicate new threats. War is becoming a high-technology affair where "information warriors" and their computers replace many of the foot soldiers. Being spotted is the difference between life and death on the modern killing fields. Viewing a target can be done at various frequencies along the electromagnetic spectrum, including infrared, visual, and radio. What can be seen can be targeted, and what can be targeted can be annihilated. As "smart" mines are developed, which can be activated and turned off and on at will, and long-range precision-guided munitions are perfected and deployed, large mobile armored forces can be reduced to rubble by an unseen opponent. Future wars may require a relatively small proportion of soldiers to programmers, scientists, and civilians.[7] Sensor-based, high-technology warfare may mean increased vulnerability as opponents seek and destroy an enemy's in-

5. A recent book on rogue states and the threats that they pose is Klare (1995).
6. See Stix (1995) on this Pentagon review. See Cohen (1996) and Stix (1995) on the future battlefield.
7. Cohen (1996) discusses this scenario.

formation assets. On a regional or global scale, information-based warfare is apt to favor preemption, in which the first to blind one's opponent's sensors achieves an insurmountable advantage. There are future scenarios where no amount of weapons can deter an attack if a preemption can sufficiently cripple an opponent's information assets.

Tomorrow's arms races can be even more wasteful than those of the past as the acceleration of technology speeds the obsolescence of weapon systems. The incentive to preempt and the ever-shortening "window" for detecting and verifying an attack can make security even more illusive no matter the size and firepower of an arsenal. Instability may characterize these arms races owing to the constant threat of preemption. In the future, a first strike may be covert in the guise of a computer virus. Outright battles would follow. As the verification window decreases over time, a preemptive strike increases in likelihood. A frightening consequence would be to retaliate against an imagined attack, thereby initiating an accidental war.

As human settlements penetrate ever deeper into the rain forest, ever-more insidious viruses, such as Ebola and HIV, may be released. Predicted increases in urbanization will then make cities an excellent place to breed and disperse the virus.[8] The global community must also contend with diseases that once responded favorably to antibiotics, but have mutated and present severe threats of plagues. Antibiotic-resistant tuberculosis is an example. Earlier generations' overuse of antibiotics has resulted in this intergenerational negative external effect as some diseases have become resistant to standard treatments. The failure of inoculation to be universal also allowed viruses to maintain a foothold prior to returning in a stronger strain. Humankind's hope in the twentieth century to purge these diseases has been dashed.

A more speculative, but no less interesting, potential crisis concerns encounters with planetesimals. Although erosion and weathering do a great job of hiding the scars of the past, the earth has been frequently bombarded with asteroids and even comets that, in the future, could have cataclysmic effects.[9] The March 1996 encounter with Comet Hyakutake within a mere ten million miles, close by

8. On urbanization and its effects on urban planning, see Rabinovitch and Leitman (1996).
9. The material in this section derives from Gehrels (1996).

astronomical standards, illustrates that the earth can be struck by such bodies. In fact, the earth's oceans are believed to be the remnants of comets that collided with the earth after it had cooled and solidified. Any water on the planet would have evaporated during the molten lava stage when the earth was hot and, thus, had to have been reintroduced by comets.

Once in every 300,000 years on average, an asteroid or comet larger than a kilometer across strikes the earth. The impact would be devastating, equivalent to millions of the times the energy released by the atom bomb at Hiroshima. The ensuing explosion would throw up dirt and debris that would obscure the sun, resulting in a "nuclear winter" with subzero temperatures, violent windstorms, massive destruction to settlements, and huge losses of life. Such a collision is now thought responsible for the sudden extinction of the dinosaurs.

What would we be able to do if such an object were hurling toward earth? If given a hundred years or more advanced notice, humankind could conceivably avert disaster by arming a vessel with explosives and sending it on a distant rendezvous in space with the intruder. At a sufficient distance from earth, the necessary explosion would be fairly small to divert the object, because even a small jolt might result in a deviation in the comet's or asteroid's trajectory sufficiently large to miss the earth by a great distance. The key is to know of the threat well in advance, so that diversionary actions can be taken. This requires that asteroids, comets, and other planetesimals that could come into the earth's path be mapped to provide the earth sufficient warning; the National Aeronautics and Space Agency (NASA) is currently engaged in a spacewatch operation to map such objects.[10] In late April 1996, a comet was discovered that has a 50–50 chance of striking the earth in some 100,000 years. Identifying these objects well in advance of collision and then doing something to divert them represents a best-shot technology. Nevertheless, the world may have to pool its efforts when the time comes if disaster is to be diverted, since one country alone may be unable to act quickly enough to design, equip, and send the vessel on its way.

10. See Gehrels (1996) on these efforts.

WITHER THE NATION-STATE?

Throughout this book, the nation-state has been assumed to be the primary player when it comes to confronting global conflicts and crises. Even though borders are no longer secure from pollutants, radical ideas, diseases, and violence, nations continue to hold onto their autonomy. In recent years, when net benefits warranted it, nations have been willing to sign treaties with others or to join in small collectives to solve common problems. These linkages are formed for specific purposes and do not indicate a trend toward the dissolution of the nation-state. For the near term, nations will continue to be the prime decision-making bodies notwithstanding the exigencies posed by pollutants, conflicts, diseases, and economics. The world stock exchanges and markets have demonstrated that capital, money, goods, and services can be traded without the need for larger political jurisdictions. For global pollutants, nations are motivated to take some corrective actions provided that there are sufficient localized effects, or else their citizens demand actions to preserve the health of the planet. In other situations, nations can sign treaties or form supranational linkages to address a *particular* concern. There is no need to dissolve the nation-state, which for many peoples provides a cultural and ethnic identity. Thus far, there is no move toward forming a monolithic state, where everyone lives without borders, despite the need to coordinate policy on some issues on a worldwide basis. A more practical approach would be to provide the supranational infrastructure to facilitate these specific transnational linkages.

Only in Western Europe has there been a serious attempt to create a superstate out of smaller states. The EU has fallen far short of the single nation once envisioned. Major obstacles still exist with respect to a single monetary union and centralization of decision making. A major motivation for creating the EU was to create an economic counterbalance to the United States – that is, a nation sufficiently large to afford significant R & D programs and to achieve scale economies. If the home market is large enough, then scale economies (low costs per unit owing to large production runs) can be supported and home industries would be more competitive in world markets. Consider the case of space exploration. The cost to any single European nation is prohibitively expensive, but it may be affordable through a united effort in which each nation shares the costs. Similarly, a common defense force can eliminate duplication and make for a more affordable defense. Although these economic principles are sound, the EU experience has shown that nations want to maintain their autonomy over defense, public safety, monetary policy, and a host of other problems.

The nation-state is here to stay for the near horizon. Thus, practical solutions for today's global challenges must adjust for this reality.

KEY CONCLUSIONS OF THE BOOK

Some key conclusions follow:

(1) The overall assessment of the world's future is less pessimistic than usually supposed. Significant challenges and conflicts of a political, economic, and health nature exist. Nations possess incentives to solve some of the challenges that represent the most harmful consequences. In other cases, loose federation of nations may prove helpful.

(2) If a contingency involves just the current generation, is well-understood, and affects a small number of neighboring nations, then the prognosis for cooperation is particularly good. If, moreover, correcting the problem provides a large proportion of localized (nation-specific) benefits, then this motivates the nation to do something. Global challenges that have unresolved uncertainty and that concern the present and future generations are especially difficult to solve.

(3) Each conflict differs along a number of dimensions – the number of nations, the proportion of localized benefits, the extent of uncertainty, the distribution of benefits – so that the need for intervention and the form of this intervention, if needed, differ among problems. There is no single blueprint or magic potion for addressing global challenges.

(4) Since many global and regional environmental challenges share common pollutants and other features, remedies must adequately account for these interdependencies.

(5) The first course of action should be to look toward independent behavior on the part of nations to confront transnational crises.

If, however, incentives are not supportive of such action, then non-governmental bodies in terms of clubs can be used to alleviate some difficulties when nonpayers can be excluded from the benefits of collective action. The mere existence of a problem does not justify the institution of a supranational linkage.

(6) During the last two decades, many international treaties concerning the environment have merely codified actions that the ratifiers had already accomplished or were soon to achieve. This was the case for the Helsinki and Sofia Protocols, which set emission limits for sulfur and NO_x emissions, respectively. Nations act when it is in their interest; to date, treaties do not reflect a global consciousness. These treaties still serve a purpose by inducing others to go along with the constrained behavior of the original framers of the treaties.

(7) Challenges with implications for both the present and future generations are more apt to attract effective collective action as compared with those with implications for just the future generations. The greater the share of the benefits going to the present generation, the larger will be its response to rectifying a problem.

(8) Some intergenerational trades can be achieved, provided that the generations are sufficiently near in time and that they share risks.

(9) If a supranational linkage is required, then it should be instituted on an ad hoc basis whenever *net* linkage benefits are positive for the group of participants *and* for each participating nation. Linkages that begin loose and that are tightened over time, as warranted, stand a better chance of formation than do initially tighter linkages. There are very few problems that would necessarily require an initially tight joining of nations.

(10) In general, the formation and operation of supranational linkages are facilitated if the international community invests in supranational infrastructure (for example, a taxing authority, an enforcement body, a science committee) that supports cooperative efforts among nations.

(11) The evolution of cooperation over time is more likely to help locally rather than globally. If, however, problems are first solved regionally, then these solutions can disperse worldwide with time. Common cultures and environments promote the evolution of cooperation on a regional basis.

(12) Regional problems involving neighboring nations at similar

points in their development are often easier to solve in a cooperative fashion as compared with problems involving nations at different stages of development.

(13) The role of income redistribution in promoting cooperative outcomes critically depends on the nature of the underlying public good and how its provision relates to individual contributions.

(14) In the near term, income distribution among nations is anticipated to become more unequal. This inequality is expected to be conducive to solving transnational challenges for which the needed public good abides by a best-shot or summation technology of aggregating the contributions. This inequality will work against solving weakest-link kinds of problems.

The world is, indeed, besieged by global challenges requiring collective action. Although the news media have characterized the world as facing imminent disaster from insidious pollutants, ghastly viruses, rogue nations, spreading civil wars, and bloodthirsty terrorists, I have taken a more-reasoned approach. In particular, I have tried to identify which collective action problems lend themselves to solutions and which are more problematic. Thus, global warming is seen as quite difficult to address on a collective basis, whereas the curing of new strains of deadly diseases is viewed as less difficult to achieve. The methods of collective action are sure to figure in an important way as nations confront regional and global challenges, now and into the future. While there are surely grounds to be concerned, the outlook is more optimistic than is usually portrayed. By analyzing the likelihood of collective action, I have identified those few problems for which a great amount of intervention is needed, since the underlying incentives are not conducive to addressing the exigency. By the same token, I have highlighted those challenges that are virtually self-correcting. I hope that this book will stimulate further work in this important area of research and that it will provide new insights for its readers.

References

Alcamo, Joseph M. and Eliodora Runca (1986), "Some Technical Dimensions of Transboundary Air Pollution," in Cees Flinterman, Barbara Kwiatkowska, and Johan G. Lammers (eds.), *Transboundary Air Pollution: International Legal Aspects of the Cooperation of States* (Dordrecht: Martinus Nijhoff), 1–17.

Alexander, Yonah, Marjorie Ann Browne, and Allan S. Nanes (1979), *Control of Terrorism: International Documents* (New York: Crane Russak).

Alexander, Yonah and Dennis Puchinsky (1992), *Europe's Red Terrorists: The Fighting Communist Organizations* (London: Frank Cass).

Amsberg, Joachim von (1995), "Excessive Environmental Risks: An Intergenerational Market Failure," *European Economic Review*, 39(8), 1447–64.

Andreoni, James (1988), "Privately Provided Public Goods in a Large Economy: The Limits of Altruism," *Journal of Public Economics*, 35(1), 57–73.

Arkin, William W. and Joshua Handler (1989), "Naval Accidents 1945–1988," Neptune Papers No. 3, Greenpeace Institute for Policy Studies, Washington, DC.

Arrow, Kenneth J. (1970), "The Organization of Economic Activity: Issues Pertinent to the Choice of Market versus Non-market Allocation," in Robert H. Haveman and Julius Margolis (eds.), *Public Expenditures and Policy Analysis* (New York: Academic Press), 23–39.

Arrow, Kenneth J. and Mordecai Kurz (1970a), *Public Investment, The Rate of Return, and Optimal Fiscal Policy* (Baltimore, MD: Johns Hopkins University Press).

Arrow, Kenneth J. and Mordecai Kurz (1970b), "Optimal Growth with Irreversible Investment in a Ramsey Model," *Econometrica*, 38(2), 331–44.

Ashlock, Dan, Mark D. Smucker, E. Ann Stanley, and Leigh Testafsion (1996), "Preferential Partner Selection in an Evolutionary Study of Prisoner's Dilemma," *Biosystems*, 37(1), 99–125.

215

Auster, Richard and Morris Silver (1973), "Collective Goods and Collective Decision Mechanisms," *Public Choice*, 14(1), 1–17.

Ausubel, Jesse H., David G. Victor, and Iddo K. Wernick (1995), "The Environment since 1970," *Consequences: The Nature & Implications of Environmental Change*, 1(3), 4–15.

Axelrod, Robert (1984), *The Evolution of Cooperation* (New York: Basic Books).

Barrett, Scott (1994), "Strategic Environmental Policy and International Trade," *Journal of Public Economics*, 54(3), 325–38.

Barro, Robert J. (1991), "Economic Growth in a Cross Section of Countries," *Quarterly Journal of Economics*, 106(2), 407–43.

Baumol, William J. and Wallace E. Oates (1988), *The Theory of Environmental Policy*, 2nd Edition (Cambridge: Cambridge University Press).

Baumol, William J., John C. Panzar, and Robert D. Willig (1988), *Contestable Markets and the Theory of Industry Structure*, Revised Edition (New York: Harcourt Brace Jovanovich).

Benedick, Richard E. (1991), *Ozone Diplomacy* (Cambridge, MA: Harvard University Press).

Bergstrom, Theodore C. (1995), "On the Evolution of Altruistic Ethical Rules for Siblings," *American Economic Review*, 85(1), 58–80.

Bergstrom, Theodore C. and Carl T. Bergstrom (1996), "Rotten Kids, Squawky Birds, and Natural Selection," unpublished manuscript, University of Michigan, Ann Arbor, MI.

Bergstrom, Theodore C., Lawrence Blume, and Hal Varian (1986), "On the Private Provision of Public Goods," *Journal of Public Economics*, 29(1), 25–49.

Bergstrom, Theodore C. and Oded Stark (1993), "How Altruism Can Prevail in an Evolutionary Environment," *American Economic Review*, 83(2), 149–55.

Bienen, H. and N. van der Walle (1989), "Time and Power in Africa," *American Political Science Review*, 83(1), 19–34.

Binmore, Ken (1992), *Fun and Games* (Lexington, MA: D. C. Heath).

Boyd, Roy, Kerry Krutilla, and W. Kip Viscusi (1995), "Energy Taxation as Policy Instrument to Reduce CO_2 Emissions: A Net Benefit Analysis," *Journal of Environmental Economics and Management*, 29(1), 1–24.

Brito, Dagobert L. and Michael D. Intriligator (1995), "Arms Races and Proliferation," in Keith Hartley and Todd Sandler (eds.), *Handbook of Defense Economics*, Vol. 1 (Amsterdam: North-Holland), 109–64.

Buchanan, James M. (1965), "An Economic Theory of Clubs," *Economica*, 32(1), 1–14.

Cauley, Jon, Todd Sandler, and Richard Cornes (1986), "Nonmarket Institutional Structures: Conjectures, Distribution, and Allocative Efficiency," *Public Finance*, 41(2), 153–72.

Coase, Ronald H. (1960), "The Problem of Social Cost," *Journal of Law and Economics*, 3(1), 1–44.

Cohen, Eliot A. (1996), "A Revolution in Warfare," *Foreign Affairs*, 75(2), 37–54.

Congleton, Roger D. (1992), "Political Institutions and Pollution Control," *Review of Economics and Statistics*, 74(3), 412–21.

Congressional Budget Office (1990), *Carbon Charges as a Response to Global Warming: The Effects of Taxing Fossil Fuels* (Washington, DC: Congressional Budget Office).

Congressional Budget Office (1991a), "Costs of Operation Desert Shield," Congressional Budget Office Staff Memorandum, Congressional Budget Office, Washington, DC.

Congressional Budget Office (1991b), "Statement of Robert D. Reischauer, Director, Congressional Budget Office," Congressional Budget Office Testimony, Congressional Budget Office, Washington, DC.

Congressional Budget Office (1992), *Paying for Highways, Airways, and Waterways: How Can Users Be Charged?* (Washington, DC: Congressional Budget Office).

Conybeare, John A. C., James C. Murdoch, and Todd Sandler (1994), "Alternative Collective-Goods Models of Military Alliances: Theory and Empirics," *Economic Inquiry*, 32(4), 525–42.

Copeland, Brian R. and M. Scott Taylor (1994), "North-South Trade and the Environment," *Quarterly Journal of Economics*, 109(3), 755–87.

Copeland, Brian R. and M. Scott Taylor (1995), "Trade and Transboundary Pollution," *American Economic Review*, 85(4), 716–37.

Cornes, Richard (1993), "Dyke Maintenance and Other Stories: Some Neglected Types of Public Goods," *Quarterly Journal of Economics*, 108(1), 259–71.

Cornes, Richard and Todd Sandler (1984), "Easy Riders, Joint Production, and Public Goods," *Economic Journal*, 94(3), 580–98.

Cornes, Richard and Todd Sandler (1994a), "Are Public Goods Myths?" *Journal of Theoretical Politics*, 6(3), 369–85.

Cornes, Richard and Todd Sandler (1994b), "The Comparative Static Properties of the Impure Public Good Model," *Journal of Public Economics*, 54(3), 403–21.

Cornes, Richard and Todd Sandler (1996), *The Theory of Externalities, Public Goods, and Club Goods*, 2nd Edition (Cambridge: Cambridge University Press).

Council of the European Communities (1988), "Council Directive of 24 November 1988 (88/609/EEC) on the Limitation of Emissions of Certain Pollutants in the Air from Large Combustion Plants," *Official Journal of the European Communities*, 50(336), 1–13.

Cummings, Ronald G., David S. Brookshire, and William D. Schulze (eds.) (1986), *Valuing Environmental Goods: An Assessment of the Contingent Valuation Method* (Totowa, NJ: Rowman and Allanheld).

Dasgupta, Partha and Geoffrey Heal (1979), *Economic Theory and Exhaustible Resources* (Cambridge: Cambridge University Press).

Dawkins, Richard (1976), *The Selfish Gene* (New York: Oxford University Press).

Dawkins, Richard (1995), "God's Utility Function," *Scientific American*, 273(5), 80–5.

de Gruijl, Frank R. (1995), "Impacts of a Projected Depletion of the Ozone Layer," *Consequences: The Nature & Implications of Environmental Change*, 1(2), 13–21.

De Long, J. Bradford and Lawrence H. Summers (1991), "Equipment Investment and Economic Growth," *Quarterly Journal of Economics*, 106(2), 445–502.

Demsetz, Harold (1964), "The Exchange and Enforcement of Property Rights," *Journal of Law and Economics*, 7(2), 11–26.

Dixit, Avinash K. and Barry Nalebuff (1991), *Thinking Strategically* (New York: Norton).

Doeleman, Jacobus A. and Todd Sandler (1996), "The Intergenerational Case of Missing Markets and Missing Voters," unpublished manuscript, University of Newcastle, Newcastle, Australia.

Downs, Anthony (1957), *An Economic Theory of Democracy* (New York: Harper and Row).

Dubner, Barry H. (1980), "An Analogy of the Law of the Seas and the International Judicial System," in Todd Sandler (ed.), *The Theory and Structures of International Political Economy* (Boulder, CO: Westview Press), 235–51.

The Economist (1995), "Global Warming and Cooling Enthusiasm," *The Economist*, 335(7908), 1 April, 33–4.

The Economist (1996a), "The Peacemakers Confer," *The Economist*, 338(7957), 16 March, 45–6.

The Economist (1996b), "Emerging-Market Indicators," *The Economist*, 338-(7960), 6 April, 110.

The Economist (1996c), "A Convoy in Distress," *The Economist*, 338(7957), 16 March, 59–60.

The Economist (1996d), "Ever More Complicated Union," *The Economist*, 338(7959), 30 March, 47–9.

Edelson, Burton (1977), "Global Satellite Communications," *Scientific American*, 236(2), 58–73.

Elster, Jon (1979), *Ulysses and the Sirens: Studies in Rationality and Irrationality* (Cambridge: Cambridge University Press).

Enders, Walter and Todd Sandler (1993), "The Effectiveness of Antiterrorism Policies: A Vector-Autoregression-Intervention Analysis," *American Political Science Review*, 87(4), 829–44.

Enders, Walter and Todd Sandler (1996), "Terrorism and Foreign Direct Investment in Spain and Greece," *Kyklos*, 49(3), 331–52.

Enders, Walter, Todd Sandler, and Jon Cauley (1990), "UN Conventions, Technology and Retaliation in the Fight against Terrorism: An Econometric Evaluation," *Terrorism and Political Violence*, 2(1) 83–105.

Environmental Protection Agency (1987a), *Assessing the Risks of Trace Gases*

That Can Modify the Stratosphere, 7 vols. (Washington, DC: Environmental Protection Agency).

Environmental Protection Agency (1987b), *Regulatory Impact Analysis: Protection of Stratospheric Ozone*, 3 vols. (Washington, DC: Environmental Protection Agency).

Fridtjof Nansen Institute (1996), *Green Globe Yearbook of International Cooperation on Environment and Development 1996* (New York: Oxford University Press).

Friedman, Daniel (1996), "Equilibrium in Evolutionary Games: Some Experimental Results," *Economic Journal*, 106(1), 1–25.

Gehrels, Tom (1996), "Collisions with Comets and Asteroids," *Scientific American*, 274(3), 49–54.

Gillis, Malcolm (1988), "Indonesia: Public Policies, Resource Management, and the Tropical Forest," in Robert Repetto and Malcolm Gillis (eds.), *Public Policies and the Misuse of Forest Resources* (Cambridge: Cambridge University Press), 43–113.

Grossman, Gene M. and Alan B. Krueger (1995), "Economic Growth and the Environment," *Quarterly Journal of Economics*, 110(2), 353–77.

Hamilton, William D. (1964), "The Genetical Evolution of Social Behavior, Parts I and II," *Journal of Theoretical Biology*, 7(1), 1–52.

Hammond, Peter J. (1976), "Changing Tastes and Coherent Dynamic Choice," *Review of Economic Studies*, 43(1), 158–73.

Hardin, Russell (1982), *Collective Action* (Baltimore, MD: Johns Hopkins University Press).

Hartley, Keith (1991), *The Economics of Defence Policy* (London: Brassey's).

Haub, Carl (1995), "Global and U.S. National Population Trends," *Consequences: The Nature & Implications of Environmental Change*, 1(2), 3–11.

Heckathorn, Douglas D. (1989), "Collective Action and the Second-Order Free-Rider Problem," *Rationality and Society*, 1(1), 78–100.

Hirshleifer, Jack (1983), "From Weakest-Link to Best-Shot: The Voluntary Provision of Public Goods," *Public Choice*, 41(3), 371–86.

Howarth, Richard B. and Richard B. Norgaard (1990), "Intergenerational Resource Rights, Efficiency and Social Optimality," *Land Economics*, 66(1), 1–11.

Howarth, Richard B. and Richard B. Norgaard (1995), "Intergenerational Choices under Global Environmental Change," in Daniel W. Bromley (ed.), *The Handbook of Environmental Economics* (Oxford: Basil Blackwell), 111–38.

Hyde, William and David Newman (1991), "Forest Economics and Policy Analysis: An Overview," World Bank Discussion Paper 134, World Bank, Washington, DC.

INTELSAT (1973), *Agreement Relating to the International Telecommunications Satellite Organization "INTELSAT"* (Washington, DC: INTELSAT).

INTELSAT (1995), *INTELSAT in the '90s* (Washington, DC: INTELSAT).

Intergovernmental Panel on Climate Change (1990), *Climate Change: The*

IPCC Scientific Assessment, J. T. Houghton, G. J. Jenkins, and J. J. Ephraums (eds.) (Cambridge: Cambridge University Press).

Klare, Michael (1995), *Rogue States and Nuclear Outlaws: America's Search for a New Foreign Policy* (New York: Hill and Wang).

Konrad, Kai A. (1994), "The Strategic Advantage of Being Poor: Private and Public Provision of Public Goods," *Economica*, 61(1), 79–92.

Landes, William (1978), "An Economic Study of U.S. Aircraft Hijackings, 1961–1976," *Journal of Law and Economics*, 21(1), 1–31.

Lapan, Harvey E. and Todd Sandler (1988), "To Bargain or Not to Bargain: That Is the Question," *American Economic Review*, 78(2), 16–20.

Ledyard, John (1995), "Public Goods: A Survey of Experimental Research," in John H. Kagel and Alvin E. Roth (eds.), *The Handbook of Experimental Economics* (Princeton, NJ: Princeton University Press), 111–94.

Lee, Dwight, R. (1988), "Free Riding and Paid Riding in the Fight against Terrorism," *American Economic Review*, 78(2), 22–6.

Lee, Dwight R. and Todd Sandler (1989), "On the Optimal Retaliation against Terrorists: The Paid-Rider Option," *Public Choice*, 61(2), 141–52.

Lichbach, Mark I. (1996), *The Cooperator's Dilemma* (Ann Arbor, MI: University of Michigan Press).

Lipsman, Michael A. (1994), *A Theory of Transportation Clubs with Special Applications to the Domestic Aviation System*, unpublished dissertation, Iowa State University, Ames, IA.

Maynard Smith, John (1982), *Evolution and the Theory of Games* (New York: Cambridge University Press).

Mickolus, Edward F. (1980), *Transnational Terrorism: A Chronology of Events, 1968–1979* (Westport, CT: Greenwood Press).

Mickolus, Edward F., Todd Sandler, and Jean M. Murdock (1989), *International Terrorism in the 1980s: A Chronology of Events*, 2 vols. (Ames, IA: Iowa State University Press).

Miller, G. Tyler, Jr. (1994), *Living in the Environment: Principles, Connections, and Solutions* (Belmont, CA: Wadsworth Publishing).

Mitchell, Robert C. and Richard T. Carson (1989), *Using Surveys to Value Public Goods – The Contingent Valuation Method* (Washington, DC: Resources for the Future).

Morisette, Peter M., Joel Darmstadter, Andrew J. Plantiga, and Michael A. Toman (1990), "Lessons from Other International Agreements for a Global CO_2 Accord," Discussion Paper ENR91–02, Resources for the Future, Washington, DC.

Mueller, Dennis C. (1989), *Public Choice* II (Cambridge: Cambridge University Press).

Murdoch, James C. and Todd Sandler (1997), "The Voluntary Provision of a Pure Public Good: The Case of Reduced CFC Emissions and the Montreal Protocol," *Journal of Public Economics*, forthcoming.

Murdoch, James C., Todd Sandler, and Keith Sargent (1994), "A Tale of Two Collectives: Sulfur versus Nitrogen Oxides Emission Reduction in Europe," Institute for Policy Reform Working Paper No. IPR98, Institute for Policy Reform, Washington, DC.

Murdoch, James C., Todd Sandler, and Keith Sargent (1997), "A Tale of Two Collectives: Sulfur versus Nitrogen Oxides Emission Reduction in Europe," *Economica*, 64, forthcoming.

Murphy, John F. (1990), "The Need for International Cooperation in Combating Terrorism," *Terrorism: An International Journal*, 13(6), 381–96.

Myers, Norman (1992a), "Synergisms: Joint Effects of Climate Change and Other Forms of Habitat Destruction," in R. L. Peters and T. E. Lovejoy (eds.), *Global Warming and Biological Diversity* (New Haven, CT: Yale University Press), 344–54.

Myers, Norman (1992b), *The Primary Source: Tropical Forests and Our Future* (New York: Norton).

Myers, Norman (1992c), "Tropical Forests: The Policy Challenge," *The Environmentalist*, 12(1): 17–27.

Myers, Norman (1993), "Population, Environment, and Development," *Environmental Conservation*, 20(3), 205–16.

Myers, Norman (1994), "Tropical Deforestation, Rates and Patterns," in Katrina Brown and David W. Pearce (eds.), *The Causes of Tropical Deforestation: The Economic and Statistical Analysis of Factors Giving Rise to the Loss of Tropical Forests* (London: UCL Press), 27–40.

Myers, Norman (1995), *Ultimate Security: The Environmental Basis of Political Stability* (New York: Norton).

Myers, Norman and Thomas J. Goreau (1991), "Tropical Forests and the Greenhouse Effects: A Management Response," *Climatic Change*, 19(3), 215–25.

Neher, Philip A. (1976), "Democratic Exploitation of a Replenishable Resource," *Journal of Public Economics*, 5(3), 361–71.

Nordhaus, William D. (1991), "The Cost of Slowing Climate Change: A Survey," Cowles Foundation Paper No. 775, Yale University, New Haven, CT.

Nowak, Martin A., Robert M. May, and Karl Sigmund (1995), "The Arithmetics of Mutual Help," *Scientific American*, 272(6), 76–81.

Olson, Mancur (1965), *The Logic of Collective Action* (Cambridge, MA: Harvard University Press).

Olson, Mancur (1982), *The Rise and Decline of Nations: Economic Growth, Stagflation, and Social Rigidities* (New Haven, CT: Yale University Press).

Olson, Mancur (1993), "Dictatorship, Democracy, and Development," *American Political Science Review*, 87(3), 567–76.

Opschoor, J. B. and David Pearce (1991), *Persistent Pollutants: Economics and Policy* (Dordrecht: Kluwer).

Organization for Economic Cooperation and Development (OECD) (1990), *Control Strategies for Photochemical Oxidants across Europe* (Paris: OECD).

Ostrom, Elinor (1990), *Governing the Commons: The Evolution of Institutions for Collective Action* (Cambridge: Cambridge University Press).

Page, Toby (1977), *Conservation and Economic Efficiency* (Baltimore, MD: Johns Hopkins University Press).

Pearce, David, Neil Adger, David Maddison, and Dominic Moran (1995), "Debt and the Environment," *Scientific American*, 272(6), 52–6.

Pearce, David and Giles Atkinson (1995), "Measuring Sustainable Development," in Daniel W. Bromley (ed.), *The Handbook of Environmental Economics* (Oxford: Basil Blackwell), 166–81.

Pejovich, Svetozar (1990), *The Economics of Property Rights: Towards a Theory of Comparative Systems* (Dordrecht: Kluwer).

Rabinovitch, Jonas and Josef Leitman (1996), "Urban Planning in Curitiba," *Scientific American*, 274(3), 46–53.

Repetto, Robert and Malcolm Gillis, eds. (1988), *Public Policies and the Misuse of Forest Resources* (Cambridge: Cambridge University Press).

Rivera-Batiz, Luis A. and Paul M. Romer (1991), "Economic Integration and Endogenous Growth," *Quarterly Journal of Economics*, 106(2), 531–55.

Roth, Alvin E. (1995), "An Introduction to Experimental Economnics," in John H. Kagel and Alvin E. Roth (eds.), *The Handbook of Experimental Economics* (Princeton, NJ: Princeton University Press), 3–109.

Runge, C. Ford (1984), "Institutions and the Free Rider: The Assurance Problem in Collective Action," *Journal of Politics*, 46(1), 152–81.

Safina, Carl (1995), "The World's Imperiled Fish," *Scientific American*, 273(5), 46–53.

Sandler, Todd (1982), "A Theory of Intergenerational Clubs," *Economic Inquiry*, 20(2), 191–208.

Sandler, Todd (1992), *Collective Action: Theory and Applications* (Ann Arbor, MI: University of Michigan Press).

Sandler, Todd (1993), "Tropical Deforestation: Markets and Market Failures," *Land Economics*, 69(3), 225–33.

Sandler, Todd (1997), "Collective Action and Tropical Deforestation," *International Journal of Social Economics*, forthcoming.

Sandler, Todd and Jon Cauley (1977), "The Design of Supranational Structures: An Economic Perspective," *International Studies Quarterly*, 21(2), 251–76.

Sandler, Todd, Jon Cauley, and John Tschirhart (1983), "Toward a Unified Theory of Nonmarket Institutional Structures," *Australian Economic Papers*, 22(1), 233–54.

Sandler, Todd and Keith Hartley (1995), *The Economics of Defense* (Cambridge: Cambridge University Press).

Sandler, Todd and Keith Sargent (1995), "Management of Transnational Commons: Coordination, Publicness, and Treaty Formation," *Land Economics*, 71(2), 145–62.

Sandler, Todd and William D. Schulze (1981), "The Economics of Outer Space," *Natural Resources Journal*, 21(2), 371–93.

Sandler, Todd and William D. Schulze (1985), "Outer Space: The New Market Frontier," *Economic Affairs*, 5(4), 6–10.

Sandler, Todd and V. Kerry Smith (1976), "Intertemporal and Intergenerational Pareto Efficiency," *Journal of Environmental Economics and Management*, 2(3), 151–9.

Sandler, Todd and V. Kerry Smith (1977), "Intertemporal and Intergenerational Pareto Efficiency Revisited," *Journal of Environmental Economics and Management*, 4(3), 252–7.

Sandler, Todd and V. Kerry Smith (1982), "Intertemporal and Intergenerational Pareto Efficiency: A Reconsideration of Recent Extensions," *Journal of Environmental Economics and Management*, 9(4), 361–5.

Sandler, Todd and John Tschirhart (1980), "The Economic Theory of Clubs: An Evaluative Survey," *Journal of Economic Literature*, 18(4), 1481–1521.

Sandler, Todd and John Tschirhart (1997), "Club Theory: Thirty Years Later," *Public Choice*, forthcoming.

Sandnes, Hilde (1993), *Calculated Budgets for Airborne Acidifying Components in Europe, 1985, 1987, 1989, 1990, 1991, and 1992*, EMEP/MSC-W Report 1/93 (Oslo: Norske Meterologiske Institutt).

Schelling, Thomas C. (1980). *The Strategy of Conflict* (Cambridge, MA: Harvard University Press).

Schelling, Thomas C. (1992), "Some Economics of Global Warming," *American Economic Review*, 82(1), 1–14.

Schulze, William D., David S. Brookshire, and Todd Sandler (1981), "The Social Rate of Discount for Nuclear Waste Storage: Economics or Ethics?" *Natural Resources Journal*, 21(4), 811–32.

Schultz, Richard H., Jr. and Robert L. Pfaltzgraff, Jr. (eds.) (1992), *The Future of Air Power in the Aftermath of the Gulf War* (Maxwell, AL: Air University Press).

Schwartz, Joel (1991), "Particulate Air Pollution and Daily Mortality: A Synthesis," *Public Health Review*, 19(1), 39–60.

Sedjo, Roger A. (1992), "Genetic Resources and Biotechnological Change," *Journal of Law and Economics*, 35(1), 199–213.

Sen, Amartya K. (1967), "Isolation, Assurance, and the Social Rate of Discount," *Quarterly Journal of Economics*, 81(1), 112–24.

Sen, Amartya K. (1982), "Approaches to the Choice of Discount Rates for Social Benefit-Cost Analysis," in Robert C. Lind et al. (eds.), *Discounting for Time and Risk in Energy Policy* (Washington, DC: Resources for the Future), 325–53.

Smith, V. Kerry (1993), "Nonmarket Valuation of Environmental Resources: An Interpretative Appraisal," *Land Economics*, 69(1), 1–26.

Solow, Robert M. (1986), "On the Intergenerational Allocation of Natural Resources," *Scandinavian Journal of Economics*, 88(1), 141–9.

Stix, Gary (1995), "Fighting Future Wars," *Scientific American*, 273(6), 92–8.

Stokey, Nancy L. (1991), "Human Capital, Product Quality, and Growth," *Quarterly Journal of Economics*, 106(2), 587–616.

Tesfatsion, Leigh (1996), "An Evolutionary Trade Network Game with Preferential Partner Selection," in L. Fogel, P. J. Angeline, and T. Baeck (eds.), *Evolutionary Programming V: Proceedings Volume of the Fifth Annual*

Conference on Evolutionary Programming (Cambridge, MA: MIT Press), 45–54.

Tiebout, Charles M. (1956), "A Pure Theory of Local Expenditures," *Journal of Political Economy*, 64(4), 416–24.

Toman, Michael A., John Pezzey, and Jeffrey Krautkraemer (1995), "Neoclassical Economic Growth Theory and Sustainability," in Daniel W. Bromley (ed.), *The Handbook of Environmental Economics* (Oxford: Basil Blackwell), 139–65.

Toon, Owen R. and Richard P. Turco (1991), "Polar Stratospheric Clouds and Ozone Depletion," *Scientific American*, 264(1), 68–74.

Ulph, Alistair (1996), "Environmental Policy and International Trade When Governments and Producers Act Strategically," *Journal of Environmental Economics and Management*, 30(3), 265–81.

United Nations (1992a), *Long-Range World Population Projection: Two Centuries of Population Growth, 1950–2150* (New York: United Nations).

United Nations (1992b), *Protocol to the 1979 Convention on Long-Range Transboundary Air Pollution Concerning the Control of Emissions of Volatile Organic Compounds or Their Transboundary Fluxes* (New York: United Nations).

United Nations (1994), *Protocol to the 1979 Convention on Long-Range Transboundary Air Pollution on Further Reduction of Sulphur Emissions* (New York: United Nations).

United Nations Development Programme (1992), *Human Development Report 1992* (New York: Oxford University Press).

United Nations Development Programme (1994), *Human Development Report 1994* (New York: Oxford University Press).

United Nations Environment Programme (UNEP) (1991), *Selected Multilateral Treaties in the Field of the Environment*, vol. 2 (Cambridge: Grotius Publications).

United Nations Population Fund (1993), *The State of World Population 1993* (New York: UN Population Fund).

United Nations Population Fund (1994), *The State of World Population 1994: Choices and Responsibilities* (New York: UN Population Fund).

United States Department of State (1994), *Patterns of Global Terrorism: 1993* (Washington, DC: US Department of State).

United States Department of State (1995), *Patterns of Global Terrorism: 1994* (Washington, DC: US Department of State).

United States National Science Board (1989), *Science and Engineering Indicators, 1989* (Washington, DC: Government Printing Office).

Vicary, Simon (1990), "Transfers and the Weakest-Link: An Extension of Hirshleifer's Analysis," *Journal of Public Economics*, 43(3), 375–94.

Walters, Robert S. and David H. Blake (1992), *The Politics of Global Economic Relations*, 4th edition (Englewood Cliffs, NJ: Prentice Hall).

Warr, Peter G. (1983), "The Private Provision of a Public Good Is Independent of the Distribution of Income," *Economics Letters*, 13(2), 207–11.

Weiss, Edith B. and Harold K. Jacobson (1996), "A Tale of Five Agreements and Nine Countries," *Human Dimensions Quarterly*, 1(4), 1–5.

Wildavsky, Aaron (1995), *But Is It True? A Citizen's Guide to Environmental Health and Safety Issues* (Cambridge, MA: Harvard University Press).

Wilkinson, Paul (1986), *Terrorism and the Liberal State*, Revised Edition (London: Macmillan).

Wilkinson, Paul and A. M. Stewart (eds.) (1987), *Contemporary Research on Terrorism* (Aberdeen: Aberdeen University Press).

World Bank (1992), *World Development Report 1992*: *Development and the Environment* (New York: Oxford University Press).

World Resources Institute (1990), *World Resources 1990–91* (New York: Oxford University Press).

World Resources Institute (1992), *World Resources 1992–93* (New York: Oxford University Press).

World Resources Institute (1994), *World Resources 1994–95* (New York: Oxford University Press).

World Resources Institute (1996), *World Resources 1996–97* (New York: Oxford University Press).

Young, H. Peyton (1993), "The Evolution of Conventions," *Econometrica*, 61(1), 57–84.

Author index

Subject index

acid rain, 3, 10, 18–19, 59, 82, 84, 90–1, 99, 114–25, 148, 158–63, 165, 177, 193, 204
  and ambient air quality, 116, 128
  and nitrogen oxides, 115–17, 121–9, 158–63
  and sulfur emissions, 115–23, 126–9, 158–63
  and volatile organic compounds (VOCs), 116, 127–9, 158–9
  see also volatile organic compounds
addiction, *see* incoherent dynamic choice
AIDS, 6, 20, 48, 50, 55–6, 73, 209
Air India Flight 182, 130
airport security, 132–5
Alfred P. Murrah Building bombing, 5
alliances, 2, 47–8, 139–40, 200
altruism, 57–60, 69, 81–3, 166, 174, 176, 178, 179–80
antibiotic-resistant diseases, 1, 6, 48, 53, 77, 82, 193, 209
arms races, 2, 28–9, 209
asteroids, *see* planetesimal
Assurance game, 34–7, 47, 174
Australia, 102–3, 105, 112, 139, 148, 180, 199
autocratic regimes, 53, 69–72, 128, 134, 148, 177

bargaining, 40–1, 97–8, 142, 152, 197
bequest value, 82, 91, 95
biodiversity, 3, 11, 43, 52, 55, 60, 68, 82, 91–3, 96
Biological Diversity, Convention of, 95–6
Bosnia, 4, 140, 195, 205–6

Brazil, 92, 95, 97–8, 178
British Antarctic Survey, 108

carbon dioxide, 2, 8, 12, 15, 61, 96, 99–106, 205
Center for Disease Control, 20
Chernobyl, 194, 199
Chicken game of, 36–9, 47, 174
  ordinal form, 36–8
China, 102–3, 112, 145, 178, 207
chlorofluorocarbons (CFCs), 3, 7, 15, 42, 44–5, 67, 84–5, 101, 104, 106–15, 141, 144–5, 147, 150, 153, 178–9, 190, 194, 200, 202
Climate Change, Convention of, 15, 101, 106
club goods, 44
  definition of, 44
  and efficient output, 44, 75–6
  and intergenerational clubs, 75–6, 83
  and private provision, 44
  and tolls, 44
clubs, 44, 75–6, 155–8, 164, 201, 213
  examples of, 44, 75–6, 155–6
  financing, 44, 76, 155–6
  INTELSAT as club, 44, 157–8
  provision, 44
  and supranational linkages, 46, 155–8, 201
Coase Theorem, 40
Cold War, 4, 7, 34, 131
collective action, 1, 14–15, 21–2, 51, 53, 55, 57–8, 69–70, 83, 85–6, 94–5, 111, 113–14, 143, 148–9, 202–7

230